D0210990

ONCE A WARRIOR

ONCE A WARRIOR

HOW ONE VETERAN FOUND A
NEW MISSION CLOSER TO HOME

JAKE WOOD

SENTINEL

Sentinel
An imprint of Penguin Random House LLC
penguinrandomhouse.com

Most Sentinel books are available at a discount when purchased in quantity for sales promotions or corporate use. Special editions, which include personalized covers, excerpts, and corporate imprints, can be created when purchased in large quantities. For more information, please call (212) 572-2232 or e-mail specialmarkets@penguinrandomhouse.com. Your local bookstore can also assist with discounted bulk purchases using the Penguin Random House corporate Business-to-Business program. For assistance in locating a participating retailer, e-mail B2B@penguinrandomhouse.com.

Insert photo credits:

Jeff Wood: pages 1 (top), 1 (center), 2 (center), 2 (bottom), 3 (bottom right), 7 (bottom left); Sarah Lenger: pages 1 (bottom), 3 (bottom left); Ray Bullard: page 2 (top); Shawn Beidler: page 3 (top left); Tim Fortney: page 3 (top right); Jake Wood/Team Rubicon: pages 4 (top), 4 (center), 5 (top); Jeremy Hinen: page 4 (bottom); Indra Wood: page 7 (bottom right); Kirk Jackson/Team Rubicon: pages 5 (center), 5 (bottom), 6 (top), 6 (center right), 6 (center left), 7 (top right), 7 (center right), 7 (center left), 8 (center left); MORE/Team Rubicon: page 6 (bottom); Ally Stepp: page 8 (top left); Jon Connors/Team Rubicon: page 8 (center right); Muna Ahmed/Team Rubicon: page 8 (bottom right).

LIBRARY OF CONGRESS CATALOGING-IN-PUBLICATION DATA
Names: Wood, Jake, 1983– author.
Title: Once a warrior : how one veteran found a new mission closer to home / Jake Wood.
Other titles: How one veteran found a new mission closer to home
Description: New York : Sentinel, [2020]
Identifiers: LCCN 2020032152 (print) | LCCN 2020032153 (ebook) | ISBN 9780593189351 (hardcover) | ISBN 9780593189368 (ebook)
Subjects: LCSH: Disaster relief. | Veterans—United States—Biography. | Philanthropists—United States—Biography. | Team Rubicon (Organization)—History | United States. Marine Corps—Biography. | Marines—United States—Biography. | United States. Marine Corps. Marine Regiment, 7th. Battalion, 2nd. | Afghan War, 2001—Personal narratives, American. | Iraq War, 2003-2011—Personal narratives, American.
Classification: LCC HV553 .W647 2020 (print) | LCC HV553 (ebook) | DDC 363.34/8092 [B]—dc23
LC record available at https://lccn.loc.gov/2020032152
LC ebook record available at https://lccn.loc.gov/2020032153

Printed in the United States of America
10 9 8 7 6 5 4 3 2 1

Book design and illustrations by Daniel Lagin

Disclaimer: Some names and identifying characteristics have been changed to protect the privacy of the individuals involved.

To my father, Jeff Wood. Thank you for all the lessons.

To my wife, Indra. Thank you for taking a chance on me.

To my daughter, Valija. Thank you for making it worth it.

CONTENTS

PREFACE   1

PART I   7

1. CROSSING THE RUBICON   9

2. MOMENTS AND DECISIONS   27

3. *POOF.* THAT'S THE SOUND THEY MAKE   37

4. RED-EMBERED MARLBORO   51

5. THE VALLEY ECHOED   67

6. EVERYTHING IS WRONG   79

7. LIFE AFTER WAR   95

PART II   103

  8. WE DO CHAOS   105

  9. EXPECTANT   113

10. WHEN THE BAGPIPES END   127

11. ROLL TIDE   143

12. HURRICANE SANDY   159

13. TORNADO ALLEY   175

PART III   191

14. TYPHOON HAIYAN   193

15. SIGNATURE WOUNDS   213

16. FIVE-HUNDRED-YEAR FLOOD   229

17. BROKEN PROMISES   243

18. WE'RE GOING TO WISH WE HAD BOATS   267

19. CLAY WOULD BE PROUD   283

EPILOGUE   297

ACKNOWLEDGMENTS   303

PREFACE

There's a saying in the military: Old soldiers never die; they simply fade away. It's poetic, but the lyricism belies an underlying sadness. What happens to a soldier after combat? In uniform they are admired and applauded, thanked as they walk through airports and toasted with beers at the local pub. But when our sons and daughters take off their uniforms for the last time, they often begin a long descent into obscurity. A higher calling lives on inside of them that no longer has a mission to pursue, and as they struggle to reintegrate, it's more comfortable for the public to look away than to take responsibility. When most people think about veterans, they default to stereotypes—and to be honest, they aren't far off. Old men, baseball caps announcing their combat campaigns perched on top of greying scalps, shuffling through crowds and feeling invisible, yearning for someone to thank them for their service. Or worse, haggard shells leaning against a brick wall, a cardboard sign propped on the sidewalk in front of them: Desert Storm Veteran—spare some change?

But what if we reframed what it means to be a veteran? What if instead of allowing our sons and daughters to simply fade away, we asked them to come home and build a legacy that would strengthen the foundation of our nation? Our communities face no shortage of problems, ranging from social division to income inequality to an increasing onslaught of natural disasters. If, as a nation, we issued a challenge to the three million men and women who have returned from tiresome wars in the Middle East to address these things, what might we unlock?

The stakes are high. My unit took some of the highest casualties of the wars during our time in both Iraq and Afghanistan. Yet when we returned home, we lost more men to their own hand than to the enemy overseas. Since 2012, more service members have died by suicide than in combat.*

It's a stunning statistic and a sobering rebuke—and many Americans have never heard it. This epidemic cannot be fully explained with clinical diagnoses of post-traumatic stress disorder. To understand, we must look more broadly to the dearth of purpose and self-worth some veterans experience upon return. Many enter communities that care little about their sacrifice and choose to treat them like liabilities, rather than the assets they are. The local minor-league baseball team will disguise a returning veteran as the mascot and surprise her family with a crowd-pleasing public reunion—an overplayed scene that gets local news anchors to peddle tropes about heroism and sacrifice. Yet that same veteran will walk from local business to local business begging for a job in management, only to be told that she lacks experience. Never mind that she commanded a supply company of two hundred soldiers tasked with

---

* Carol Giacomo, "Suicide Has Been Deadlier Than Combat for the Military," *New York Times*, November 11, 2019, www.nytimes.com/2019/11/01/opinion/military-suicides.html.

making daily runs to far-flung forward operating bases along highways riddled with IEDs.

Think about that for a moment. Imagine our country recruited you out of high school and invested hundreds of thousands of dollars into your training. We give you a uniform and a rifle and a rank. Perhaps most importantly, we give you a mission and a band of brothers and sisters that would do anything for you. We send you to war, where you fight for our flag, and, perhaps for the first time in your life, it feels like your existence matters. You execute a difficult job in impossible circumstances, gaining experience and confidence. You come home and we pin a medal on your chest and cheer for you at stadiums and arenas. But eventually that ends and your time in uniform is done. You take it off for the last time and the Army hands you a piece of paper and says, "Good luck, soldier." But before they've even finished wishing you good luck, they've turned their attention to the next body in a uniform, because they have a war to win. You walk off base and into your next chapter, eager and maybe a little scared. One thing is certain: your mission, community, and sense of identity have faded.

Stripped of this scaffolding, you might begin to feel listless and alone and fear that you are sinking like a battleship to the bottom of a harbor. Memories of the friends killed alongside you reoccur in your dreams. Perhaps you're plagued by a sense of failure after seeing the cost in blood and treasure of the U.S. military intervention in Iraq and Afghanistan while some of our communities at home rot in front of us. Despite having served more than most, you feel you still have a debt to pay.

What's more, civilian life confounds and frustrates you. Were people always so self-involved? Instead of protecting life and liberty, you're supposed to muster enthusiasm for socializing with your coworkers with an eye toward that promotion. But this new set of norms feels like a step in the wrong direction. It's hard to form bonds with people who are more interested in greasing the wheels of their career than forming a real brotherhood. You knew your fellow soldiers would die for you; you're fairly sure these people would plant their Italian loafer on your back as they stepped over you onto the ladder's next rung.

But there is hope in this battle. We can reignite a sense of purpose in our veterans by providing them a new mission that rivals their wartime sense of duty. In the decade since I've left the Marine Corps, I have seen countless men and women become better versions of themselves by serving with Team Rubicon in disaster zones around the world and here at home. Through this continued service, they have found within themselves an immutable sense of purpose and a tightly knit tribe. They gain these things not by focusing on themselves, but by turning their focus outward—on others. They don Team Rubicon's iconic grey uniform and help their neighbors restore order amid chaos. The mission gives them hope that their best days are before them, not rusting at the bottom of the sea, as they'd feared.

This story explores both the harrowing cost of military service and the path to healing upon return. On the most basic level, it's my memoir of returning from two bloody tours in Iraq and Afghanistan, founding Team Rubicon with no money or experience, and mobilizing over one hundred thousand volunteers to help communities on their worst day. On a higher level, this is the story of America's veterans and the battles they continue to fight. Some prevail; others do not.

I refuse to believe we are destined to fade into nothingness. Instead, our wartime experience should serve as the prologue to long, fulfilling lives, propelling us forward to become beacons of strength and leadership in our communities. Our nation finds itself in a battle for the narrative that will define an entire generation of men and women sent to fight.

Will we tell them that they are pitiful, empty shells of their former selves? Worthy of our sympathy and charity, but not capable of leading us? Or will America slam its gauntlet onto the table and issue a challenge—one that inspires this generation and flips the narrative, recognizing veterans as our best bet in restoring the America we love?

PART I

CHAPTER I

CROSSING THE RUBICON

I was halfway through Bolivia when my Marine buddy Tim called. "Charlie is dead," he said, no context required. We'd gotten to know Charlie in sniper school. He was a special operations Marine, and I spent the majority of sniper school in awe of him. He was a machine, invincible. He died in an ambush, Tim said. I'd later learn that he'd been shot through his lung while rushing forward to save some wounded Afghan allies. He'd still managed to drag the Afghans to safety. Later, his Silver Star citation would state that he fought ferociously until his final breath. He was a warrior, after all, he'd always said. And what do warriors do if they don't fight wars?

Charlie bled to death on some meaningless Afghanistan mountain-side. Meanwhile, when I received the news, I was half a world away drinking pisco sours in the Andes, my Marine Corps uniform taken off for the last time three months prior. I felt a touch of shame.

My girlfriend, Indra, who was with me, had never known Charlie, so she couldn't join me in mourning. It was my first suspicion that, now no longer in the Marines, I'd forevermore be grieving alone. I wasn't truly alone. Indra and I were fast in love, and back home in Iowa I had two supportive parents and three sisters. They were always there for me, eager to support in any way possible. But the reality was those people, who knew me better than anyone, no longer understood me. Iraq and Afghanistan had changed me.

I was one of the lucky ones. After four years of war, the tattoos on my shoulder and arm were the only scars of combat I bore. So many men I served with had come home with real scars. Scars that proved their commitment and sacrifice. Dozens came home in flag-draped coffins. Their sacrifice would never be in doubt. Had I done enough?

My decision to get out of the Marines was complicated. My deployments with the 2nd Battalion, 7th Marine Regiment (2-7), to Iraq and Afghanistan were challenging, and our unit took some of the highest casualties of both wars in 2007 and 2008. I was proud of my service but became conflicted about our progress toward a mission I couldn't easily define. The sense of urgency to go and fight our nation's enemies in foreign lands waned as I found myself in firefights with disenfranchised youth as often as with radical ideologues. Nonetheless, my sense of duty compelled me to consider reenlisting and going back overseas. After some quiet reflection, I decided that I didn't want war to define my life, and I chose to leave the Marine Corps on my own terms, rather than in a box escorted home on an empty cargo plane.

Though I knew I no longer wanted to be in the fight, I wasn't entirely sure what to do next. I took the standardized test for graduate business school programs and scored well, so I applied to some top MBA programs with the hope that two years of school would give me time and space to figure things out. After finishing my applications and anxious to put Iraq and Afghanistan in my rearview mirror, I disappeared to

South America with Indra. We crisscrossed the continent in planes, trains, and automobiles, immersing ourselves in history and culture. I relished not having to wonder if the foreign-speaking men and women smiling at me in restaurants were only being kind and generous because of the assault rifle strapped across my chest or the missile-laden jets I could call overhead. Yet the trip left me wondering if I was truly ready to become a civilian, especially after learning that Charlie was dead. Part of me missed having that rifle.

Back home in Los Angeles, I peeled off my damp gym clothes. I had the apartment to myself. Indra coanchored the morning news program at KABC Los Angeles and was a rising star in broadcast meteorology. Even as a young child, Indra knew she wanted to predict the weather and had spent her whole life in pursuit of that career. I admired her singular pursuit of that dream. I was twenty-seven years old and, no longer a Marine, totally unsure what to do with my life. Outwardly I projected confidence that after business school I would launch into a successful career, but inwardly I doubted I would ever find what Indra had: a job that felt like it was what I was put on this earth to do.

I turned on the TV and waited for the audio to come to life as I returned to the kitchen. Hunched over three frying eggs, I heard the first hint that my typical morning was about to take a turn.

". . . officials here are stating that initial estimates are as many as ten thousand people may have been killed in last night's earthquake, but a quick survey of the scene indicates that it could be many times more than that number . . ."

I slid the eggs onto a plate and moved over to the couch with a mug of coffee. Prior to going to bed the night before, I'd read headlines about an earthquake in Haiti—or was it Cuba?—but no journalists were yet on the ground to report with any accuracy. Now, as the sun was rising over

California, I watched a reporter sweating amid a pile of rubble. He motioned to the devastation behind him and continued, *"Experts estimate the earthquake was a magnitude 7.0, with an epicenter just outside the Haitian capital of Port-au-Prince."**

CNN began playing a shaky cell phone video. I took in the scene. Every building appeared to have had a 2,000-pound bomb dropped on it in an airstrike. Throngs of men, women, and children, their dark skin covered in chalky white powder, stumbled like zombies through the streets. They surged past the camera, desperate to get anywhere but where they were.

". . . aid organizations throughout the world are mobilizing their response units, but sources say an effective response might take days . . ."

I watched and watched and watched. The images—eerily reminiscent of my wartime experiences—cracked my hardened exterior. My heart broke for every infant I saw being rushed away in a mother's arms, and it broke again for every father I saw digging through rubble with his bare hands. There it was again, on channel after channel, along with instructions on how to text to donate. I looked at my phone, but felt so inadequate, so removed from the situation.

Chaos. Destruction. Hopelessness. It seemed . . . familiar. I reached for my phone and, clicking it on, noticed hours had passed. I looked at the eggs and coffee, untouched and long since cooled. I punched in the ten digits and waited. *". . . due to heavy call volume . . ."* And then, finally, a voice.

"Yes, ma'am. My name is Jake Wood. I just got out of the Marine Corps after four years and two tours. I'd like to go with your organization

---

* "Haiti in Ruins: A Look Back at the 2010 Earthquake," NPR, January 12, 2020, www.npr .org/sections/pictureshow/2020/01/12/794939899/haiti-in-ruins-a-look-back-at-the -2010-earthquake.

to Port-au-Prince. I can help you with any number of things and you won't have to babysit me. I've got all of the necessary equipment, my inoculations are up-to-date, and I can leave immediately."

"Thank you, sir, but we're not taking any volunteers right now. If I may direct you to our website, where you can make a donation..."

I hung up in despair. *I should do something. I must do something.* I had not felt an impulse this strong since waking up a decade earlier on September 11, 2001. I looked at the empty coffee mug, sitting atop an envelope. Inside the envelope was a rejection letter from Stanford Graduate School of Business. I picked the phone back up and dialed a familiar number. Clay Hunt was one of my best friends. He was smart and handsome, and wavered between foolish optimism and the belief that humanity had decayed beyond redemption. A restless youth, Clay had spent several years after high school bouncing between attending college, working at youth camps, and bumming on ski slopes before joining the Corps. Down his left forearm was a tattoo reading *Not All Who Wander Are Lost.* He wasn't the first person to use the phrase, but it fit him unusually well.

We'd served together in Iraq and Afghanistan and endured sniper school together as partners. That meant that for ten weeks we were never more than an arm's length away from each other. Clay had left the Marine Corps a few months before me and enrolled at a local university. Despite having deployed on the same tours and fought the same battles, our wartime experiences were different. Every warrior sees a different image through their scope. Similarly, our experiences after coming home seemed to be diverging. Clay was struggling to adapt, and his marriage was faltering. To be fair, having been out of the Corps for only two months, perhaps I hadn't had enough time to flounder. Perhaps it was only a matter of time. With my elbows on my knees, I held the phone against my head. After two rings, a familiar voice answered.

"What's up, Wood?"

"Clay, do you want to go to Haiti with me?"

"Uhh, well, I got school, but when were you thinking?" Clay asked. "Is Haiti even a nice place to visit?"

He had no idea what I was asking him to do. "Clay, turn on the news. Haiti got rocked yesterday by an earthquake. It's Fallujah down there."

"Oh. Sorry, man. What are you thinking? What are you trying to do?" Clay was always down for an adventure.

"I don't have much of a plan, but I know we can help if we can get there. I want to leave now, tonight. Get on the ground, set up shop. We can do triage, logistics, security . . . anything."

"Shit, I can't, man. Sorry. You know I'd be there if I could, but I'm leaving tomorrow for a wedding in Houston. My family would kill me if I skipped out."

"Damn. Alright, man. Well, I'm gonna run. I need to see if I can get someone to go with me."

"You know it. And call Tim—he's not doing anything up in St. Louis. Maybe he can go."

I found Tim's number.

"Well, well, well, if it isn't Mr. Jake Wood. Ladies and gentlemen—"

"Hey, Tim. Real quick—I'm trying to get a team of guys together to go to Haiti. You in?" I said, cutting him off before he could launch into his standard string of crude jokes.

"What's going on in Haiti?"

"Do none of my friends watch the news?" I said, maybe a little angrily.

"Whoa, sorry. I'm sorry some of us are going to school and doing something with our lives. I am going to ask you again, and you better respond nicely. What's going on in Haiti?"

I couldn't help but crack a smile. Tim was always a smart-ass. "Tim, Haiti got hit with an earthquake last night. They're saying as many as fifty thousand people might be dead, and it's complete chaos—looting, gangs, everything. I want to go down and help. You in?"

"Looting? Gangs? Hell yeah, I'm in. Just one thing—I don't have a passport."

My eyes widened. I never even considered that the U.S. military deploys millions of troops overseas, but never requires them to carry a passport. "You seriously don't have a passport?"

"Nope. Recent experiences have led me to hate other countries. You know that."

"Alright, man. Well, that's not going to work. I'll talk to you later." I hung up the phone and tossed it onto the couch, mentally assembling a list of people I could call. I tried my old college roommate, Jeff. We'd played football together at Wisconsin and Jeff was now a firefighter in Milwaukee.

"Woody, what's up, buddy?" he answered.

"Jeff, I can't stop watching what's going on down in Haiti. I'm calling to see if you want to go help." I held my breath, unsure whether to give up if Jeff said no.

"Sure, man. When do you want to leave?"

I breathed out sharply. Finally, I had a simple yes. For the next few minutes we confirmed and reconfirmed and triple confirmed that we were going to do this. After the call I grabbed my computer and logged onto Facebook. If Jeff and I were going to go to Haiti, we would need a few more people and some help paying for it. I clicked on my status update and hesitated, unsure what to write. A minute went by. Finally, I punched some keys.

ATTENTION *I am legitimately trying to find a way to get to Haiti to help with disaster relief. I think it will be possible to fly into the Dominican Republic and cross the border overland. IS ANYONE WILLING TO HELP?*

It wasn't Hemingway, but it felt clear enough. I clicked "post" and sat back, staring at the screen. Five minutes later, an unknown number called. "Hello?" I asked.

"Wood, it's McNulty." Thinking I'd misheard, I asked the caller to repeat himself. "McNulty," I heard again.

"Who?"

"Mc—Nulty," the voice said forcefully. I struggled to place the name. Then it hit me. William McNulty was a Marine I'd been put in contact with when I came home from Afghanistan. He'd had some business opportunities that he'd wanted to run by me. We hadn't spoken but for a few times, and that had been twelve months earlier.

"Oh, hey, man. What's going on?"

"I saw your Facebook post. I want in."

"Alright, you're in. We could use another Marine."

"So, what's the plan?"

I laughed. "I'm not gonna lie to you, William—I don't have a clue. They just shut down the airport, so my initial guess is we either get there by boat or we fly into the Dominican Republic and go overland. I figure we get as many medical supplies as we can, plus some tents and water purifiers, and we get down there to assess the situation. After that . . ." I let the silence speak for itself. William and I discussed plans and logistics for the next hour.

After getting off the phone, I walked into the bedroom and lifted the mattress off the bed frame. Underneath was my old patrol ruck. Next to the bag sat a pair of dusty, tan combat boots, a dog tag still laced into the left one. I grabbed all of it, swatting at the tops of the boots to knock the dust off.

Unbuckling the ruck, I turned it upside down. Out tumbled a pile of gear that I had considered selling to a surplus store—a tent, canteens, my combat knife, paracord, water purifiers and flashlights, among other items. Almost all of it bore traces of grime from Iraq and Afghanistan. Some things just never wash out.

I sat at my computer late into the night, attending to the myriad of details that piled up as the operation grew in complexity. Jeff added another fireman, Craig Parello—also a former Marine—to the team. William had secured lodging at a Jesuit compound in the middle of the city that was willing to let us use their facility as a base of operations in exchange for medical care and help with security. My girlfriend's brother-in-law, Ryan, offered to buy our plane tickets. I had plotted our method and details of transportation—fly to Santo Domingo, take a bus to the border checkpoint at Jimaní, cross on foot, and then secure local transportation on the other side. Our flight left in twenty-four hours.

William called again.

"This is getting big. I mean, we're raising money, we're building a team. People are following what we're doing." Friends were sharing our posts all across Facebook and donating funds to my personal PayPal account.

I leaned back. "Yeah, it's crazy."

"I think we should name it."

"Name what?"

"This, name this. I think that this has gotten big enough that we should give it a name, something to rally around."

I rubbed the stubble on my chin and looked at the ceiling. "Okay. Have any ideas?"

"I do. I just emailed you a list of names I debated using for the company I just incorporated. Open it up." I clicked on the email and looked over the list. There were about fifteen names. In true military fashion, there was a heavy emphasis on Latin words.

"I don't even know what half of these mean. Like this one, *Hastam*. What's that?"

"It's Latin for 'spear.'"

"Nope. How about this one—Rubicon?" I was only familiar with the term as it related to off-road vehicles.

"It has something to do with Caesar. I don't exactly remember the story behind it."

I typed the term into a search engine. "Alright, sounds like it was a river in ancient Rome . . . No Roman generals were allowed to cross it with their armies . . . Caesar marched his army across it and toppled Rome . . . Now used commonly to refer to a point of no return, as in 'crossing the Rubicon.'" I shuffled through papers on my desk until I found the map I'd printed. I traced my fingers along the thick black route I'd drawn from the Dominican Republic to Haiti, stopping it at a small border crossing named Jimaní. "That's it, man—that's the name. That's what we're doing! Jimaní sits on the edge of Haiti's largest lake, and the Artibonite River flows right out of it. That's our Rubicon."

I could practically hear William thinking. "I like it," he allowed.

"Operation Rubicon?" I asked.

"No, not 'operation.'" William paused. "Team. Team Rubicon. That's what it has to be, Team Rubicon. We're a team, not an operation."

"Alright, Team Rubicon it is."

We hung up, not knowing in that moment that the name we'd chosen would extend far beyond the four individuals packing their bags and preparing to leave at sunrise. Over the coming decade, Team Rubicon would scale to a size that none of us ever could have imagined and touch the lives of tens of thousands of people—survivors, veterans, and beyond.

* ● *

JIMANÍ, DOMINICAN REPUBLIC

"Listen up! Everyone gather up here at the lead truck for a patrol brief," I shouted above the clamor. Our Toyota Hilux pickups were parked outside a small, nondescript government building, an anxious crowd seething around us.

McNulty looked up from his BlackBerry, where he was receiving a steady stream of unclassified intelligence reports from friends in the Marine Corps, each one grimmer than the last.

My mind raced with the mission's parameters. Enough food and water for five days. Medical supplies for an estimated hundred patients. Uncertainty around reports of violent criminal networks exploiting the vacuum of a defunct government. No quick reaction force. That last one was the most unsettling. The moment we crossed the wire, we were on our own. There would be no one on the other end of the radio if we found ourselves in trouble. Then I realized we didn't even have radios.

I looked up and down the convoy. All our equipment and supplies were secure in the backs of the vehicles, cross-loaded in case one of the trucks got separated—or worse, hijacked—en route to our destination.

The team assembled around the truck's hood. The white dust around us was as thick as gun smoke. I found my waterproof notebook and retrieved a map that I'd torn out of the back of the *Wall Street Journal* on my flight down.

"Alright, just to review. We are going to proceed through this gate here"—I extended my arm and pointed beyond the truck—"and make our way along this main road here." I traced the route along the map. "We expect this road to be heavily congested with traffic in both directions, and there are reports of armed bandits. I have instructed our drivers to blow through any nongovernmental checkpoint—we're not stopping for anyone that doesn't have both a badge and a gun." I looked around at all seven faces.

"Maybe we should stay on this side of the border and set up a clinic where it's safer?" Dr. Eduardo said, anxiety giving him a stammer. Jeff had met Eduardo for the first time on his flight down to the Dominican Republic, and Jeff's infectious enthusiasm convinced Eduardo to join our small team.

"No chance. We're pushing forward," I replied. "Doc, this is your last chance. Once we cross that line"—I again pointed toward the gate—"we are committed. The team won't turn back." Eduardo nodded his head, tacitly reenlisting onto the team. I spent the next five minutes briefing the team on our movement into Port-au-Prince before turning it over to Mark Hayward.

William had met Mark while waiting for his own flight to the Dominican Republic, sitting on the tarmac at Dulles International Airport. After recognizing William's camouflage pants, Mark leaned across the shuttle bus and quietly whispered, "Semper Fi." He asked William if he was going to Haiti. When William replied he was headed down with a group of former Marines, Mark introduced himself as a retired Army Special Forces medic and current emergency room physician assistant with experience in Haiti. Mark said he was heading to Haiti as well, and looking for a team of guys he could trust. I'd later learn that Mark's trust didn't come easy, and while speaking to William he was frantically emailing friends in the intelligence community to see what they could dig up on a "William McNulty" or this "Team Rubicon" he'd never heard of.

"Mark, can you please give a quick refresher on our medical emergency plan?" I asked.

"Sure thing, boss." Mark stepped into the circle and held up a homemade medical kit. "Alright, as you'll recall, last night we made each of you an IFAK, or individual first aid kit. The primary purpose of this kit is bleed control. Should this team sustain casualties, this will be our first line of defense." Mark was matter-of-fact, as if telling us our catered lunch might not arrive until after twelve thirty. "Inside you will find a tourniquet and various pressure bandages. I will serve as the primary medic for Vic One. Dr. Griswell here—" Mark gestured to Dr. Griswell, a Vietnam-era veteran and emergency room physician I met at Santo Domingo's baggage claim. "Doc will serve as the primary medic for Vic Two."

Griswell nodded enthusiastically, hands on hips. Unlike Eduardo, who was dressed like a hiker on the Appalachian Trail, Doc Griswell wore light blue hospital scrubs. With highlighted hair and a hoop earring, he didn't fit the mold of a grizzled former Army military police officer. But when he approached me at the airport, he'd been quick to inform me he'd responded to numerous disasters with the Red Cross and could handle life in the field.

"Thanks, Mark." I looked up at the sky. Getting to the Haitian border had taken longer than we'd anticipated, and I began worrying about dwindling daylight. Making the trip in was dangerous enough. Doing it after dark carried incalculable risk. "Alright, everyone know their vehicle assignments?" Heads nodded. "Okay. Mount up!"

As I was walking to my truck, someone grabbed my arm. It was Jim Boynton, a Jesuit brother from Michigan who had recently been assigned a teaching job in a village north of Port-au-Prince. William, a graduate of a Jesuit high school in Chicago, had called and arranged for Jim to meet us at the border to serve as our guide.

"Jake," Jim said.

"Yes, Brother Jim?"

"You're not going to get me killed, are you?" Jim had already demonstrated a fun-loving personality, but when Mark had given a class the night before on how to apply a tourniquet to a hemorrhaging femoral artery, Jim looked like he'd seen a ghost. Jim was a teacher, not a warrior. "Actually, let me rephrase that. Please don't get me killed."

I mustered as much confidence as I could. "Jim, I promise you, everything is going to be alright." I turned away, not wanting my eyes to betray my growing unease. Hopping into the bed of the truck, I smacked the roof, signaling for the driver to roll out.

As the sun sank, our team crossed its Rubicon. The truck's tires chewed the white rock into dust as our convoy approached Port-au-Prince. We encountered more and more Haitians walking in the opposite direction, toward the Dominican Republic, until finally we had to physically remove people from the backs of our trucks. The sea of arms and hands was pinching, grabbing, yearning for something, anything. Children put their hands to their mouths or patted their stomachs in hunger. Women held up their sick children and begged us for medicine. Many of the men eyed our supplies longingly. "Look the men in the eye so you don't appear weak or vulnerable, but don't do anything that can be misconstrued as a threat," I said to the team from the truck bed. "If they ask for handouts, tell them it's for the embassy so they assume we're on official business."

My mind flashed back to 2007 when I'd landed at an airbase in Iraq. Another Marine unit had picked us up and convoyed us through the city of Fallujah, scene of the fiercest battle of the war. Like Fallujah, Port-au-Prince appeared to have had heavy artillery and 2,000-pound bombs dropped on it for weeks on end.

Driving farther, we reached the city. The scope and magnitude of the destruction increased with every city block until, eventually, it was absolute. Wails of agony emanated from unseen victims. The rancid smell of death and decay hung in the air like a putrid mass grave—which Port-au-Prince had just become. "Dear God," I muttered. Survivors were clawing through the rubble. Even now, four days after the earthquake, they were calling out the names of loved ones, shouting into the cracks and crevices.

The congestion forced our vehicles to slow down, and another wave of people tried to climb into our truck beds. "Push them back! Push them back!" I yelled, planting my palm firmly on the chest of a teenage boy while holding on to the packs behind me. Our eyes connected momentarily. He was terrified. I pushed him backward, where he was swallowed by the crowd. "Don't give out any supplies! We could start a riot!"

Finally, with the sun nearly at the horizon, we reached the Jesuit compound we'd arranged for shelter. William and I pounded on the sheet metal door and shouted the only thing we could think to say that wouldn't have someone on the other side open fire on us: "Open up! The Americans are here!" After a few moments of uncertainty, a series of rusty bolts rotated and slid back, and the gate swung back a few inches. Two bloodshot eyeballs appeared, looking us up and down. Once. Twice. Three times. Finally, the gate swung all the way open.

The Jesuit compound, known as a novitiate, was expansive. It served as an academy of sorts for aspiring Jesuits. A quick walk around the perimeter revealed it to be well secured, with a high exterior wall topped with barbed wire. Perhaps more importantly, it had a working fresh-water well, crucial to our survival, but potentially detrimental if it became widely known and people outside became more desperate. We pitched camp in the novitiate's open field, erecting tents and establishing an area for supplies. As the light waned, Doc Griswell and Mark tended to our first patient, a little girl with a broken leg. They had no anesthesia. I used a cheap, battery-powered lantern to check and recheck the lines and stakes of our various tents, trying to remain focused as the blood-curdling scream of a young girl having a limb-threatening fracture set cut through the air.

I found one tent stake that needed to be pounded farther, and I hammered it until it disappeared into the ground, my jaw tight.

We had arrived.

• • •

When people ask me how Team Rubicon was formed, I often tell them it was by accident. The organization, I say, wasn't conceived on a conference room whiteboard, or as a class project for business school. It was born out of an impulse to act. But that's still not the full story.

We didn't go to Haiti expecting to launch and build an industry-disrupting disaster response organization. Our ambitions were much humbler. Our hope was just to help as many people as we could for as long as we could. After that, we would come home and return to our normal lives, perhaps recounting our adventure to friends or strangers at dinner parties.

But while in Haiti we began to sense that Team Rubicon could be something much bigger. That sense came in moments when our experience as military veterans helped us rise to the occasion, like when one of our teams discovered a small community trapped at the bottom of a steeply cut valley. Before the earthquake, crudely built homes had clung to the valley's walls, only to turn into a deadly avalanche of cinder block, tin roofing, and human bodies when the earth shook. Hearing the desperate shouts from below, we packed as many supplies as possible onto our backs and gingerly climbed our way down. Or like when we called to mind the counterinsurgency manual we'd used in Iraq and Afghanistan and relied on its instructions to set up a triage clinic in a crime-ridden corner of the city, liaising with and empowering local leaders.

We certainly didn't anticipate that Haiti would be a spark for a veteran community returning from the Middle East, war weary and searching for purpose. Those veterans, once warriors, would serve as the kindling that would fuel a roaring fire dedicated to bringing warmth and comfort to people who've had their lives upended by natural disasters and humanitarian crises. I remember watching my friend Clay, who would join us later, fashion rudimentary crutches out of tree limbs. A Texas flag bandana tied around his neck, Clay used duct tape to weld the two pieces together. When he handed the crutches over to Mark to give to his patient, Clay's face spoke volumes. He was at his best when he was in service to others.

That spirit of service—unflinching in its effort to make a difference—is perhaps what has distinguished Team Rubicon above all else.

So, while we often say that Team Rubicon began in Haiti, I would argue that it really began when millions of men and women raised their hand to serve their country overseas, and in the process learned that service was in their blood.

CHAPTER 2

MOMENTS AND DECISIONS

Nearly three million American men and women have deployed to Iraq and Afghanistan since 2001.* All of their efforts are woven into the tapestry of the longest-running wars in America's history. Many of them fought. Some of them bled. All of them lost something—to be there for the birth of their son, the opportunity to build a career, their limbs or their sight or their hearing, their life. Each of them volunteered, and in doing so they left behind family and friends and futures unknown.

My decision to enlist wasn't spontaneous, nor was it a complete surprise to those who loved me. It was the culmination of a series of moments in my life, beginning when I was seven years old and first discovered the true meaning of evil and the definition of hero. Oftentimes we don't recognize these moments for what they are when they happen.

---

* Niall McCarthy, "2.77 Million Service Members Have Served on 5.4 Million Deployments Since 9/11," *Forbes*, March 20, 2018, www.forbes.com/sites/niallmccarthy/2018/03/20/2-77-million-service-members-have-served-on-5-4-million-deployments-since-911-infographic/#6c38f37d50db.

But they shape us. They define us without our knowing. And sometimes we wake up and realize we are trapped in a version of our life that our moments didn't intend for us. Only then can we look back and appreciate those moments for what they were—the universe showing us our life's book and affording us the opportunity to read how the story should end.

Eventually I enlisted in the Marine Corps because the seven-year-old version of me whispered in my ear about a moment we had shared and compelled me to do what my heart thought was right: join my fellow citizens in the fight of our generation. That decision became yet another moment that would forever define my life.

● ● ●

AUSTRIA, 1989

My father, mother, two sisters, and I trudged uphill in near silence, unusual for us. At seven years, I was old enough to know that something terrible had taken place here, but young enough to need time to figure it out. The towering stone walls and imposing guard towers were not unlike the castles I'd seen during our time in Austria. I always looked at those castles and dreamt of kings and princes and knights. Of noble armies defending the land or marching off for the Crusades. I'd often imagine myself among their ranks, my polished armor shining bright in the Middle Eastern sun, the walled city of Jerusalem rising in the distance, behind which sat God and country's enemy. I would pick up sticks and they would become swords, and I would spend hours in the yard clanging make-believe steel against make-believe steel, locked in mortal combat.

But this wasn't a castle. The high stone walls and towers were not designed to keep unwanted people out. They were designed to keep unwanted people in. This place was called Mauthausen, my father told me on the car ride over.

"What's a Mauthausen?" I asked naively.

"It's a place that the Nazis built to send the Jews. It was a terrible place."

"So why are we going?"

"Because you and your sisters should understand what happened there."

Walking up the ramp, I kicked a rock. It skipped off the road and careened down the rocky hill, breaking the stillness. My father shot me a stern glance behind thick-rimmed glasses. He didn't have to say anything; I knew I wouldn't be kicking any more rocks.

We proceeded through the gate into a wide-open courtyard, eventually walking into a windowless room with a wall of red bricks in the middle, rising from the floor to the ceiling. I heard my mother stifle a gasp and looked anxiously around to see what was upsetting her.

"These are the ovens," my mother murmured to my father. I glanced back at the bricks. They sure were funny-looking ovens.

"This doesn't look like a kitchen," I observed.

"Honey, this is where the Nazis would burn the bodies of Jews who died."

A chill—the growing awareness of evil—crept upward from my toes.

We shuffled past chains, gallows, and gas chambers. Each stop revealed a universal truth to a young boy: humans are capable of unimaginable horror.

When we reached the final exhibit, a strange expression spread across my father's face, the way he might look if he was stepping back to admire a successfully completed home project. I recognized it as a good look but didn't know at the time that it was pride. He read aloud from a plaque the story of the camp's liberation by U.S. Army soldiers who'd battled their way through Nazi lines. I looked in awe at the photographs of Americans riding through the gates of Mauthausen on top of tanks, skeletal prisoners reaching for them with gratitude and relief. There were pictures of Army medics empathetically treating prisoners on death's doorstep, and soldiers gingerly carrying out the bodies of those who could not hold on so that they could be buried with dignity.

My father paused his reading. He reached up under his glasses and wiped his eyes. "Thank God for such men," he said.

We walked down the hill in silence. Halfway down, I tugged on my father's arm. "Dad, when I grow up I want to join the Army."

He continued walking. "Let's hope there are no Mauthausens when you grow up, Jake."

· ● ·

TWELVE YEARS LATER
MADISON, WISCONSIN

The alarm grew louder as my mind resurfaced from sleep. Reaching out, I slapped the clock clumsily. In the silence I rolled onto my back and stared at the popcorn ceiling. My entire body ached. My shoulders, back, hips, and knees all protested as I pushed myself up and swung my legs out of bed. I rubbed my eyes and sat there, waiting for my body to wake up.

It was still early fall and I already felt like I'd been in fifty car crashes. I had spent the entire summer on campus working out with the football team and was bigger, faster, and stronger than I'd ever been. But nothing really prepares an eighteen-year-old to repeatedly smash into an All-American defensive tackle. During the first week of camp, when only incoming freshmen were practicing, I'd held my own, even excelled. But once the varsity team showed up, I learned what I was in for. I'll never forget lining up for the first time against Wendell Bryant, a future first-round draft pick. I was on the scout team, running offensive plays against the starting defense. Wendell was lined up at tackle. When the ball was snapped, Wendell exploded off the line and hit me so hard that I was sure he'd knocked my teeth loose. As I stumbled backward, Wendell ripped my jersey forward with his hands, whipsawing me onto the ground. I swear he stepped on my back on his way past.

Four weeks later, I stood up tenderly, pulled on my Wisconsin Badgers football sweatshirt, and walked down to the cafeteria for breakfast. The coaches wanted me to gain another fifteen pounds; eating was less a luxury than a chore.

Normally the room was abuzz with conversation and laughter, but this morning it felt like a funeral wake. A large group of students huddled in front of the television. One sat in a chair, arms tightly crossed over her chest, rocking back and forth.

"What's going on?" I asked. No one answered. I looked at the screen. Smoke billowed from a building in lower Manhattan. *Was that ... yes, the World Trade Center. What's going on?* Footage of bewildered New Yorkers wandering the streets ran side by side with anchors in studios telling America that a plane had struck the World Trade Center. Suddenly one anchor reached up and inserted his earpiece more forcefully to listen to an unseen producer. His demeanor shifted from stoic and concerned to shocked and terrified.

"Ladies and gentlemen," he said, "we've just been informed that a second plane has been flown into the World Trade Center. It would appear these events are not accidents, but rather deliberate acts of terrorism." The station cut to footage of an airplane effortlessly piercing the steel facade of the south tower. The cafeteria erupted. Many in the room were from New York and New Jersey; some even had relatives who worked at the towers.

31

We'd soon learn that a plane had hit the Pentagon and that another was hijacked over Pennsylvania.

We were at war.

I watched as firefighters jumped off big red trucks and ran into the burning World Trade Center. I imagined them having to run up all those stairs in all that equipment, and suddenly my aching muscles ached a little less. Down below, police officers worked to keep the crowds safe and calm, though their faces betrayed their own unease. *Thank God for such men,* I thought.

No longer hungry, I retreated to my room. A year prior, as a senior in high school, I'd received a letter from Iowa senator Chuck Grassley nominating me for a prestigious appointment to the United States Military Academy at West Point. I'd swelled with pride, knowing how proud my father would be. Staring at the letter, I knew I'd soon face the most consequential choice of my life. I put the letter in a drawer on a stack of other letters—offers of full athletic scholarships to places like Stanford, Nebraska, Iowa State . . . and Wisconsin.

Perhaps I made the wrong decision, I wondered as the television played images of fighter jets scrambling to defend America's skies.

* ● *

FOUR YEARS LATER

Leaning back with my eyes closed, my helmet *thunked* the wooden locker behind me. In an adjacent room showers were springing to life, their hiss a welcome white noise.

I reflected on my football career. It wasn't what I'd hoped for. I chose Wisconsin as a senior in high school because it had the best offensive line program in the country. It was a veritable factory for producing NFL draft picks at my position. I walked onto campus a highly touted recruit but would leave just a two-time varsity letter winner who never really lived up to his potential. The injuries didn't help. I'd blown out both my shoulders numerous times and had one reconstructed. It also didn't help that the team recruited the country's top offensive line prospect during my sophomore year. The moment Joe Thomas stepped on campus I knew my shot at NFL riches was over. The future NFL Hall of Famer would carry on the Wisconsin legacy, not me.

I stared at the helmet on my lap, trying to accept that I'd just played my last football game—a bitter loss to Georgia in a New Year's Day bowl. Lost in thought, I failed to see Joe walk over. "It's been fun playing with you, Woody. What's next?"

Joe probably assumed I'd just take my business degree and enter the business world. But earlier that spring I'd committed to a much different plan. I was done ignoring my childhood desire to serve. I'd gotten good at silencing that voice: I made excuse after excuse for why I should head to class or practice instead of Iraq or Afghanistan with my fellow Americans. I had a flag sticker on my car and supported the troops. I was doing my part, right? But there were moments when I felt guilt watching, say, a line of uniformed Americans make their way across the tarmac, bags slung over their shoulders, to board a plane headed overseas.

Then, the previous April, while visiting back home in Iowa, I saw a headline scroll across the bottom of the television: "Former Arizona Cardinal Pat Tillman Killed in Afghanistan."

I didn't need to be told who Pat Tillman was. Fellow football players knew his story well. After September 11, he'd left behind a multimillion-dollar NFL contract and enlisted alongside his brother with no fanfare. The station flashed a photo of Pat in his Army uniform. His chiseled jawline was tight, his eyes fierce. I was with family when the news broke, and, sensing emotions that I could not control, I excused myself and took the stairs two at a time up to my bedroom.

I locked eyes with myself in the mirror, pulsing with shame. Pat Tillman was the man I'd dreamt of becoming. The type of man who answered the call. Who gave without counting the cost. How had I become a young man concerned only with enriching himself? Where Pat had been selfless, I had been self-centered. Where Pat took action, I was happy to stand on the sidelines. Where he found courage, I found fear.

Staring at my reflection in the mirror, I made a decision that would forever change my life.

Back in the stadium's locker room, I looked up at Joe. "I'm joining the Marines."

• ● •

I enlisted in the Marine Corps infantry, intent on doing my part. I would serve for five or ten years, I thought, and then get out and get on with my life. I didn't appreciate then just how dramatically this decision would change my life.

In joining the Marines, I embraced a legacy that stretched back two centuries. In the Marine Corps, we're taught something called the Rifleman's Creed. During boot camp, drill instructors would sometimes make us recite it in bed as we held our rifles before lights out. The creed starts like this:

> *This is my rifle. There are many like it, but this one is mine.*
> *My rifle is my best friend. It is my life. I must master it as*
>   *I master my life.*
> *Without me, my rifle is useless. Without my rifle, I am useless.*

And so it goes. The creed reinforces that only two things will keep Marines alive on the battlefield: their rifle and the Marines on their left and right. I learned that lesson over the next four years as I served two bloody tours in Iraq and Afghanistan.

It's no surprise that all Marine rifles are alike. They are the same caliber, have the same barrel length, the same range, the same lethality. But they're also unique. Each has its own serial number, memorized as keenly as its owner's blood type or social security number. Each rifle shoots just a little differently, as the rifling in its barrel erodes with each round fired. Of course, they also get their own unique dings and scratches. There are many rifles, but only one is yours.

Upon leaving the Corps, I turned in my rifle for the last time. In the decade since, I've often reflected on the journey my rifle and I traveled together. Boring stretches on watch, long patrols under moonlit nights, hellacious gunfights. Sometimes I tell those stories—to my family, my friends, sometimes just to myself. And I've come to realize that my story of service is like my rifle. There are many like it, but only one is mine.

I joined three million of my fellow Americans in the War on Terror. My story is not that different from theirs. Sure, I might have served in a different branch, in different cities, or in a different role, but we all served the same mission, all for the same flag. We all came home and wondered what was next, what our story would become after war. Some of us picked up the pen and wrote the story of our lives after war; others waited for their story to be written for them. I chose to write mine.

This is my story. There are many like it, but this one is mine. Without me, my story is useless. Without my story, I am useless.

CHAPTER 3

POOF. THAT'S THE
SOUND THEY MAKE

War is hell. At least that's what those of us who have seen it are supposed to say.

Is war hell? Yes, but not only for the reasons people assume. They know about its outer circles: complex ambushes and insider attacks and young limbs vaporizing in the summer twilight. Those moments are hell, but they are easy to overcome because we can fight them together. We were trained for them. The Marines on our left and right will close ranks and lock shields like the Spartans of old. Our platoon leaders will shuffle down the line and slap us on our helmets, directing our fires and offering words of encouragement. War is almost easy when it resembles the hell we trained for.

The mission of the Marine Corps rifle squad is simple: *To locate, close with, and destroy the enemy by fire and maneuver, or to repel the enemy assault by fire and close combat.* That mission, however, collapses when the enemy can't be located. When he melts into the countryside or hides among a crowded marketplace. Or, when he is feeling more sinister, fights behind children thrust forward as human shields. We weren't prepared for that hell, because that wasn't in the movies or the training manuals. No one had told us about this darker underbelly.

But those are not the only circles of hell. We also faced stretches of mind-numbing boredom and dangerous incompetence. The long stretches of nothingness, pockmarked by violent combat, wreak havoc on young Marines' limbic systems, driving them toward mental and emotional exhaustion. These experiences are layered atop inexplicable decisions made by unseen politicians and generals, governing our hell from their angelic perch ten thousand miles away. Those decisions result in ridiculous rules of engagement, or inadequate equipment, or steak and lobster night at the big forward operating bases. Because steak and lobster win wars.

Travel deeper and one uncovers the maddening reality of a muddled mission, complete with unclear objectives and end states. Overseas, troops stumble into this ring of hell like a complex ambush and quickly learn they can't fight their way out. By 2007 and 2008, the years of my wars, we looked with envy toward those who had fought in the invasions of Afghanistan and Iraq in 2001 and 2003. Those Marines had phase lines and objectives and timelines. They could capture cities and raise flags and cheer their victories. Of course, they didn't capture bin Laden or find weapons of mass destruction, and that was probably hard for them, but at least they still had hope that those things were possible.

No, my wars lacked all those things that bring closure. That bring victory. We were simply there. We joked that we were winning when we left, but a decade later, with Americans still dying on the ground in both countries, that joke has become harder to chuckle at. We clung to clichés to make it easier. We'd say we were fighting for each other, not for some ambiguous mission or the politicians and generals back home. Perhaps a cliché, but it was true. Even when it was hard to define what our job was, we didn't fight any less fiercely or bleed any less freely. We were Marines, and we would never let the Corps down.

Eventually we were brought home. When they pinned medals on our chests and told us we'd written ourselves into the annals of Marine Corps history, we assumed hell was behind us. Most of us left the Marine Corps after a couple of tours. Not because we were angry or bitter. We were just tired, and the long march to victory extended beyond the horizon.

We took off our uniforms for the last time and put those medals in a drawer. Justifiably proud, our heads were high and our eyes clear when we walked off base toward our next chapter.

That's when War sprung his final ambush. War doesn't let you walk away, many of my brothers and sisters learned. It stalks some long after, hiding in the shadows of their mind. Some wanted to call all of it post-traumatic stress disorder. "You were in intense combat, so you must be fucked up," they would say to some, eagerly scribbling prescriptions for a cocktail of powerful drugs. A lazy and negligent approach that often did more harm than good.

Drugs don't cure survivor's guilt. "Why did Johnny die, and I live?" is every combat veteran's daily meditation. Steel bracelets became the scarlet letters of combat veterans, their shiny surface etched with the names and dates of friends killed in action. The anniversaries of those deaths are observed at nondescript tombstones with six-packs of beer. "Only the dead have seen the end of war," I once read—perhaps another cliché, but also true.

After the Corps many of us would return to our hometowns. Some married high school sweethearts; others went to college or pursued careers. Almost all of us discovered that life had lost its flavor. The sense of purpose we'd previously felt was missing, and our newfound nine-to-five couldn't replace it. Family and friends from our past had moved on and couldn't understand why we couldn't do the same. And when we looked in the mirror we no longer swelled with pride. Our sense of identity, so closely tied to the Corps and its mission, was gone.

At night, when we closed our eyes, we yearned for war.

• ● •

FEBRUARY 18, 2007
AL-ANBAR PROVINCE, IRAQ

Poof. That's the sound they make. Or so I'd heard. I read it was called auditory exclusion. It was some physiological magic trick your body performed in combat. During attacks, your body would narrow your ear canals. Booms became poofs, bangs became pops. After only two weeks in Iraq I had yet to truly experience it and, frankly, I wasn't sure I believed it.

I was in a Humvee in Iraq's al-Anbar Province with the 2nd Battalion, 7th Marine Regiment, or 2-7 for short. Two-Seven was a historic battalion, best known for its actions at the battle for the Chosin Reservoir in the Korean War. It was 2007, and 2-7 was now deployed as part of America's surge strategy. It was an attempt to pacify a deteriorating Iraq by flooding it with five additional brigades of troops and employing a new strategy: counterinsurgency, or COIN. Developed by General David Petraeus, COIN required American troops to build relationships with locals, show restraint in the use of force, and eventually apply pressure for insurgent groups to lay down their arms by reducing their influence over local populations.

Outside of Fallujah, in al-Anbar, we found ourselves fighting a three-way war. Al-Qaeda in Iraq, or AQI, had deeply entrenched itself even after their brutal defeat in the Second Battle of Fallujah. Likewise, local Sunnis, many of them Baathists, were organizing into a highly effective insurgency. We'd fight each group weekly, and they'd fight each other just as frequently. That meant that 2007 would become the deadliest year of the war in Iraq, with an estimated 6,700 insurgents killed—almost twice as many as the prior year and over three times as many as the following year. Of course, that came at a cost, as the U.S. military lost 904 Americans the same year, the highest total of the war. Tonight would be more of the same.

I looked out the window and scanned the roadside. The last rays of daylight glittered off trash strewn everywhere. *Stay alert. Watch for that copper wire on the road. What are the chances I see an IED before it sends me packing?* I wondered. *Even if I do see it, even if I do spot it in all this trash, it'll probably be too late. The boom will have already hit.*

Just then, a glint of light. My eyes snapped shut and my heart missed a beat. My shoulders tensed and my asshole clenched. A wave of nausea overcame me. The backs of my eyelids became a projector screen as my hippocampus assembled and played a slideshow of my life. A moment passed. I realized there had been no boom. Not even a poof. The fear of death faded. My limbs tingled. I was alive. One at a time my eyes unglued themselves and fluttered open. My heart rate returned to normal. *Lub-dub. Lub-dub.* Fifty-four lub-dubs per minute.

It took several minutes before my ass began to unpucker. The sphincter was always the last physiological response to normalize. The subconscious fear of shitting oneself in front of comrades is so strong and innate that the muscle refuses to take chances. *Probably better that way,* I mused.

"Arguello, did you see that tire on the side of the road? I swear on my life there was a wire." Arguello, reading glasses perched on his nose, squinted over the Humvee's steering wheel and shook his head.

Tires always raised suspicion. Bad guys loved planting bombs in tires. The bombs were called IEDs, or improvised explosive devices. But it wasn't just tires. They also loved planting bombs in boxes and bags of rice. In the ground and under bridges. They would plant them in broken-down cars and dog carcasses. They came in all shapes and sizes—triple-stacked one-five-fives, double-stacked eighty-ones, single-lay anti-tank mines with fifteen pounds of HME (homemade explosives). They could be remote detonated with pagers, cell phones, two-way radios, garage door openers, or car alarms. They could be command detonated with copper wire. They could be victim initiated with pressure plates, anal beads, Christmas tree lights, or trip wire. They could be fuel-enhanced to burn victims or use Iranian-designed shaped charges to penetrate armor. They could be stuffed with nuts and bolts for secondary shrapnel or made slightly smaller to intentionally maim instead of kill. They could be strapped to a young girl's chest and ridden up to us on a bike. They had a host of federal-agency-sounding names—IED, VBIED, SVBIED, RCIED, FEIED. All I had seen was a tire and a wire. And it terrified me.

Up ahead, Howey's truck turned onto an unmarked road and drove toward a bridge. Normally we'd get out and scan the bridge for IEDs, but we were already late for our mission. The mission itself was mundane. Another platoon had been out on a patrol and one of its Humvees got stuck in the mud. My squad was on QRF, or quick reaction force, and was called out to provide additional security and assistance in getting it pulled out. It was hardly the door-kicking adventure I'd signed up for.

Without warning, the truck in front of ours was outlined by a brief, fierce orange glow. A second later I heard a poof. Just ahead, Williams's truck rolled gently to a halt. The brake lights looked like haunting red eyes against the plume of white smoke that rose into the night sky.

"What the hell?" I growled. I paused. I couldn't hear my own voice. In fact, I couldn't hear much of anything. As if someone had pressed a "mute" button.

In the turret, Bullard dropped down into a squat. The volume dialed up to a dull roar as he screamed, "—y're hit, they're hit! They hit an IED!"

FUCK. I pulled the latch and plowed my shoulder into the Humvee's heavy steel door. It swung open, and my nostrils filled with the smell of cordite and smoke and just a hint of flesh, though I didn't know that at the time because I'd never smelled scorched flesh. My boots hit the ground as a wave of heat blasted my face like a furnace. I twisted rearward to pull my rifle from inside the cabin, while yelling for Arguello to move the truck forward and left so we could cover a sector of fire beyond the burning vehicle. The flames and the shadows and the sparks all danced leisurely. A second ticked by, maybe two. A third, perhaps, but not likely.

I sprinted toward the wreckage, yelling at Doc Campanali to follow. As I ran I could see Latcher ahead, struggling, willing himself out of the smoking and burning turret. On the passenger side I could see Payne pulling and kicking a door. On his second attempt he stumbled back, and Sergeant Rosenberger, whom we called Rose, emerged, seemingly thrown forward by an impossibly thick cloud of smoke. Rose staggered toward me, seemingly unaware that his lower leg was shredded. At the Humvee Latcher finally escaped, hurling himself over the thick armor of the machine gun turret and onto the roof. My lungs burned as I reached the halfway point, weighed down by gear and dread. Payne and Latcher were dragging Howey out of the driver's seat. They collapsed only a few feet off the road, still within the radius of the truck's oxygen-consuming blaze. Getting back up to their feet, they just stood there looking down at Howey. *Come on, guys,* I screamed inside my head. *Start working on him! Get your kits out, grab some bandages, check his breathing. Just do something.*

I danced through burning puddles of oil and fuel on the bridge before I reached them. Payne outranked me, but his eyes were glazed over from the blast. He was in no condition to take charge. I heard myself issuing instructions. "Latcher, get security fifteen meters down that way, make sure no one tries to hit us again." I turned to Payne. "Payne, do me a favor and go down this little road along the canal twenty-five meters and do the same. Let me know if you see anything."

"I'm on it."

Kneeling beside Howey's motionless form, I fumbled with my first aid kit. My eyes, burning and tearing from the smoke, slowly came into focus on his face.

"Oh my God," I muttered as I slumped backward onto my rear. "Oh Jesus."

Doc arrived behind me. Gasping for air over my shoulder, he asked, "How is he? What's he need?"

"Nothing."

"Nothing?"

"Nothing. He's fucking dead."

I felt Doc's hand on my shoulder. "Let me have a look," he said gently. Howey's legs were covered in blood, missing flesh. His right arm lay at an impossible angle, mangled and charred. His flak jacket was scorched black and torn open, revealing a chest peppered with shrapnel. But all that still looked vaguely human. It was his face that no longer bore any resemblance to the carefree California kid we all knew. The blast had warped the size and shape of his skull but cruelly left his features intact, so that what remained looked humanoid, but not human. He looked monstrous and disgusting. It was an image that would intrude upon my thoughts in subsequent years, visiting at times that seemed natural, like every February 18, but more often in moments that made no sense. Like on a conference call or on the treadmill. Or during the birth of my daughter. Sometimes I would curse the image and the pain that it brought. Other times I would embrace it. The pain reminded me I was alive. Of course, that meant Howey was dead.

Williams and I dragged Howey's body off the road and helped Latcher and Payne with security. The bridge was now engulfed in flames and impassable, cutting us off from the rest of our squad and leaving us vulnerable to a secondary attack. We waited for what seemed like hours while the shadows cast by the fire mercilessly haunted us. Off in the distance the sound of helicopters grew louder and louder. Suddenly the *whomp-whomp-whomp* of a CH-46 filled the air above. The rotor wash caught me full blast and I struggled to stay upright.

A stranger emerged from one of the birds, running awkwardly as he battled the violent rotor wash. When he got closer, I could see that he'd pulled his flight suit out of the laundry today at Camp Fallujah. I glanced down at myself and then over at Williams. We were filthy. Mud and soot and blood covered us from head to toe, caked in layers on our uniform and our gear and our skin. The rivers of cold sweat running down our faces had formed a patchwork pattern in the filth.

"You boys alright?"

"Yeah, but we're ready to get the hell out of here."

"Where's the litter?"

"Over there with our corpsman, Doc Campanali." I nodded my head in the direction of Doc. Four more crew members raced toward where Doc Campanali squatted next to Howey's body. When they reached Doc, I motioned for him to step aside and make his way toward the helicopter.

He stood, gathered his things, and, after a final look at Howey, marched away.

Eventually I turned toward the birds. Their twin rotors were still spinning fast, each blade chasing the one in front in a never-ending game of catch. Williams and I trudged toward the first helicopter. Inside, two members of the flight crew were busying themselves with preflight checks, scurrying back and forth between this gauge and that lever. Inside, seated atop the cargo webbing, were Payne, Latcher, and Doc.

Twisting around, I saw the rest of the flight crew struggling to carry Howey's heavy litter through the muddy field toward the other helicopter. *Howey doesn't want to go,* I thought. *He knows that the second he's on that bird he's gone.* "Fight it," I whispered. *Fight it. Load the damn thing up with us. Bring it over here.* Finally, the gaping mouth at the rear of the second helicopter devoured the stretcher.

Dismayed, my eyes dropped. Something glinted at the top of my left foot. I knelt down and smeared away clumps of wet earth. Underneath I found my dog tag, tied neatly into the laces just like Sergeant Rosenberger had taught me. I used my thumb to clean off the remaining filth. The fire behind me reflected intermittently off the crisply stamped letters.

WOOD J. A.

365 25 8280

A POS M

CHRISTIAN

Could have been you. My thumb was trembling. I forced myself to walk briskly up the ramp. Inside, I tripped over a fire extinguisher bolted to the floor and tumbled into one of the seats. I could sense the door gunner weaving and bobbing behind his suspended machine gun, scanning the darkness outside the helicopter for targets. In his mind he was fighting off hordes of enemy insurgents. In reality, he was wasting his time.

"There's no one out there," I said under my breath.

We had waited for them to come. The bad guys. Waited and waited and waited. Waited with our knuckles white around our weapons. But they never came. I screamed over the roar of the engine, "Get this fucking thing off the ground!"

He just looked at me and shrugged—he wasn't the one flying the bird. I ripped off my helmet and stared at an irrelevant bolt on the ceiling until the bird finally lifted off and struggled into the night sky.

Slowly, very slowly, the clamor of mechanical parts faded. I became numb to the vibrations and bumps. Sleep was pulling me by the arm, promising me that I would wake up and it would all be a bad dream.

As I drifted off, my mind returned to the bridge. To the sights, the smells, the acrid taste that still permeated my mouth. I felt odd but couldn't place it. Then, abruptly, I knew what I was feeling. I was feeling relief. Relief that I was alive. Relief that it was not me riding in the other helicopter, floating through the night sky alongside us. Relief that I would see another sunrise. Relief that I would again love a woman. That I would drink beer and watch football and care about careless things. Relief that I could return to a life without war, without rifles, without insurgents. Relief was replaced with guilt. *You selfish son of a bitch,* I thought.

The helicopter touched down on an asphalt runway. One by one we rose, gathered our gear, and shuffled toward the ramp. Reaching the exit, I paused and looked out. The tarmac was buzzing with activity, mechanics working on helicopters, refueling trucks driving every which way, and a group of medics rushing toward us. A frantic swarm of medical personnel met us at the bottom.

"Where's the wounded?"

"We were told there were nine urgent-surgicals!"

"Who's in charge?"

"What's your unit?"

Someone handed me a cup of cold water. "Here, drink this," she said with concern. I grasped the Styrofoam cup.

"Lance Corporal Latcher here is wounded," Doc Campanali stated matter-of-factly, his hand placed in the small of Latcher's back.

I looked for the second helicopter. I found it resting on the asphalt near a building across the way. Ignoring the poking and prodding of the medical staff, I stared. Soon the gaping mouth that had devoured Howey back in the field spit him out as four men carried his body down the ramp and through the large doors of a nearby building.

"Goodbye, brother," I whispered softly toward the deaf ears of my fallen friend.

• ● •

Thirty miles away, Clay Hunt sat in the company's operations center, listening to the radio. Long stretches of infuriating static were interspersed with barely intelligible updates. Sergeant Rosenberger's initial transmission had set off the medevac and diverted two tanks into the area to provide security. It wasn't long before Rose was pulled off the radio for his own medical treatment. He would be sent home due to those wounds. Subsequent radio traffic confirmed the names of the Marines who'd boarded the medevac, including mine—but instead of relaying that we'd walked onto the helicopters, we were reported as urgent-surgical casualties.

Clay spent hours on the radio, fearful that I was lying on a cold aluminum operating table, intubated and in surgery. As word spread that

Howey was dead, Staff Sergeant Kortje walked into the platoon's hooch and began gathering Howey's things to ship home. The Marines didn't need to stare at reminders of his death. Finally off radio watch, Clay returned to the hooch and lay down in Howey's now empty rack. Closing his eyes, he wondered what would become of his friend Jake.

CHAPTER 4

RED-EMBERED MARLBORO

THREE WEEKS LATER
MARCH 11, 2007
AL-ANBAR PROVINCE, IRAQ

"Wood, I know you don't smoke, man," Little said as he cupped his hand around his mouth and raised a Zippo to his lips. "But if you feel like you need one, let me know."

The tip of his red-embered Marlboro flared as he shut his eyes and inhaled. He leaned back and held the smoke in. He looked calm. Watching him, I felt the pulse pounding louder in my head. I was anything but calm. I was clenching and unclenching my fists, trying to force the shaking to stop. I had never smoked in my life, but I reached across the Humvee for Little's cigarette. He took one last pull and handed it to me.

I let the smoke into my lungs. I felt it seep into every vein and cell inside me. It whispered sweet nothings and my body relaxed. I shut my eyes and laughed.

"What the hell's so funny?" Little asked as he reached for the cigarette.

I kept laughing.

"What the goddamn fuck is *so funny*?"

"I never smoked before . . ." I said, "because this shit will *kill* you."

We both laughed. We laughed until we didn't know if we were laughing or crying. Little took the Marlboro and gave it an odd look. There was a red smear on the filter that looked like lipstick. Looking down at my hands, I saw the blood on them. Little saw it too but ignored it. He took a pull.

"Today was fucking crazy," he said.

I agreed. Looking out the window, I watched a stray dog sniff the carcass of another dog. "Fucking crazy."

"Do you think he's alive?" The question hung in the air. "I mean, do you *really* think he's alive?" Little asked, begging for the truth.

"I don't know," I said. "I don't know. I think so. I hope so," I said, replaying the scene in my mind. "I mean, *fuck*, he was alive when we put him on that bird." My voice drifted off. "I think."

Little nodded, trying to convince himself. Still nodding, he reached under the seat for a water bottle. Unscrewing the cap, he dropped the dying butt into the bottle. It landed with a hiss. Not missing a beat, he put his hand in his cargo pocket and extracted a red-and-white pack of Marlboros.

"Fucking crazy, man," he muttered, slapping the pack into the palm of his hand. *Whap, whap, whap.* "Think we killed any of those hajjis back there?"

I looked back at the dogs. One alive, one dead. I remembered the sound of the first shot, *CRACK*, and all the gunfire that came next, my rifle tight against my ear, beating a rhythm on my shoulder, *pop, pop, pop*.

I thought about the white car and the spiderweb on its windshield. I thought of Ray Ray Bullard, about pointing at the car and shouting something to him, and the *tat-tat-tat* of Ray Ray's M-249 machine gun and the *clink-clink-clink* of his shell casings. The red puddle.

"I don't know, man," I said, trying to rub the fatigue from my eyes. "I hope we smoked some of them."

• ● •

FIVE HOURS EARLIER

"We're gonna hit them hard and fast as soon as they gather this morning," Lieutenant Clevenger told us. "First Squad, you guys are going to take outer security. Second Squad, you guys are going to step off for a foot patrol at 0700 and establish a presence at the house located *here*." He pointed to a spot on the large map hanging on the cinder-block wall. "Third Squad will initiate the raid . . ."

"Roger."

"Check."

"Your squad is taking point because you owe these motherfuckers. Detain all military-age males. We expect maybe one to two high-value targets will be present, so don't be surprised if there's some resistance."

My squad of thirteen Marines would lead the raid. I gathered with Williams and we issued orders and tasks and left the men to prepare. Morale within the platoon was low. Howey's death had rattled us, but more demoralizing was our total lack of control. The COIN tactics we were employing left us feeling vulnerable. Every day we patrolled by vehicle or by foot, seemingly waiting for an explosion to go off. Our small forward operating base would get mortared every Tuesday, bombs raining from the sky. We were incapable of fighting back. This wasn't how we imagined winning a war.

I grabbed my rifle and found a quiet corner in the Iraqi home we'd turned into a temporary patrol base. As I cleaned my rifle, I imagined a war that was good and right and that we were capable of fighting. Where bad guys wore uniforms and attacked in formation and didn't hide in dark fields to explode bombs under bridges. Where Marines charged uphill under machine gun fire and threw grenades. Where the victors marched home to ticker-tape parades and strangers bought them beer and they married prom queens.

I let myself believe that the day's raid would be such a battle. We would enter the market and kick in doors and find the enemy's weapons and IEDs and maybe, just maybe, Osama bin Laden himself would be attending a meeting with his top leadership, and we would butt-stroke him with our rifles and drag him to New York City. We would put him on trial before the whole world, and when he was found guilty, my squad would be selected to conduct his execution. We would line up in a pretty row and we would shoot him. We would shoot him not just once, but twice for good measure. And then the citizens of New York would lift us on their shoulders and march us through Ground Zero and shower us with rose petals and confetti.

I let my imagination make me a hero. I let it make me think I could stand in a hail of bullets and strike a pose and scream something like, "Come on, you sons of bitches, do you want to live forever?" But that was no good, because they'd taught us in boot camp that it had already been screamed in some earlier, probably more righteous, war.

I imagined these things because they were better than the reality of my war, where the enemy wore no uniforms and refused to fight on honorable terms. Or on our terms, rather, which I presumed were honorable.

A war without epic battles but with plenty of SigActs, or significant actions—one of the benign-sounding names the colonels and generals came up with to describe the short-lived events that maimed and killed Marines. A war where we simply waited to absorb whatever the insurgency gave us, hoping to survive and perhaps kill one of them with a drone strike or automated counterbattery fire from a howitzer miles away. A war that found us driving with our assholes clenched tight, afraid of the things that go *boom*, things that can take our legs and our arms and our balls and paint the ceilings of our Humvees with them.

"What's up, Wood?" Clay Hunt stood in front of me, beanie pulled low on his forehead. Three weeks prior, when I finally rejoined the platoon after being evacuated with Howey's body, Clay had walked up and embraced me in a way he never had before. It wasn't friendship; it was love. The kind of love warriors have written about for thousands of years.

I kept scrubbing. "Not much, buddy. Getting ready."

"So you assholes get point on the raid, huh?" he said, sitting down alongside me.

"Looks like it. We're stoked."

"Yeah, I'm obviously not," Clay said, crossing his arms. Clay's assignment was driving one of the vehicles for the raid. If there was to be any action today, he'd only be able to watch it.

I laughed. "We can't all go kick the doors in, Clay."

"Yeah, but I'll be behind a steering wheel. Not even in the turret. Shit, my truck won't even be facing the market. I'll be stuck watching cows chew grass while you're nabbing the guys who killed Howey." He leaned against the wall and pulled the beanie over his eyes. "I fucking hate this place."

"We all hate this place, bro." We sat in silence.

"Start loading up!" The call came from outside. A throaty rumble filled the air as a seven-ton truck engine came to life. I stood and helped Clay to his feet.

• • •

The truck swayed back and forth on the rocky dirt road. *A few more minutes, that's all it should take,* I thought. Sporadic chatter filled the intersquad radio in my ear. *Be advised . . . Approaching . . . Third Squad, get ready to move . . .*

"Get ready, gents." I looked around at the rest of the men. Clenched jaws, steely eyes.

Third Squad, GO GO GO!

I slapped Arguello on the back of his flak jacket. "Move move move!" I followed him off the back of the truck, dropping the last three feet to the ground. I pushed him forward to clear the ladder area and raised my rifle, pointing it into the crowd gathered in the market.

"Marines! STOP!" I shouted over and over in Arabic, sweeping my M-16 back and forth, looking for threats.

We ran to the cinder-block-and-tin structure we had designated Building Bravo. "Stack up!" As the words left my mouth, Bullard and Cartwright slammed into the wall behind me. "Stack up!" I repeated. Seconds ticked by. I heard Williams's team breach Building Alpha. That was our cue.

"Arguello, *go.*"

He stepped in front of the doorway and I raised my rifle. He looked at me and I nodded. Then he kicked the door with all his might. Nothing. "Again! Harder!" He kicked again. Again, nothing. He raised his leg for a third try. "No, move back. We'll use the shotgun."

He moved aside and I took aim with our Italian-made Benelli. The lock exploded. This time the door flew open when Arguello kicked. I raised my rifle and entered, passing through the haze created by the shotgun blast.

We cleared the shop, grabbing unarmed men and unceremoniously throwing them into the center of the market where other Marines were waiting to detain them. We could hear Marines shouting "Clear!" from adjacent buildings until finally a definitive "Clear, All Clear! All Clear!" echoed off the walls. Inside Bravo we tore through drawers and bins and boxes, desperate to find some piece of incriminating evidence that would allow us to claim a small victory in a fight we couldn't help but fear we were losing.

Nothing. Well, not nothing—we found bootlegged cigarettes and DVDs, but no bombmaking material or illegal weapons. I went outside to find the lieutenant.

"Sir, there ain't shit in our building," I announced with less tact than intended. The lieutenant's face indicated he was getting similar news from the other assault teams.

"Alright, we'll remain in place and have the interpreter interrogate a couple of these military-age males. In the meantime, I need you to take a team to that rooftop and see if you can get the Combat Operations Center (COC) up on the radio. We haven't been able to get any situation reports (SitReps) out for the last twenty minutes."

"Roger that." I grabbed four Marines and maneuvered them across a freshly tilled plot of land toward the house, passing by an Iraqi woman and her two little girls. I asked her whether we could use her roof but knew her answer wouldn't change the outcome. Bullard offered the girls candy anyway.

We hurried onto the roof, where the heat rose in waves off the tar. From our perch we could see the market and the Humvees and seven-ton trucks blocking the three roads leading into the market. There was laughter below and I leaned over the parapet to look. The two little girls were running in circles, the one in front clutching a piece of Bullard's candy. The girl being chased reached her mother and hid behind her billowing garment. In one swift movement the girl unwrapped the candy and plopped it in her mouth, raising her hands in glee. The mother looked down and smiled.

A Marine exited the driver's seat of the lead vehicle. A bead of sweat rolled into my left eye, blurring my vision. "Shit," I said, wiping it. "Cartwright, you got comms with COC? We need to get off this roof." I was getting uneasy about how long the platoon had remained at the market.

"Just got 'em, Corporal Wood. What info am I passing?"

"Basic SitRep." My eyes followed the Marine as he walked to the rear of his armored truck and began yanking on the handle of the rear compartment. With a heave, the Marine unlatched the trunk. Losing his balance, he stumbled back two steps. Readjusting his helmet, he stepped forward to peer inside.

Suddenly he lurched, as if someone had yanked a string attached to a puppet.

CRACK, the sound came a split second later. I blinked. The Marine remained standing.

Blink. His knees buckled as he reached up and grasped at his throat.

Blink. A fountain of red erupted and sunlight reflected off raindrops of blood.

Frame by agonizing frame I watched the Marine fall, his hands desperately trying to seal the leak that had sprung from his carotid artery. The frames clicked by until, finally, his body came to rest on the asphalt. With that, life came roaring back to full speed.

Rat-tat-tat-tat. The sound came from our right. *Rat-tat-tat-tat,* a second chorus from our left. "CONTACT RIGHT! CONTACT LEFT!" I screamed.

"CARTWRIGHT, MAN DOWN! GET A NINE-LINE MEDEVAC UP NOW!" Gunfire erupted from our Humvees, turret gunners leaning into their machine guns and chewing up targets with copper-coated teeth. Bright tracers passed each other in opposite directions, some arcing over our heads on the roof.

"Arguello, Crass, keep looking north, those rounds aren't aimed at us. Make sure nobody's coming in on our six."

"Who's hit?" Cartwright yelled.

"Don't know! Send up a nine-line. One urgent-surgical, litter, extract at—" My mind raced to visualize the patrol map. Where could we land a helicopter? "Intersection of Mobile and Pirates, no special equipment, ZAP unknown."

"Roger." Cartwright relayed the message. I looked down at the Iraqi mother gathering her children in her arms. The woman's eyes betrayed no fear, only fatigue. My eyes locked on a white sedan facing our convoy, doors open on both sides, men standing behind the doors.

Flash. Flash. The men were firing from behind the car. I turned to Bullard, positioned behind his M-249 SAW machine gun. "Bullard!"

"Yo?"

"White sedan, two hundred meters direct front. Open doors. Three males."

"Got it."

"Light that motherfucker up!"

I refocused, forcing the illuminated reticle in my scope to hold still on the center of the car door, behind which knelt two men. I knew my ammunition would shred right through it.

Breathe, breathe, breathe. Squeeze, squeeze, squeeze. *Click-bang.* The first round tore through the door.

Breathe, breathe. Squeeze, squeeze.

Click-bang. Click-bang. Click-bang. The rounds became easier to fire.

Bullard's machine gun roared and the *clink-clink* of his shell casings bounced off the roof. "Cease fire, cease fire!" I yelled. I looked through my scope. A spiderweb crept across the sedan's windshield as smoke poured through bullet holes punched in the hood.

"Nine-line is up, birds on the way!" Cartwright yelled.

"We gotta get off this roof and back to the platoon," I shouted.

We flew down the stairs and huddled at the corner. Looking at two hundred yards of open field, I jostled my ammo vest up and down, trying to get comfortable. I explained that we would have to rush in pairs across the field, providing cover fire for each other every ten yards. The rate of fire was increasing and there was no place to hide once we stepped off. It could become a killing field for the enemy machine gunners. But I didn't tell them that. Instead I turned and asked, "You guys got it?"

"Yeah, we got it," they said. An instant willingness and obedience to orders is what made Marines, well, Marines.

I sprinted forward, propelled by adrenaline. After eight strides I dropped to a knee and raised my rifle. A moment later Cartwright reached his position to my right. "SET!" we screamed.

The reply came from behind. "MOVING!"

And so it went. We rushed and set and moved and shot. We held our breath and said our prayers and clenched our jaws tight. When the rounds began splashing the dirt by our boots, we thought about how it would feel and hoped it would be quick. We bargained with God, swearing off sex and booze and Lord knows what else. Until finally, at long last, we collapsed into that earthen berm next to the trucks and celebrated life. We slapped each other's backs and exchanged high fives and shouted "Fuck yeah!" at the tops of our lungs. We had cheated death and, in an abrupt reversal, had never felt more alive.

I crawled up and down the line, directing the Marines' fires, shouting words of encouragement. Eventually, with Bullard providing cover fire, we climbed the ladder attached to a seven-ton truck. The firefight continued raging outside. Wrapped in relative safety, I melted into a corner and closed my eyes. Minutes passed. Minutes filled with back slapping and chest thumping. The others swapped stories, one-upping each other. I sat and listened—not to the stories but to a lingering thought in the back of my head. *That shit was . . . amazing.* I suddenly realized my life would forever be defined by combat. There would be life before being shot at and after.

Bullard's voice came into focus. ". . . and then Corporal Wood was like 'Light that motherfucker up' and I was like 'Fuck yeah' and I fuckin' put a burst in that fucking car like you wouldn't believe." He laughed. "I swear I ain't ever rocked a SAW like that—*tat-tat-tat-tat*!" He held up his hand, pulling an imaginary trigger.

Suddenly I remembered that we had a dying Marine.

"Why aren't we moving?" I shouted. Then realized I was talking to a truck full of men whose only answers came from me. I told Arguello and Bullard to get ready to move. I dropped the magazine from my M-16 and slammed home a fresh twenty-eight rounds. I looked outside, judged the distance to the ground, hopped off, and tumbled forward. The air around me sizzled with bullets.

"Bullard, Arguello! Stay put!" I yelled, concerned that the enemy would anticipate more Marines. "Don't jump! I can make it to the lead truck." I ran in bounds, pausing behind each truck's massive wheels or armor plating to catch my breath and wait for lulls in shooting. At one point I found myself huddled next to Jeff Muir, who was frantically trying to account for all his Marines. "Don't get shot," he shouted when I sprinted away. Finally, I reached the lead Humvee.

"Lieutenant Clevenger, sir, why aren't we moving?" I said between labored breaths.

"We haven't stabilized the casualty."

Sergeant Lyons and Doc Lacea tended to the Marine's body. I looked at his face. It was Windsor.

In the turret of the Humvee above us, Lance Corporal Wherry unleashed a burst of hatred from his .50-caliber machine gun. The noise was deafening. Lacea pressed gauze deeper into Windsor's neck and grabbed Sergeant Lyons's hands, instructing him to do the same. "What do you need, Doc? What do you need?" Lyons kept asking.

"Pressure, just pressure. Just press."

Windsor's face was ghastly white. His lips bore the slightest hint of blue, speckled with flecks of red. The gurgling wasn't coming from his lips; it was coming from the hole in his neck. I watched as pink bubbles frothed from the wound, expanding and dissipating with each painful gasp.

The lieutenant's voice broke my stare. "Wood, I need you to protect our flank to the front of this Humvee." Beyond the Humvee, just off the road, a patch of reeds swayed in the wind. The shadows and the rustling looked like people could be moving through it.

I climbed onto the truck and slapped the turret gunner, Wherry, on the helmet. His face was smeared with machine gun grease. He cocked his head, signaling me to speak.

"RIGHT FLANK!" I yelled. Wherry swung the .50-caliber toward the road and let loose a long burst into the reeds. The concussion knocked me off balance and I fell to the ground. My hand reached out to brace the fall and slapped into the puddle of Windsor's blood. "Fuck," I said, and ripped both gloves off, tossing them aside. My hands were stained a deep red. I loaded a grenade in the breach of my launcher and lobbed it into the reeds for good measure.

Lacea finally hollered that Windsor was ready to be moved. We decided I would get the high-back, which was on the other side of my seven-ton. The high-back is a Humvee designed like a typical truck, with a large, armored cargo bed. I ran and ran and ran, thinking to myself, *There's too much of this running bullshit in combat.* Finally, I reached the high-back and found Sergeant Little leaning behind his rifle on the hood. I yanked open the driver's side door and jumped in while Little climbed in the other side. It took ten seconds to get back to Windsor. I slammed on the brakes and threw the door open.

WHACK. A bullet struck the door's bulletproof window. "Holy shit!" I yelled, ducking and looking up to see the bulletproof glass cracking outward from the strike point. That's when I first heard helicopters in the distance.

Lieutenant Clevenger shouted, "Those are our birds! Mount up. Move out."

I waited, hoping the lieutenant's truck, with Wherry's machine gun, would take the lead, and ours, with Windsor clinging to life in the back, could follow. Little smacked the dashboard. "Screw it, Wood. Don't wait—just go!" Three minutes later, I pulled into a field and parked. The only hint Windsor was still alive was Doc Lacea's soft voice telling him to hang on.

"Who's got smoke?" I shouted, turning in a circle as other trucks pulled up.

Wherry shouted my name and tossed me a canister. Tugging the pin, I hurled it with all my might. With a pop and hiss the grenade spewed yellow smoke. The helicopters were close, their double rotors *whomp-whomp-ing* the air. Flashes of Howey's evacuation on Route Reds three weeks prior played in my mind.

We pulled Windsor to the edge of the truck as the first CH-46 banked over the landing zone (LZ), billowing the yellow smoke outward. "One, two, three." We lifted Windsor's deadweight and carried him to the center of the field where the bird gently touched down. Once inside he was surrounded by flight medics. I reached down to touch his arm.

"Good luck, brother," I whispered. I ran down the helicopter's ramp and looked around at the solemn faces of the turret gunners, all leaning on their warm, smoking weapons, watching the helicopter speed toward the horizon. I walked to the idling high-back. Little was inside. I slid in.

"Wood, I know you don't smoke, man," he said as he cupped his hand around his mouth and raised a Zippo to his lips. "But if you feel like you need one, let me know."

• ● •

Windsor died en route to the surgical center. A few days later, only hours after we held his memorial service, Clay Hunt was shot. An insurgent sniper shot him through the wrist while his chin rested on it, a bullet clearly intended for his head.

I wasn't with Clay when he was hit, and when the call for a medevac first came over the radio we didn't know who was wounded. Thus began the worst thought exercise known to every combat veteran—if one of my thirteen friends is dead or wounded, who do I hope it is? Of course, that's not quite how you play it. It begins with who you hope it isn't. It was an emotional game—you know one of your friends is hurt, and you assign a hierarchy of who you hope most is safe. The names jostled for position in my head, like the leader board at a golf tournament. Hunt was one of my best friends; I hoped desperately it was not him. Lyons was a good leader; they would need him to survive the deployment. Garza had been an early mentor to me in the fleet. Vicencio had two young children back home. Villareal, everybody loved Vill. It can't be Vill.

The Marines have a name for games like this. They're called mind fucks. When it was first passed that the casualty was Clay, my body went numb. I imagined him bleeding to death in a field like Windsor. Fortunately, Clay would survive.

After being sent home, Clay was assigned to a headquarters element on our base in California while he recovered. Each day he would have to take a shift manning a phone at the Battalion Command Post. It was a special phone. It only rang when someone was wounded or dead. Clay would later say that manning that phone was ten times worse than getting shot. Every time it rang—and it rang frequently for 2-7 over the course of that tour—he would answer it wondering whose name would be transmitted by the voice on the other end. Would it be Muir? Wood?

Two-Seven fought for six more hard months, taking daily contact with the enemy. The war didn't get any easier. More often than not, our attackers were invisible. Their explosions and gunfire and rocket-propelled grenades were real, but the people behind them seemed like ghosts. Sometimes they would stick around and fight, and in those moments we'd think the war was fair. Then we'd drop a 2,000-pound bomb on their position. I'm sure the enemy didn't find that too fair. But we didn't care, because we were winning in those moments, and the only unfair fight is the one you lose, the Marine Corps taught us.

We came home to California that fall with fewer men than when we'd left. We held our heads high when we stepped off the buses to greet our families, finding pride in the small victories we'd achieved. But not many of us sustained the illusion that whatever we accomplished in Iraq was worth the price we paid. Inside we were tired and hurting. Some wondered why or how they'd made it home at all; others wished they hadn't.

I met my family on the grassy field. My mother barreled through the crowd, her high-pitched scream only quieting when she buried her face into my chest. Two of my sisters were right behind her, and I caught my father patting at wet eyes as he awaited his turn. It was good to be home. When my father released me from his grip, Clay approached. "Welcome home, brother. Been waiting for you guys."

CHAPTER 5

THE VALLEY ECHOED

JUNE 2008
HELMAND VALLEY, AFGHANISTAN

I rolled over on top of the cardboard box serving as my bed, tugging on the corner of the blanket to reclaim as much fabric as possible from Shawn, who was sharing it. The increasing frequency of our night missions had destroyed our sleep patterns, and we'd become accustomed to taking brief naps to compensate. Tonight we were slated to sneak into an enemy-controlled area and set up a firing position for a large Marine operation the next day. Being on the verge of operations like that made it hard to snooze, and my mind raced.

I was now part of a Marine scout-sniper team, having joined the sniper platoon upon my return from Iraq. After several months of training, the platoon sent me to the Corps' legendary sniper school, notorious for its high failure rate. Clay and I were paired together and endured the school's grueling physical and mental tests, all while struggling to meet the high standards demanded in skills like shooting and stalking. Finally, after ten weeks we graduated, though over half of our peers were gone. At the ceremony we were welcomed into the Marines' most exclusive fraternity and awarded our Hog's Tooth. Snipers were known as Hogs, for "hunters of gunmen," and wore the Hog's Tooth, a sniper bullet dangling from parachute cord, around their necks in place of dog tags. Snipers believe that there is a bullet destined for every warrior on this earth, and superstition holds that the Hog's Tooth is the bullet meant to kill its bearer. So long as a sniper wore his own bullet, the enemy did not possess the bullet that could kill him. He became invincible.

My team was now in Sangin, a small city in Afghanistan's southern Helmand Province. Helmand was a bastion of Taliban strength, due in no small part to its lush poppy fields. Helmand's poppies supplied most of Afghanistan's harvest, which in turn fueled most of the world's illicit opium trade. Eighteen months earlier, control of Sangin was wrested from the Taliban by the British, who had assaulted the town out of helicopters, eventually fighting their way to the District Center. For weeks they repelled counterattacks from Taliban fighters, until they finally cemented their position. In the year since that time, the Brits had lost dozens of troops in Helmand, and the British public were demanding the country's withdrawal.

In the hopes of convincing the United Kingdom to stay, the United States deployed two battalions of Marines. Two-Seven, only nine months removed from our bloody tour in Iraq, was one of the two slotted to go. I learned news of the deployment while at sniper school, and those of us there from 2-7 rejoiced. Everyone preferred a deployment to Afghanistan over a return to Iraq, which many of us still doubted was worth it. Afghanistan was the good war. The right war. Unfortunately, because this was not a preplanned deployment, 2-7 did not deploy as an Air-Ground Task

Force, as was customary for the Marine Corps. That meant that 2-7 would lack integrated close air support, helicopters, tanks, and artillery. Effectively, the Pentagon threw a thousand Marines into the bloodiest province of Afghanistan, told them to hold the line, and wished them luck. Two-Seven didn't mind. Cocksure after staring down an insurgency in Iraq, the Marines of the battalion almost relished the fight coming our way. The daily violence we encountered there did not disappoint.

That night, the Afghan platoon that shared our small patrol base invited us to join them on the roof for a Ramadan feast. Warm bread and juicy mutton and all manner of spices and relishes were laid out on a carpet surrounded by our sniper team and a half dozen Afghan soldiers. We spent an hour talking through an interpreter, exploring the differences in our lives and cultures. It was a humanizing experience, and those were hard to come by for a group of Americans whose primary interactions with Afghans were filtered through a high-powered scope from five hundred meters away. Of course, that normalcy didn't last long.

Machine gun fire echoed in the distance. Down below, too far away to cause us to flinch, a stream of tracers streaked across the valley floor. "I wonder who that is," I said.

"I don't think Echo Company would be down this far this early," Shawn said, dipping a piece of bread in hummus and popping it in his mouth. Echo was the infantry company our team was tasked with supporting. Between chews, he continued, "Might be a British unit, or maybe some Special Ops guys." Not knowing the radio frequency of the unit below, we had no way to reach them.

The first tracers, which were green, were answered with streaks of red, originating from multiple locations. Back and forth the fires went. I poured myself another cup of chai, and we sat together peaceably, watching two groups of men trying to kill each other. How strange, I thought, that I could not feel any real concern for the mortal engagement below. There, off in the distance, a mother's son was being killed. The killer's reasons were unknown to me. They could have been born of ideology or patriotism, desperation or anger. The dying, it seemed to me, was far less complicated than the killing, despite their inseparable coupling. Slowly, over the course of ten minutes, fewer and fewer green tracers were fired until, finally, we sat in silence.

"Well, looks like the good guys won," Shawn said, reaching for another piece of bread.

• ● •

Looking back, I'm amazed at the ease with which violence was normalized. I don't say that with regret. I'm not sure I would have survived Iraq and Afghanistan if I hadn't become comfortable with death.

The military has become quite adept at desensitizing its troops. In the Marines it begins at boot camp, where recruits acknowledge orders by shouting *"KILL!"* at the tops of their lungs and joke about blood making the grass grow. Target practice is no longer conducted on targets of concentric circles but on "Ivan targets" shaped like men. In the sniper community, we rarely spoke of shooting or killing human beings. That was too personal. No, rather we would "whack tangos," or "smoke hajjis," or "eliminate threats."

Before we knew it, we could go on a mission that had us patrolling deep into insurgent territory, picking our way through areas known to be littered with land mines and IEDs, and never find our heart rate elevated. Our own mortality was rendered inconsequential. Constant fear was exhausting, and so our minds coped. In order to shut down the fear, we had to shut down our other feelings. That's just the way we survived.

The problem, though we didn't know it at the time, is that once that emotional switch was turned off, it was really hard to flip it back on.

• • •

THREE HOURS LATER

Shawn roused our team from a brief and fitful slumber. We groggily donned our gear, cinching down straps to ensure nothing rattled. The slightest noise would carry on the wind at night. Shawn moved among the men, checking equipment and asking questions, making sure everyone was ready for the mission. He reached me. "What do you think? Finalize our route?"

I pulled out a laminated map that I kept stuffed between my magazine pouches and body armor. Clicking on a small red flashlight, I stepped close to Shawn. "I think we'll maneuver here along this canal," I said, tracing the map with my finger. "At this crossing here, I'll move us across the road and up this ridgeline." My finger paused. "The problem, as we discussed, is this wadi. The moon's bright tonight, but we can't avoid walking across it. Satellite imagery shows no vegetation. We'll be out in the open, asses in the wind." Shawn shrugged. He knew we had no choice.

Ninety minutes later we paused at the edge of the wadi, staring out across four hundred yards of naked terrain. A bright moon reflected off ankle-deep sand. It looked like the moon's own lunar surface. Normally reticent to leave traces of our movements, we knew that there would be no way to mask our boot prints, short of dragging a net behind us like a field crew at Dodger Stadium. An ambush in the valley would allow the enemy to cut us down like grass. But we had Marines who needed us to cross that wadi, because in the morning they'd move into hostile territory expecting to have snipers keeping them safe from above. We hastily made our way across and then up the steep side of the valley, arriving at the target compound's exterior wall an hour later.

I handed Shawn my rifle and pulled out a pistol. Being six foot six helped in these moments. I hoisted myself up onto the wall and pointed the pistol into the courtyard, scanning with my night vision goggles. Nothing moved. Shawn passed my rifle up and I hopped into the compound.

We moved through the courtyard together. A cough rang out. My rifle's infrared laser shot past the barrel and danced along the compound wall until it came to rest on a man's rising and falling chest. As we drew closer, we could see the rest of the family lying on mats near him, a wife and three children. This was always the worst part of missions like this—having to wake a family at gunpoint in the middle of the night. As far as we knew, this family was innocent of any wrongdoing. Their only crime was having a home on a cliff that provided ideal angles for sniper fire in support of the morning's operation.

Tiptoeing around slumbering children, I stood over the man. Looking down, I felt a twinge of guilt. *No wonder these people hate us,* I thought. Shawn bent over and smothered the man's mouth with his hand. His eyes fluttered open. It took only a moment for him to realize he was staring at the barrel of my rifle, behind which sat a painted face faintly illuminated by the soft glow of night vision goggles. Shock turned to terror, which turned to rage as the man's eyes first widened and then narrowed.

"Shhhhhhhh," Shawn whispered, bringing his finger to his lips in the universal sign for quiet. The man spoke no English and we had no interpreters, so we motioned for the man to quietly wake his wife and children. The wife's vitriolic glare could have melted me, and I avoided crossing it a second time. The children rubbed sleep from their eyes, unsure why they were being roused. We ushered the family into their own home and found a windowless room. Inside, we cracked ChemLight sticks and placed food, water, and mats for them to sleep on. We locked the door from the outside.

Shawn began issuing assignments. He and Josh, our team's best shooters, would set up a firing position in a room overlooking the small village that was the morning's target. Thenn and Davis would take a machine gun up to the roof. Wheeler had the radio. Clay would be a utility player and help with spotting. My job was to secure the compound's rear, which had wide entrances on three of the courtyard's exterior walls. It wasn't the job I wanted. I wanted to be up where the action was, lying behind the .50-caliber sniper rifle I'd just hauled in on a four-kilometer insert. But it wasn't up to me.

I worked to set a claymore mine near the most vulnerable entrance. It was right off the road and just wide enough for a truck laden with explosives to drive right through. The claymore, a breathtakingly deadly anti-personnel mine, was a simple device. Packed full of six hundred tungsten steel balls embedded in a pound and a half of C-4 explosives, the mine could shred anything in front of it. Despite its simple design, I diligently read the raised print on the back: *REAR TOWARD FRIENDLIES.* The front read *FRONT TOWARD ENEMY.* I didn't want to screw that up.

• • •

The sun was rising, and long shadows began to creep across the courtyard. In the distance, the faint sounds of clanging pots and pans and baying farm animals rolled over the outer wall. The radio cackled. "Echo is on the move."

Our job today was simple, but dangerous. From our vantage point, behind the enemy front line, we would have a perfect view of the unfolding operation. We would report enemy movements and alert the incoming troops of potential ambushes, and, when the opportunity presented itself, we would take out targets without revealing our hiding spot. Of course, if the enemy learned where we were, our small team could be overrun within minutes.

"Stand by for shots," Wheeler's voice said matter-of-factly over the radio.

Seconds later I heard Clay's voice in the other room. "I have control, I have control, I have control. Firing on the 'T' of two. Five . . . four . . . three . . . two—" *Crack-Crack.* Two suppressed rifles fired shots simultaneously. They were quickly followed by three more rounds. And then silence.

Seconds and then minutes ticked by. Machine gun fire sounded in the distance. Sporadic reports coming through on the radio portrayed a small but growing battle underway, out of my field of view. Our snipers continued to watch, reporting the movements of locals in the area and advising of potential traps being laid for the advancing Marines. One of them fired a shot at two fighters on a motorcycle, an RPG tube—a rocket-propelled grenade—lying across the lap of the passenger. The shot missed, but the rider lost control of the bike and the RPG careened into a patch of tall weeds.

"Thenn, can you see those kids that keep running from the front line back to the rear?" Wheeler asked. Thenn was on the roof.

"Intermittently, but someone is definitely directing them. The same kids keep going back and forth. It looks like one of them is going to make a run for that RPG." There was dread in Thenn's voice. If the child went to retrieve the weapon, our shooters would be faced with an impossible choice.

"Keep an eye on them and see who their handler is. We need to take him out."

The enemy fighters were using kids as runners and scouts, sending them back and forth across the battlefield to bring ammunition or messages from a Taliban leader who didn't want his radio chatter intercepted. It wasn't uncommon. I had seen it a few weeks prior when I was in the District Center's tower covering the withdrawal of a British unit that was under fire. A little girl, no older than nine or ten, had stood on a pile of rocks, hand shielding her eyes from the sun, yelling back the unit's movements to a man in the shadows below. We couldn't see the man clearly, but knew he was there. We'd debated sending a round into the rocks at the girl's feet, hoping to scare her off the pile, but decided the risk of hitting her was too great.

Shawn came on the radio. He identified the man responsible for directing the children and described in detail a middle-aged Afghan with dark hair, a traditional beard, and wearing a grey tunic. Shawn stated the man was holding an Icom radio—notoriously used by Afghan fighters to communicate on battlefields. Shawn indicated he would seek permission from higher to engage him.

"Echo-Six-Actual just confirmed. Next time we see the kid-runner we are cleared to engage. How copy?" Shawn's voice reported the information matter-of-factly, void of emotion. I gripped the handle of my rifle tighter. I would enjoy killing him.

The Marines advanced for another hour, until the enemy decided they'd had enough. Fighters became farmers. Young scouts became playful kids. Women returned to their crops, feigning ignorance of the dead Afghan men lying in their fields. Our shooters covered Echo Company's withdrawal, serving as unseen guardian angels. Finally, the call came for us to move. Normally we would wait until dark and slip out as silently as we had slipped in, but there was an attack helicopter circling overhead to cover our egress.

We spent fifteen minutes returning the house to complete normalcy, scouring every inch for evidence of our presence, taking care to pack it up and hump it out. Outside, the team was finally letting the owners of the home emerge. The woman quickly hustled the children down the steps and around the corner of the building. The man lingered to express his disdain, waving his hands and yelling in Pashto. I walked up to him and extended a bag of beef jerky. He brushed my arm aside contemptuously.

Finally, we stepped out of the house and into the sunlight, and the shooters who had been operating deep in the shadows of the home cringed. I glanced left and turned right, walking forward with my eyes sweeping the ground in front of me. Shawn stepped out behind me and spun to cover my six before following. That's when his voice stopped me dead in my tracks.

"Wood. Hold." I brought my rifle up, feverishly scanning for whatever threat Shawn had seen. "Is *that* the motherfucker?" he asked in disbelief. "Down to our left. Is that the fucking kid-runner?"

We lowered into a crouch and signaled the rest of the men to stay in the house. I peered through my scope at the man Shawn had indicated. There, just outside a small mud home, stood a dark-bearded man in dark grey garb. Surrounding the man was a group of children listening to him preach with animated arms.

"I don't know, Shawn. I didn't have eyes-on earlier. Looks like he meets the description I heard you guys pass, though. And the fact that he's surrounded by five kids . . ." My voice trailed; the connection was obvious.

"Wheeler?" Shawn called.

"Yeah, boss?"

"Get out here and check this guy out."

Wheeler emerged and peered through his scope. A few moments passed. "That's him, Shawn. Sure as shit."

"This stupid mother . . ." Shawn whispered. His body relaxed as he melted into his rifle. "Whaddya say, Wood?"

He wasn't seeking permission. Or assurance. He was the team leader, after all. He was seeking complicity. Shawn needed me to share in the moral burden of what we were about to do. I studied the man's face through the small four-power magnification of my scope. The man would scowl, yell, point to a field, and then to a boy, and then back to the field. I struggled with shooting a man, even this evil man, in front of the children. I realized I owed Shawn an answer. "If this is the guy"—I paused to emphasize that we had to be certain—"then let's smoke him."

"I hear ya," Shawn said, slowly rotating the magnification ring on his scope back and forth. Finally, he settled on a setting. "Wheeler, tell Echo-Six-Actual to stand by for shots." Behind us, Wheeler put the PRC-119 radio to his ear and relayed information to Echo's company commander. Above, the Cobra pilot circled lazily, oblivious to the imminent kill below.

"Alright, Shawn, nice and easy," I said. "You're just shy of two hundred yards. No wind. Elevation negligible. Hold center mass. Easy shot." Then I added, "Watch the kids." I looked at the little girl sitting on the ground, her legs crossed. A lump formed in my throat. Slowly, my eyelids closed. When they opened, the children remained.

"On target," Shawn said.

"Fire when ready."

Crack.

The man jerked as if punched in the chest. Behind him the muted wall exploded in color as his heart erupted out his backside. As he dropped to the ground, Shawn's rifle shot reverberated off the valley walls, back and forth until it faded to nothing. That nothingness was filled by the bloodcurdling screams of five children who, after a moment of disbelief, fled in every direction. For several painful seconds the valley echoed with the sounds of their terror. Finally, my scope was empty.

"Hit. Tango down," I said calmly.

• ● •

In the decade since that shot, my mind has revisited it countless times. It's probably a good thing I'd grown callous by that point in my military career. Our survival depended on our ability to take those moments—to take our decisions and actions—and bury them deep within ourselves like radioactive waste in a Nevada desert. We had to cover four kilometers of open terrain after that shot to get back to safety. If ambushed on the way home, empathy and compassion for those children were not going to make the enemy's bullets bounce off me. Guilt and shame were not going to make it easier for me to spot an IED set along our path.

People sometimes ask me what war was like. What they really want to know is whether I did or saw anything terrible. Sometimes I'm tempted to tell them that whatever I did, they paid me to do it. Of course, I never tell them that and I usually just say that we always made the right choice, no matter how hard. My answer always feels truthful, but the truth is rarely simple. Is there ever a right choice among only bad options? "We came home with our honor and integrity intact," I'll say as my mind wanders back to the screams of those children echoing off the valley walls.

CHAPTER 6

EVERYTHING IS WRONG

My flip-flops slapped against the bottoms of my feet in a steady rhythm as I walked back to the tent. The smell of urine faded mercifully as I put distance between myself and the shallow trench we had been pissing in for five months.

"Hey, Wood. What's up, man?"

I looked up and saw Clay sitting on a pile of lumber, smoking a cigarette with a single earbud blasting music from an iPod. "What's up? Haven't seen you in a while, buddy." I made my way in his direction. Clay had been working up north with another team, out of a small outpost called Patrol Base Downs, manned by a platoon of Afghan soldiers. "How've you been?"

Clay flicked an ash and shrugged. Something was bothering him. I decided to push him. "What's wrong, man?"

"*Everything* is wrong."

"Tell me."

Clay took one last pull off his cigarette and deposited it in an empty ammo can. He reached into his pants and pulled out a tin of chewing tobacco and began smacking it with his finger, packing the contents. "All this bullshit, man. Like, what the fuck are we doing here, Wood? Seriously, what the hell are we trying to accomplish?"

"What do you mean? On what level?"

"Any level. I just spent four days at PB Downs. You know what we accomplished?" I didn't, so I remained silent. "Nothing. Not a goddamned thing. Nothing—seriously, nothing." He shook his head. "We got into a firefight. Well, more accurately, Downs got attacked by a bunch of guys with guns and RPGs, and we shot back and forth for an hour. But for what?" Clay pulled his lower lip out with his fingers and placed a pinch of tobacco between his cheek and gums. He wiped his hand on his pants and squinted up at the setting sun.

"You just feel like we're wasting time, huh? Like we should be getting out on better missions?" I knew it was deeper than that, but I wanted him to talk it out.

"No, man. It's so much more. Better missions? What's a better mission? At this point, I want out. I want nothing more to do with this bullshit war. If someone walked into the District Center tonight and said anyone could raise their hand and get a ticket home, I'd be on the helicopter before they could finish the sentence."

"Really?" I asked, a bit surprised.

"Man, Wood, I realized it when Washington and Crass got killed. Here you got these guys . . . take a guy like Washington, young, smart, good-looking, and now what? He's dead. Why? He drove down the wrong road. You think whoever planted that bomb would fly to America and set it off if we left here? No way. Why are we doing this to ourselves?"

"Dude, we all signed up. Washington loved this shit. It was the only thing he ever wanted to do. You too—you knew what you were getting into." I sat down next to him and cracked my knuckles, debating how to proceed. Clay spoke next.

"What's the goal? We're here for four more months. We're going to go on more missions, kill more people, roll the dice with our own lives every day—and, in the end, what? When we leave, is Afghanistan safe? Helmand? Sangin? Fuck, will the District Center be safe? No. None of it is going to change. But then a new unit will rotate in. They'll lose their Washington and their Crass, they'll lose limbs and kill Afghans, some of them even Taliban, many of them not, and none of them al-Qaeda, and seven months later it will repeat. It has been repeating now for seven years." If only we knew then that it would repeat for a dozen more. "How many more Washingtons do we have to lose? How many more Mrs. Washingtons will receive a knock on their door, answer it, and be told that their son has been killed in a country that nobody back home gives a fuck about?"

"So what?" I asked.

"What do you mean, 'so what'?" Clay retorted defensively.

"Dude, you're one of my best friends, and you know I love you, but I don't like what I'm hearing." I shook my head and cast my eyes to the ground between my feet. "You've got a job to do, Clay. Regardless of what you're saying right now. You have a duty."

"I have a duty to myself to question these things, Jake. Our commanders couldn't define our mission if their lives depended on it—meanwhile, *our* lives *do* depend on it. And the whole time America is out to the mall," Clay said. Bending down, he picked up a handful of rocks and threw them one by one at the sandbags.

I watched in silence. In the three years since we'd met, Clay and I had become fast friends. We spent every weekend back home together, raising hell in the beach cities of Los Angeles. When Clay was shot and wounded on our deployment to Iraq, his perspective on life understandably changed. He began questioning authority, military and otherwise. It didn't help that the global economy was also beginning to melt down around us, leading him to question the motives and competence of decision makers even more. He'd grown moodier and more distant. Nevertheless, I loved him like the brother I never had.

Our time in Iraq, though progress was made, was fought under the unspoken shadow of doubt cast by the false pretenses that had started it. This war, Afghanistan, was supposed to be the righteous war, the war waged to avenge September 11 and protect America. It was supposed to be easier to pull on boots each day and risk our lives for this cause. Several months into Afghanistan, however, this war's veneer of nobility had begun to erode. Our frequent firefights were often with disenfranchised teenage farmers, not hardened Taliban, and certainly not al-Qaeda. Each day it became more and more evident to me that bullets and bombs alone would not secure peace.

Clay depleted the supply of rocks in his left hand and bent down to scoop up more.

I reached out and grabbed his wrist. "Clay, listen to me. I need you to listen. I need you to be very honest. You have five guys that count on you every time your team leaves the wire. Five guys with mothers and wives and children at home. Five guys and me, because every time you go out, I lose sleep. And if you get killed, you know who hands that flag to your mother? Me. If your head—I don't give a shit about your heart—isn't one hundred percent in this, I need to know right now." The words came out harsher than I'd intended, and I winced.

After a moment I continued, eager to provide some measure of support. "Brother, listen—we can't choose our war and we can't change our mission. The only thing we can control are the decisions we make. You don't have to sacrifice your honor and integrity for anyone, and nobody is asking you to." It was true. Shawn, my team leader, took as much pride in the times he showed restraint and didn't pull the trigger as in the number of bad guys he bagged.

Clay dropped the rocks and turned to me. A hint of wetness, barely visible, caught the sun at the corners of his eyes. "Wood," he said, the muscles in his jaw flexing outward, "you know I'll do my job. I just need to vent."

"Good," I said, standing up. "Now let's go play some cards."

• • •

TWELVE HOURS LATER

I took careful steps across the loose rocks. Toe, heel. Toe, heel. Down the berm we stalked through the cornfield, potential danger all around us—and beneath us. I relied on Shawn to watch my twelve o'clock, over my shoulder, as I scanned the ground in front of me.

I continued to glide, not allowing myself to rush. Tonight was a hunting mission. We had no objective other than to go out and stalk prey, to find someone doing something bad and kill them. The truth was, that person might be around the next bend, on the other side of the wall beside us, or fast asleep in bed. Finding them was a matter of us stumbling onto them or them stumbling onto us. Yet, despite the level of insurgent activity in Sangin, the odds of us finding someone doing something bad were maddeningly low. My conversation with Clay played in my head. I was surrounded by mortal danger—an ambush around every corner, an IED underneath every step. Yet Clay's voice forced me to wonder whether this night's mission, or any of the missions we'd run over the past month, was going to change the tide of a decade-long war. Or whether one of us would simply have our life snuffed out and our remains stuffed in a box and shipped home, joining the expanding casualty count that had become nothing more than noise to a distracted American public. As I had learned to do, I silenced the doubt and forced myself to focus on the task at hand. To doubt was to die, and to feel was to falter. I scanned the fields stretching out before me.

The cornfields in Afghanistan were different from the ones back home in Iowa. In Iowa, farmers took care to plant the corn in nice uniform rows, spaced exactly apart, leaving enough room for a man to walk between. In Afghanistan they didn't care. It was as if they planted the corn by dumping sacks of seed out of a low-flying airplane. Entire acres of it were so densely packed that the only way to maneuver through was to walk on the raised berms that haphazardly crisscrossed the fields.

I glanced down at my watch. It read one a.m., and I decided to give myself six minutes to rest. I sat on the berm, flipped down my night vision, and scanned for movement ahead. Nothing stirred. Then a cornstalk snapped in the field and six helmets swung in its direction. I held my breath and listened. I closed my eyes, straining to filter the baseline sounds and amplify anything out of the norm. I forced my heartbeat to slow so I could hear more clearly. The tips of my fingers tingled, and my right index finger curled around the trigger. Behind me I heard Davis raise his SAW, the belt-fed ammo making the softest clink as it rose off his leg.

We waited. And waited. No more sound. Finally, after several minutes had passed, I forced my heels into the ground and stood up off the berm. Once standing, we waited again. A minute passed, then another. Still nothing. Convinced we were alone, I walked forward. Toe, heel. Toe, heel. A dozen steps later we heard it again. I froze. The hair rose on the back of my neck and triggered a chill down my spine. The unease was palpable, and I anticipated someone screaming "Chargers," which was our code for "Get the fuck on the ground." If someone yelled "Chargers," everyone would drop and start hurling grenades while Davis unleashed his entire belt of ammo in a 360-degree circle. I didn't hear the signal, although I screamed it repeatedly in my head.

I hastened my step, anxious to find the end of the path. Finally the berm ended, running into a wide dirt road that followed alongside a swift canal cut from the Helmand River a few miles away. I approached the intersection, cognizant that the sound of running water could drown out dangerous men shuffling through the cornfields on either side of us. Kneeling just shy of the road, I examined the tracks and footprints marring the clay and dirt path. The tread seemed relatively fresh.

We decided to follow the footprints to the left and skirt the stream along the road. Tracing the road through the cornfield was not an option: we wouldn't be able to see past our noses or hear anything above the sound of our own movement.

Moving forward, I halted, foot in midair. *Crunch.* Yes, there it was again. Only this time, the crunch was different. This was the distinct sound of a shovel being thrust into the earth. *Crunch.* Yes, someone was digging. And from the sound of it, they weren't digging in a field, but on a road. Digging in fields at night could be forgiven, maybe. Digging on a road meant only one thing: IEDs. Digging on a road could not be forgiven, and the punishment was death. *Crunch.* Then a distant, frustrated voice.

I hopped off the road and into the cornfields. I waited until Shawn reached my shoulder. "You hearin' what I'm hearin'?" I whispered.

"Yep. What're ya thinkin'?"

I turned to look at him. "It sounds like they're close. Hundred, maybe two hundred meters? Could be on the other side of that wall up ahead." I paused and strained to get a better view. "Looks like the road goes up to that wall and swings left, but the sound seemed like it is up and to the right." Shawn's eyes narrowed as he nodded, thinking. "Want me to take us up to the wall and we can reassess?"

Shawn lifted a finger to silence me. I looked at him quizzically, cocking my head to the side. Silence. The sounds had stopped. Completely. "No more sound," Shawn mouthed, not making a peep. We didn't move. The white noise of the cornfield—the rolling stalks of corn, the singing insects, the rippling water—were deafening in the absence of the voices and shovel.

Finally, I asked, "Think they heard us?"

Shawn shook his head. We waited several minutes until the digging resumed, an indication that whoever was digging thought they were alone. Shawn prodded me forward. We moved cautiously, careful to note any changes in the noise patterns, which faded as we moved farther away. Eventually I found a break in the wall and discovered that corn had been planted so close to the opening that it practically spilled out into the road. Reaching the break, Shawn looked at it with disgust. It was clear that moving through the dense cornfield would impede our effort to double back on the diggers. He made his decision and pointed for me to move into it. I slung my rifle to the rear, grabbed both edges of the gap with my hands, and hauled myself over the three-foot ledge and into the waiting maize.

I grabbed a stalk with my hand and gently stepped on its base with my heel. I repeated this again and again, making my way through the corn as quietly as possible. Then I noticed the silence. The digging had stopped again. I faced the area where the noise should have been coming from and waited. Nothing. Around us the corn swayed lazily, almost in concert with our nervous breathing. Suddenly the sound of someone rustling through the corn caught my attention. It was exactly the sound we had just been making, except that we were not moving. I looked to Shawn. A simple twitch confirmed my fear. Someone knew we were there.

I reached rearward and grabbed my gun, slowly swinging it to the front. The nylon sling that held it to my body groaned and I grimaced, trying desperately to get the weapon in place without making more sound. Behind me, one by one, I heard five faint clicks as weapons were switched from safe to fire. It was entirely possible that we had been tracked from the moment we'd left the District Center. Our entire team had just funneled into a walled-off field and we had no sense of its size or avenues of approach. There was a good chance we had just walked into a well-laid trap. My thoughts became foggy and I realized that I was hold-ing my breath. I forced air in and out through my nostrils. In and out. In and out. I prepared to fight a foe I could not see through the dense field. We had no air support and were out of the range of the District Center's mortar teams. I wasn't sure we could win this fight.

"Get us out of this fucking cornfield, Wood," Shawn whispered behind me.

• • •

EIGHT HOURS LATER

Opening one eye, I stared at the roof of the tent. In front of me, Tim looked up from his SAW.

"You're awake," he stated matter-of-factly. "I was beginning to think you were a lazy piece of shit." He held his SAW barrel up close to his eyes and examined it, finally looking at me and cracking a smile. "Heard you guys had an interesting night last night."

I rubbed my eyes and looked down at the black, brown, and olive drab smears on my hands. I realized that I still had greasy paint on my face from the night's mission. The river had been too cold to wash in when we walked back into camp at dawn. "Dude, I'm telling you . . . last night was . . . like a horror movie."

Tim laughed, still working the Afghan dust out of the tiny crevices of his weapon. "So your other missions have been romantic comedies? What happened?"

I shrugged, not sure where to begin. "It was like any other night op. Went out, set up some ambushes, followed some trails. But . . ." I drifted, thinking back to the cornfields and the game of hide-and-seek.

"But what? You got spooked and ran back here to me?" he asked sarcastically.

"Man, I'm telling you—I'm not sure I have ever been so pants-shitting scared." Reaching between my legs, I pushed my ammo belt and a claymore mine aside and grabbed a canteen. Wetting my throat, I continued, "For the first time I felt what it was like to be prey." I wanted to change gears. "How'd your team do last night?"

Tim shrugged. "Didn't shoot anybody." He looked up. "And we didn't find the boogeyman either, so not quite as successful as you."

"Dude, last night was fucked up."

He chuckled. "Aren't they all fucked?" *Fucked* is a crude word. Certainly not a word I would use in front of my mother. But it's a necessary phrase in war. Equal parts verb, adjective, adverb, noun, and conjunction, *fucked* adeptly conveyed the unconveyable. Things being fucked up had become an odd status quo. It wasn't just the violence—though, as the days turned to weeks, and the weeks turned to months, the team had grown increasingly desensitized to it. Only a few days prior, a local had arrived at the District Center in a truck, its bed full of arms and legs and torsos, each separated from the other by an Apache helicopter. Turns out that the helicopter's 30mm chain gun chewed up humans like a chain saw. Observing the Afghan army haul the parts away, someone made a joke. How do you fit three Afghans in a wheelbarrow? he asked. One limb at a time, someone replied, laughing. That was fucked up.

Fucked up also meant some colonel thought sending a helicopter full of cheap steaks and nonalcoholic beer would boost dwindling morale— never mind the fact that our company was dangerously low on water and fuel for the generator. Of course, *fucked up* also summarized those moments we just couldn't comprehend, like when one of Echo Company's Marines got shot through the ear lobe in an ambush. *Zip*, right through the cartilage. His ear pierced by an AK-47. How's that for fucked?

I walked over to an upside-down crate and turned on battery-powered speakers. Hundreds of artists scrolled past on the iPod until my thumb randomly selected a playlist. I lay down and closed my eyes as Bob Marley told me everything was gonna be alright. The wind gently flapped the tent's sides. With the heat and the reggae, it could almost be mistaken for a palm tree swaying in the breeze. I imagined I was far away. In a cabana. On a lounge chair.

A dull explosion in the distance, outside the safe walls of the District Center, pulled me back to Sangin.

Wheeler poked his head through the tent's back entrance. "That wasn't us. Somebody set off an explosion in the market and started shooting. We don't have any patrols in the area. Don't know anything else as of now."

With Bob Marley still jamming on the cheap speakers and my moment of Zen ruined, I organized the stuff around my cot, picking up my gear and laying it out for inspection. I hummed the tune of the song as it played.

All around the tent guys played cards, dusted off gear, or read tattered paperbacks, humming the lyrics or bobbing their heads to the music's rhythm. I picked up a grenade, inspecting the pin and turning it over in my hand, looking for imperfections, whistling the chorus through pursed lips. Satisfied, I placed the grenade back in its pouch and clipped it in. I was reaching for a second grenade when Wheeler's voice cut above the song.

"Hey! Cut the music!" Someone reached over and pressed "pause." "They need medics up by the front gate. The Afghan police are bringing in a bunch of casualties from the market." I could hear a commotion brewing a hundred yards away, in the direction of the gate.

Tim, Wheeler, and I reached the front gate and found a row of empty stretchers lined up. A handful of Corpsmen and British medics stood ready to man them. Soon, Afghan men and women struggled in, many carrying wounded children in their arms. Each was hastily patted down by a guard to ensure they weren't wearing suicide vests. The first man, old with a long grey beard, came through carrying what might have been his grandchild. He laid the child on a stretcher, only to reveal that he himself had been shot. Soon all the Corpsmen and medics were gone, having carried the first batch of wounded away. Another young boy came in, shot through the thigh. I took a moment to try to calm him down, but soon realized that I didn't need to—his eyes were glazed with shock and he wasn't making a sound.

As Wheeler and I carried his stretcher toward the small field hospital near the District Center's landing zone, I looked at the boy. He looked back at me. His leg was bleeding through the T-shirt that had been tied around it. We tried our best not to tip the stretcher to one side or the other as we jogged across a gravel lot.

We reached the small tent that served as the casualty collection point. Six or seven other stretchers were spread out, each with two or three men kneeling alongside. The battalion surgeon emerged from the tent, snapping latex gloves onto his hands as he walked forward. Soon a shirtless British medic with tattoos covering his chest and arms leaned in to look at the boy. I knew him from several missions we'd run with the Brits. He was a fierce fighter. The medic grabbed the boy's shoulder. "How ya doin', lad?" he asked, his appearance softening.

Wanting to be helpful, I handed out bottles of water to those tending the wounded. Approaching one stretcher, I could see that things were bad. I looked over the shoulder of the battalion surgeon to see another young boy, maybe eleven or twelve, with two bullet holes in his torso. The boy's breathing was shallow and his eyes were rolled back into his head. "We need to get this kid into surgery now," the surgeon declared. He marched back into the tent to prepare, the medics hauling the dying child in after him.

I returned to the boy I had carried. I asked the medic how the kid was doing.

"Ehh, he'll be alright. The bullet missed his femoral artery, although it was bloody close." He continued cleaning the wound. "Lucky bastard— if it'd hit, he'd be dead. This lower leg looks like it may be broken, though. Maybe he fell after getting hit." He reached down with a bloody hand and showed me the tender spot on the boy's tibia. Looking to the kid, who was still stoic, I smiled encouragingly and uncapped some water. I brushed back his hair while he sipped it.

"There we go, kid," I said softly. "Let's get some more water in ya. Then we're gonna go for a little ride in a helicopter. Have you ever been in a helicopter? They're fun, real fun. You've probably seen them up in the sky before." I held up my hand and made a hovering motion while attempting a helicopter sound. The boy's eyes widened. I couldn't tell whether he was excited or terrified. The surgeon walked back through the maze of stretchers, surveying the scene. A medic asked him what had happened to the boy with the wounds. The surgeon just shook his head.

"Hey, mate. Mate? Let's get this kid ready for a stick, eh? He could use some fluids." He whistled for someone's attention and shouted, "Hey, we need a bag of lactated Ringer's over here."

I grabbed the kid's hand. "Wow," I said with fake wonder, "look at this!" I held up our hands in front of his face, showing him how much bigger mine was. Behind me, a child's scream pierced the crowd. I could hear men trying to calm the little girl down, but she was hysterical with pain, screaming for her mother in Pashto. I looked at the boy, concerned the hysteria would spread. "We're not going to cry, are we? You're a tough little kid, right?" I rubbed his palm, trying to keep him calm. Another medic knelt with a needle and grabbed the boy's left arm. The boy looked at the needle with horror. I grabbed the boy's chin and forced him to look at me. "Hey there, kid, you just got shot by an AK-47—that little needle ain't gonna hurt at all. You're gonna be just fine," I continued until I saw the medic slide the catheter into the vein and pull the needle out.

I looked at the boy. "You're gonna be okay, kid, alright? You hearin' me? They're going to take you to the big city and stitch you up and before you know it you'll be right back here." He didn't understand a single word I said, but as I stood, he smiled gently.

Turning around, I got a clear view of all the casualties. Twenty feet away medics were still working frantically to stem the flow of blood on a now silent little girl. Off to the side of the clearing was a stretcher covered in white sheets. A helicopter landed, and the dead and wounded children were loaded up. "Goddamnit," I whispered, ripping off my gloves and walking toward the ramp that would take me back by the river. I was joined by Wheeler, Tim, and Clay.

"Well, that was fucked up," Tim said. Another chapter written in an expanding tome of *fucked.*

"I'm over this," Clay said under his breath.

CHAPTER 7

LIFE AFTER WAR

A hush swept through the crowd as the first *thwump* echoed in the distance. We gazed skyward—searching, waiting for the bomb burst. Then it came, a brilliant red explosion high in the sky. A series of far-off *thwumps* followed as the red embers floated to the ground. Soon a mesmerizing display lit up the night.

Indra leaned into me. I'd met her three weeks before, upon my return from Afghanistan. I was spending Thanksgiving with two good friends I'd made in Los Angeles, Joe and Mike, brothers about three years apart. She'd gone to high school with them and that weekend attended a small reunion they were hosting. It took me awhile to work up the courage to approach her, paralyzed with cowardice despite having just returned from a war zone. Tonight, we were on our first date, the holiday fireworks show in Manhattan Beach.

"So why do you like fireworks so much?" Indra asked.

I smiled sheepishly. "I don't know. It's tough to say. I've loved them since I was a kid." That was only part of the truth. The full truth was they reminded me of a sense of patriotism I'd felt since I was a young boy, of the Star-Spangled Banner and the promise that it confers on our nation, and of the men I'd served with. I loved America deeply; it's why I chose to serve. But all of that was too deep for a first date.

Under the intermittent flashes of red and white and blue, I clenched my jaw and thought about the war. I welcomed it. In fact, I longed for it. To be transported back. To think of Mike and Layton and Nathan and Blake alive. To feel the thrill of combat. The imminence of death. The taste of life. The memories weren't peaceful, but they were what I wanted to remember.

I felt a tear form and I shut my eyes hurriedly, careful not to let my emotions show. Conscious of Indra's presence, I tilted my chin slightly away. But I wasn't ready to leave my memories behind just yet. I needed to feel them.

After a moment, I felt a cool, smooth hand reach up and cradle my elbow. I hid a small smile and moved closer, inviting her to hold my arm more tightly.

A few weeks later Tim and I were transferred from 2-7 to Camp Pendleton, where we joined the instructor cadre at 1st Marine Division's Pre-Scout Sniper Course, a grueling precursor to the ten-week sniper school Tim and I had graduated from before Afghanistan. Our group had been the first Marine Corps sniper teams to operate in Afghanistan in several years, and the Corps thought we could help share the lessons we'd learned operating in that unique threat environment with the next generation of snipers.

The weeks were long and physical; our goal was to weed out as many Marines as possible that we didn't feel could hack the full course. But as soon as we cut the class loose each Friday, I would hop in my car and drive north from the base, eager to see Indra. In the months since that first date, we had fallen fast in love.

But a choice loomed on my horizon. In many moments, maybe even most moments, I was anxious to finish my Marine Corps enlistment and put the military and war behind me. When I returned from Afghanistan, my parents once again greeted me at the airfield. As my father embraced me, he whispered that my mother had repainted the living room ten different colors to occupy herself while I was gone. He couldn't bear the thought of her enduring another deployment. And Indra made no effort to mask her wish that I get out. She admired my service but could not imagine enduring the long stretches of loneliness a military marriage would bring. She wanted a husband and father who would be present.

But despite the lingering doubt about the wars and our ability to win them, I felt an insuppressible urge to return to them. In quiet times my mind would drift to the men we'd lost. I imagined sitting at a table drinking whiskey with them. What would they say? Go finish the job? Or get out and move on? Would they call me a coward? And if I did move on and the job was left unfinished, would their sacrifice have been a waste?

Not knowing those answers caused me great distress, and I would often think to myself that the only way I could find peace was by returning to war. And then the opportunity came. A handful of my senior instructors from my time in sniper school were transferring over to a battalion that was preparing to rotate into Afghanistan. They were assembling an all-star sniper platoon from across the 1st Marine Division, and one of the staff sergeants invited me to join. It would require me to extend my enlistment by a full year, but it gave me the chance to go back to Helmand and finish what we'd started. Or at least that's what I imagined.

Two hours later I walked into Indra's apartment. She ordered a pizza and I made cocktails and eventually we settled onto the couch. We'd only chatted for five minutes before Indra cut me off.

"What's wrong?" she asked. Her capacity to read people always unnerved me. I deflected and told her I was tired, that we'd really smoked the pre-sniper students that week. She would have none of it. "No, something else is wrong. What is it?"

Stammering at first, I told her about the sniper platoon being pulled together and my invitation to join it. I considered lying and telling her that I was getting orders to go but couldn't bring myself to do it. Re-upping and going back to Afghanistan with the battalion was a choice, and a choice that only I could make.

Indra asked a hundred questions, each of them designed to poke a new hole in my logic. Each of them designed to reframe how I thought about my war experience and what, if anything, I still owed my country and my brothers.

"I just don't know," I said, shaking my head and closing my eyes.

"Well, I'll tell you what I know," she responded, her voice firm. "You going back to Iraq or Afghanistan is not going to win the war. I'm sorry, but no one is that special. And it definitely won't bring any of your friends back. I know you feel guilt, but you'll only see more friends get hurt. The cycle won't end. I love you, but I can't sign up for that."

After Indra went to bed, I sat on the couch alone for several hours, contemplating what Indra had said. She was right. My urge to go back to war was not born of idealism or patriotism or a defense of good versus evil. It was driven by guilt and fear. Guilt that I'd come home unscathed. Fear that I would never be able to honor and make sense of my friends' deaths.

But I knew that couldn't be true, and in that moment, I chose to get out. I didn't know what I would do with the rest of my life, but I would not have it defined by war.

• • •

What will become of me? It's a natural question to ask when you know you can't go back to who you once were. It leads to other questions: Who was I? I was a warrior—I think. But what is a warrior, anyway? It's easy to look at those who have been to war and call them warriors. And perhaps that is fitting. I once drank whiskey until the sun rose with two men that were on the Osama bin Laden raid. They were no doubt warriors, kin to the Vikings, the Aztecs, or the Zulu. But if they are the yardstick by which warriors are measured, then maybe I wasn't one.

Though if I was a warrior, the transformation probably happened when I extended my palm and the drill instructor with the lantern jaw placed an Eagle, Globe, and Anchor on it, making me a Marine. In that moment I became part of a legacy of warriors that stretched back centuries.

Or perhaps it could have been when I learned to thrust a bayonet into another man's body and practiced that in the sun and the sand against a stack of tires, screaming "KILL!" with every attack. The Marine Corps was adept at training us to fight and kill. Were we made warriors then?

If not then, then certainly when I carried a rifle and wore a uniform and stalked bad men in foreign lands. Maybe not all Marines are warriors, but I would like to think I earned my stripes when I first loaded a grenade into my launcher's breach and lobbed it with a *thwump* at an insurgent machine gun position. Those moments seemed sufficiently war-filled to earn me the right to call myself a warrior.

Yet perhaps I was using the wrong measure. The Greek philosopher Heraclitus said that the warrior is defined by his responsibility to bring others home from war. Interestingly, Heraclitus makes no mention of the warrior's physical prowess or formidability in combat, only that sacred duty to look after others. If that is true, then I have been looking in all the wrong places to burnish my warrior claim.

The bracelet on my wrist has four names: Blake, Nathan, Mike, and Layton. They didn't come home. Well, they did, just in flag-draped coffins. Still others came back but lost their battles here. Bojorquez and Hilbert and Pak were fierce warriors in their own right, but they chose to board with the boatman on the River Styx. For them, home was the grave. If a warrior is judged by his ability to get his brothers and sisters home safely and keep them safe, then it seems I failed.

I know that there are two versions of me. Me before war, and me after. War took away some of my most precious possessions. It snuffed the life out of friends I loved dearly. It also ripped a simplistic and ignorant worldview out of my hands and ground it underneath the heel of a combat boot. Perhaps that was a gift. Now I see the value of life, my own and others, with new eyes. Sunsets no longer mark another day I have survived. Now they mark another day I have lived. If that makes me a warrior, then I am proud. Of course, no gift, no lesson, is worth the price of hundreds of thousands of lives. Nonetheless, I owe who I am, in part, to war.

Still, sometimes I ask, *What if?* What if I had pursued a different path, one that didn't involve going to war? If I wasn't a warrior, then my mother wouldn't have to wonder about the battles her son fought. She could forget the sleepless nights and haunted days. She wouldn't have to remember how fearful she was that the doorbell might ring and bring with it uniformed Marines, standing there stoically to inform her that her son had died in service to his country.

My wife would no longer have to endure those awkward moments when new friends learn that her husband was a sniper, their silence clear indications of where their minds were racing. Movies would be easier to watch because she wouldn't need to sneak glances at me when characters bled to death on battlefields or city streets.

I wouldn't nervously await the day my daughter tugs on my arm and asks me about the wars. Never have to look at her and wonder about all those little girls in Iraq and Afghanistan, and wonder if they're alive today—or worse, wonder if anything I did brought them harm. Of course, I know better. I know that we killed breadwinners and emboldened the Taliban and probably destabilized the regions I served for decades to come.

Those things would be convenient, but would they be worth the cost? Being a warrior has given me a deeper appreciation for the value of honor, courage, and commitment. Hollow words to so many but hallowed by warriors. I know that honor means adhering to what's right, regardless of personal cost. That courage is not the absence of fear. Far from it. It is having the fortitude to endure for one moment more, moment after moment after moment. And commitment is an ironclad resolve to see one's obligations through to the very end.

Many veterans struggle with who they are or what they will become when they leave the military. But they shouldn't. Being a warrior is not as much a job as it is a way of life. Not a role, but a perspective of the world. Not a title, but a responsibility to others. The burden we may bear is lightened by the calling we can answer.

We were warriors once. And we will always be warriors.

PART II

CHAPTER 8

WE DO CHAOS

PORT-AU-PRINCE, HAITI, DAY TWO

In front of me, anguished faces squirmed in the hot Caribbean sun. Old men, their knees and elbows knobby with age, groaned in pain. Women threw their arms in the air and prayed loudly in Creole. Scattered between all the legs and torsos were the children. The only thing keeping the peace was a long, thin piece of military paracord tied between two tree branches. We were at a camp called Manresa, having made our journey across Port-au-Prince that morning on the advice of our Jesuit hosts. Sparse trees provided little respite from the heat. The field sat nestled between what were once buildings and were now piles of rubble. Dozens of bodies were likely buried underneath. For miles all around, Port-au-Prince lay in ruin. Haiti, with a per capita GDP of $900, is one of the poorest countries in the Western Hemisphere. It is a nation virtually without building codes, with a dysfunctional emergency services system, and a corrupt government. All of this created a perfect storm following the earthquake. No other organizations were present at Manresa, which was less an indication of their effectiveness and more an indication of the overwhelming need all across the city.

". . . So let's grab our chlorhex, our gauze, our—" Mark Hayward paused as he looked at the pile of supplies laid out on the poncho. "And that satchel full of silver sulfadiazine, and let's move it over here to set up." Three novice Jesuits from the novitiate had joined our team and were now herding the most grievously wounded into the makeshift triage area.

I knelt in front of a plastic chair and began to align and realign the rows of gauze, disinfectant, and bandages that made up my cache of materials. Over and over again I picked up the boxes of ointment and turned them, ensuring all their labels were facing forward, like a craps shooter with his die. I couldn't admit it to myself at the time, but the chaos was nearly overwhelming, and organizing my supplies brought, for me, some measure of order. I collected myself and waved the first person in line forward. A woman hobbled toward me, aided by two men. She was breathing heavily and grimacing in agony. I wasn't a doctor, but I had seen this before. A massive piece of flesh had been torn off her lower leg, revealing tissue, muscle, and bone.

Every Marine infantryman learns basic battlefield medical procedures—like how to stop arterial bleeding or stabilize a sucking chest wound or conduct a needle thoracentesis. On top of that, I had been sent to an advanced lifesaver course multiple times. Of course, none of that training matters if you can't recall it and perform it under pressure. But by this point in my life I was as comfortable with a tourniquet as I was with a remote control. I could do enough to at least save her from losing her leg to infection.

Gingerly placing my fingertips around the wound, I began probing, switching my eyes back and forth from the wound to her eyes, judging her reaction to every touch. With the bottle of chlorhexidine in one hand and a piece of gauze in the other, I looked up at her and said in a calm voice, "Miss, I'm going to be as gentle as I can but this is going to hurt like hell, okay?" She seemed to understand. I squeezed the chlorhex into the wound.

The woman leaned back and howled. I used the gauze to scrub away the dirt and gravel and pus occupying the wound. Her screams rose until one of the men pulled her face into his chest and buried her screams in his tattered shirt. Back and forth I went. Scrub. Chlorhex. Scrub.

"Hey, Mark!" I hollered over my shoulder. "I need you to check out this patient before we let her go. She probably needs antibiotics."

"I'll be right over there. Gotta finish this amputated hand first."

Holy shit, I thought. We had been at Manresa for only thirty minutes, and people were coming in like the wounded at Gettysburg.

Finding another open chair, I knelt and aligned and realigned the gauze, chlorhexidine, and bandages. The columns and rows of supplies looked to me like a company of Marines crisply standing in formation. I snapped back to the present, raised my arm, and waved the next patient forward. Two crusty feet stepped under my field of view. The feet, cracked and weathered from decades walking barefoot along the rough streets of Port-au-Prince, belonged to an old man, eyes yellowed from years under the sun. He said nothing; he simply looked down to the bundle in his arms. He was cradling a trembling little boy, maybe five or six, his small hands balled up into fists underneath his chin.

"Hey there, little guy. How ya doin'?" A pretty stupid question to ask five days after a catastrophe. I reached out and grabbed his forearm. "What's wrong with you, tough guy? Can I have a look?" I turned to the old man, who I assumed was his grandfather. I wondered if the kid's parents were buried under a mountain of rubble somewhere. The man shifted the boy to reveal a leg wrapped in a rag stained with motor oil, pus, and blood. The kid turned and buried himself in his grandfather's armpit. I squeezed his forearm gently and placed a hand on his head. For a moment I forgot everything, struck with the urge to direct every ounce of compassion that remained inside me toward creating some better outcome for this boy, even a minute of respite from the pain. Finally, the child nodded his tacit approval.

"Alright, I'll be gentle. I promise."

The yellow stain expanded as each layer of cloth was removed. I told myself not to react. The kid had a hole straight through his leg, steadily oozing multicolored pus. If he hadn't already contracted staph, he was probably only hours away. I slapped him playfully on the shoulder and pointed to the wound. "That little thing? That's what you're crying about? Come on, kiddo. I thought you were tougher than that."

I pointed to my chest. "My name is Jake. J-A-K-E. Jake, can you say that?" The kid just stared. "What's your name?" I asked, pointing to his chest. Nothing. Pointing back to myself, I repeated my name. Finally, the child's lips moved, and an almost inaudible sound escaped. I pressed on. "I was a Marine. Marines are tough. I bet one day, because you're so tough, you can be a Marine." I let the offer hang. "But I need you to prove how tough you are for me. I'm going to squeeze all this nasty pus out of your leg, and I need you to be a strong boy and let me do it, okay?" I flexed my arm to demonstrate the strength I needed from him.

I looked to the grandfather for permission to begin. He tightened his hold on the boy and nodded. I reached up with both hands and grabbed the child's thigh. My fingers nearly wrapped all the way around. Placing my thumbs just below the wound, I clenched my teeth as if I were the one about to feel the pain. "One . . . two . . . three . . ." I squeezed my thumbs inward. A river of pus and blood streamed from the hole, down the boy's leg, and onto the old man holding him.

The child screamed, cutting through the din of the encampment.

"It's okay, it's okay. It's going to be over soon." But it wasn't over. I squeezed again.

Again, the child screamed.

I squeezed again and again. The river of pus began to wane.

The screaming continued, and when I finally looked the boy in the eyes, I saw fear, pain, and betrayal. Betrayal because I was Jake, and I was supposed to help him, not hurt him. I motioned for the man to stay put, and I stood, ripping off the latex gloves. Looking around behind me, I found Mark and made my way to him.

"Mark? Hey, Mark, do we have any local anesthetics we can stick this kid I'm working on with? Looks like he fell and drove a rusty spike all the way through his leg, and I was hoping to numb him up before I start probing and cleaning it."

Mark turned to face me, revealing his patient. A man was missing three fingers and half his palm. It was like he'd placed his hand down a garbage disposal. Mark's eyes caught mine and locked them in, so I didn't look back at the hand and cause the man to panic.

"I saw some lidocaine in one of the bags, but we don't have much." He raised his forearm up to his forehead and wiped the sweat away from his eyes, careful to keep the bloody gauze he was holding from touching skin. "Let me ask you this—is the boy going to lose his leg?"

"I don't think so. I think I'll be able to get it under control and keep the infection away."

"Then I'm sorry, the kid's going to have to deal with the pain."

I nodded.

"Do me a favor, though. Make sure Doc Griswell checks him out before you send him off so he can prescribe antibiotics."

"Roger that, boss," I said.

"You're the boss, Jake. I'm just the medic," Mark said and mockingly offered a salute with a gloved hand. I turned and walked over to the pile of supplies, realizing halfway there that I had not seen Doc Griswell since we'd started seeing patients.

I yelled back to Mark. "Hey, Mark. Where is Doc Gris?"

"Delivering a baby somewhere."

A baby? In this? Even if it was delivered alive, would it live to see February? I scanned the area for Griswell. He was on his hands and knees facing away from me in the shade of the only trees around. His baby blue hospital scrubs were framed by two legs, split wide open in the air. Doc Gris was indeed delivering a baby, the mother lying flat on a dislodged wooden door repurposed as a hospital bed. I closed my eyes and said a quick prayer. A prayer that the mother and the child would survive and that, somehow, they would escape Manresa, and Port-au-Prince, and maybe even Haiti altogether.

I opened my eyes and walked over to the pile of supplies. Brother Jim was there, rummaging through the different piles in search of something. He looked up and smiled.

"Welcome to Haiti, my friend," he said. I laughed. "How are you doing? You good?"

"Yeah, I'm good, Brother Jim. Thanks. You?" I couldn't believe how composed he was.

"Can't say I've ever seen anything like this before, but I'm good," Jim said. "I'll make sure we send some interpreters on a beer run later so we can relax and reflect."

"Jim, you're beginning to make me think you were a Marine in a prior life."

"Jesuits aren't saints, Jake," Jim said with a devilish grin. We both laughed, in a moment that separated us from the present world. "Alright," Jim said, clapping his hands. "Back to work. The beer can wait."

Digging into the pile, I found a box of sterile cotton probes. Grabbing the supplies, I walked back over to the young boy. I reached into my pocket and grabbed a bottle of water, offering it to the boy. The child looked cautiously at his grandfather, who smiled and nodded. Reaching out with both hands, he brought the bottle to his dry, chapped lips. The water poured out of the bottle and into his mouth and down into his tiny belly and, for the first time in five days, the kid drank without fear of where his next drink would come from.

I put a new pair of gloves on my hands and ripped open a cotton swab. Reaching up, I continued working on his leg.

Later that night Brother Jim sat us in a circle at our camp. Dr. Griswell miraculously produced a bottle of Hendrick's gin, while our interpreters returned with cardboard boxes filled with Presidente beer. I looked around for an opener. It took a few seconds to remember where I was. I would have to improvise. The killed-in-action memorial bracelet I wore on my right wrist was inscribed with the names of four Marines I'd lost overseas— Blake, Nathan, Mike, and Layton. Below them was the phrase *Frater Infinitas,* Latin for "Brothers Forever." Placing the steel bracelet between my thumb and the bottle, I popped off the cap and took a long swig.

For the next ten minutes I led the team in a swift after-action review of the day's events. It was second nature for the veterans in the circle to brutally recount the mission's successes and, most importantly, the failures. We would have to improve in the coming days, and we could only do that by relentlessly probing our mistakes. After the AAR, Brother Jim spoke up.

"I want to ask everyone to take a moment and reflect on what happened today," he said. "We just spent ten hours in perhaps the worst situation imaginable, and the images you saw today will likely be seared into your memory for the rest of your lives. It's important for us to talk about that. Some of you will want to share bad memories, some of you good ones. But I'd ask that you share them."

Silently, we nodded.

Brother Jim went on to talk about what had impacted him that morning in Manresa, and slowly, one by one, everyone in the circle talked about their experience.

As I sat listening to the group, my mind drifted back to the young boy. He had been so similar to the Pashtun boy I'd worked on a year and a half prior in the Helmand Valley. The wounds the same, their age and size as well. That earlier day had had a profound impact on me. I left the Marines in part because I never again wanted to see a young child needlessly wounded like that. Yet here I was. Somehow this felt different. Not necessarily good, but . . . what? Pure? I would think about it later.

I realized the circle was silent. William had just finished speaking, and it was my turn. I smiled apologetically. With another swig of beer, I stared at the ground and cleared my throat. "There was this boy today . . ."

CHAPTER 9

EXPECTANT

O ur horn blared as we wove our way through teeming streets toward Port-au-Prince's largest hospital, where a currently dysfunctional emergency room needed extra hands. "Holy shit," I said, pointing to a charred carcass lying in the middle of the street.

"Is that from the earthquake?" someone asked.

"No, that's gotta be gang related," I said. My squad had once stumbled on a makeshift grave with a half dozen bodies. Retribution killings had a distinct look and feel.

"We're here," the driver said. Hundreds of Haitians were gathered outside the hospital walls, shouting and waving their arms, each convinced their ailment warranted immediate entrance to the compound. Behind the bars of the gates stood two young, clean-shaven white kids, eyes hidden behind dark Oakley sunglasses. Their grayscale camouflage indicated they were U.S. Army.

"The 82nd Airborne is here!" I called. I pulled myself through the crowd and thrust my old military ID through the gate. "Hey, Specialist, over here," I shouted. "We've got three trucks and five casualties who need to be in surgery within the hour or they'll die. The operating room is expecting us." The last part was a lie, but the type of lie specialists are used to hearing and saying to get things done.

The soldier walked over and peered suspiciously at my ID. He studied the ragged Marine boonie hat that sat on top of ten-day stubble. The green camouflage of my boonie hat didn't match the desert camouflage of the pants I was wearing, and neither matched the navy blue Milwaukee Fire Department shirt on my back. "I've got orders not to open this gate except for Red Cross officials or U.S. Army personnel."

"You gotta trust me, man. I've got three vics, five friendly pax, and five casualties."

He looked around nervously, desperately hoping his lieutenant or platoon sergeant would show up and tell him what to do. "Hey, listen, man," I said. "You need to do this. I'll go to bat for you with your lieutenant."

He nodded and stepped back from the gate, giving a thumbs-up to a soldier sitting in the booth. "These guys are good to go. Let them in."

I walked behind the last truck as it maneuvered through the small courtyard and parked. The entire complex was in disarray, with gurneys being frantically wheeled to and fro, doctors crisscrossing and running into each other, a pile of bodies stacked up near one wall. Behind me I heard someone yell my name. Turning, I saw William walking toward me briskly.

"Hey, Wood. Glad you guys made it," he said.

"So, what's the deal here?" I asked. "Brother Jim came back to the clinic and said you guys wanted to shift the mission here."

"We got here with that first batch of surgical cases and the place was total chaos," William explained. "There's a pretty well-stocked emergency room with no doctors over there"—he pointed back in the direction from which he'd come—"and a quasi-functioning operating room over there," he said, pointing in the opposite direction. "The problem was that nobody was taking charge of the ER, and, as a result, people weren't getting to the operating room. So Mark and I decided to put Doc Gris in charge of the ER, since he runs one in DC." It was a lot to take in. *Did we just take over an emergency room?*

It was obvious that the hospital needed people willing to make quick and tough decisions. William led me through an alley. "This is the back entrance," he said, sidestepping a pile of bloody gauze and soiled clothing. "Nobody's established a plan for the biohazardous waste, so it's piling up back here." A myriad of diseases must have been baking in the open sun.

Double doors leading inside were propped open so that a large fan could blow air into the emergency room. I saw Mark Hayward pick up a syringe and walk back toward a table.

"Oh, Wood, you made it," he said. "I guess I should give Marines more credit." Holding a syringe with somewhat sterile hands, he awkwardly offered me his elbow to tap. "I've got to go stick this huge needle into a little boy's leg and then cut hunks of rotting flesh from his gangrenous wound. Would you like to join?" I'd come to appreciate Mark's dry humor. It masked a deep concern for his patients.

"Thanks for the offer, but I think I'm going to ease into it here."

Maintaining a constant hum, the fan in the doorway drowned out the monotone whimpers and sobs. Metal chairs screeched on dirty floors while, nearby, a Haitian nurse spoke in hushed Creole, most likely about an impending amputation. Across the room an aluminum bedpan crashed to the floor with a loud curse, spewing piss and shit and blood. Beside me a young man slapped the cold metal top of his table with the palm of his hand, grimacing in pain as Craig Parello, a Marine veteran and firefighter, removed infected tissue from his other hand.

Doc Griswell touched my shoulder. "Good to see you, Jake," he said.

"What do you need me to do, Doc?"

He put his hands on his hips and pursed his lips, looking back and forth across the room. "Well, I tell you what—we could really use someone cleaning up these floors. We're going to start getting people infected if we don't clean up this mess."

"You got it." I found gloves and trash bags in what seemed to be a supply closet and started picking up pieces of gauze stained with blood, mucus, pus, iodine, chlorhexidine, and burn gel. Each piece had a story behind it—a little boy's bleeding leg, crushed while escaping his cinderblock home. An old woman, raped while struggling to survive alone in postapocalyptic Port-au-Prince. A young man's oozing hand, infected because he'd been defecating next to his makeshift shelter for days. I reached down to pick up a pile of sheets, only to drop them quickly before the noxious smell made me vomit. "Holy shit!"

"What?" I heard Jeff ask above. I pointed at the pile. "It's just a pile of shit, dude. It won't bite." Jeff bent down and scooped up the mound of soiled linens, his thick-muscled forearms bundling up the linens and stuffing them into the garbage bag. I walked out the back door and tossed it in the alley, remembering that no one had yet set up a system for the biohazardous waste. We would have to figure that out. Soon.

The floor, while clear of gauze, was obviously no more sterile than when I'd begun. I found a gallon of bleach and a yellow mop bucket on rickety wheels. Swabbing it back and forth, back and forth, across the floor was oddly soothing. For the first time in days, my mind started to clear.

Years later, as Team Rubicon grew and my job evolved, I would think back to that moment. As the team leader, it was equal parts humbling and gratifying to be assigned such a seemingly menial task. I was a highly trained Marine, a veteran of two wars, yet my best use at that moment was scooping up soiled linens and mopping the floor. I didn't know it at the time, but that spirit of just getting the job done would become a defining aspect of Team Rubicon's culture and help mark an organization that is as humble as it is proud.

"Wood, we need your help."

I recruited a young Haitian boy to finish the mopping for me, then walked over to where Hayward and Griswell were standing. "What's up, guys?"

"I need you and Mark to turn this woman over. She's completely immobile. I think she has a back injury," Griswell said.

I looked down at the woman. She was old, very old. Dark cracks crisscrossed her face, and matchstick limbs, impossibly frail, poked out of a dark, tattered robe. I looked to Hayward for guidance.

"Alright, Wood. Grab her here and here—" He pointed. "Be careful of her neck." I placed my hands where he pointed and looked up. "Okay, one, two, three." Her body was light as goose down.

"Okay," Griswell said. "Let's cut away her clothes. Looks like she's got some bleeding on her hip."

I unstrapped my combat knife and paused to look to her for tacit approval. Her eyes were expressionless. I realized just how far gone she was. As the blade ripped through the cheap fabric, I remembered the phase of my life when I carried this very same blade in case I had to pull it across a man's throat. I forced the thought away.

The open robe revealed a naked skeleton clinging to life. Each shallow breath drew her skin taut across her rib cage. The flesh that once covered hip bone had long rotted away. Lower down, her vagina and legs were covered with sores that oozed a milky substance. "Oh shit," I whispered, completely unsure what to do next.

"Gentlemen, be aware," Griswell stated clearly. "This woman's condition is indicative of full-blown, late-stage AIDS. Be extremely careful."

I went a little numb. Hayward and Griswell leaned in and began probing the wound on her hip. Without thinking, I snapped a second pair of latex gloves over my first, naively hoping the added layer would protect me from infection. "What can I do?"

Hayward stood up and grimaced, thinking. "She's in desperate need of fluids. Can you start an IV?"

I tied a latex glove around the woman's arm to better expose her veins. Her arm was no thicker than two of my fingers. How would I ever be able to start a line? I smacked her forearm, turning it this way and that to look for a vein. Finding nothing, I grabbed her hand and balled it into a fist, intermittently squeezing it. I looked into her eyes, hoping I could get her to realize that I needed her to squeeze her forearm to pump blood into her veins. She was too far gone to understand. Finally, I found what looked to be a suitable vein and prepared the needle. I thought back to my training: in at a thirty-degree angle, puncture, then fifteen degrees, wait for blood, gently slide the catheter in. Simple. I breathed slowly to steady my hands, forcing the fear of infection to the back of my mind. Puncture. The needle was in. I gingerly probed, hoping to find my way into the vein. Nothing. I reset, working to find another location. Puncture. Probe. Nothing. "Mark?"

"Yeah," he responded.

"I got nothing. This woman's blood volume is so low it's impossible." I stepped away from the table and cursed silently. Mark and I looked at each other, both thinking the same thing.

"Whaddya say, Doc?" Hayward asked Griswell.

"Well, she's in incredible pain," he said, continuing to poke and probe. "She needs a catheter inserted into her bladder or she's going to be in horrific pain. That said, I don't think she will last more than a few more hours."

"I agree. She's expectant," Mark said. *Expectant* was a military term. It meant someone was expected to die. It was a sterile way of saying there was nothing we could do. "We need to focus on people we can save." I nodded, calmly accepting the decision to let the woman die on the table.

I followed Mark across the room. A mother had draped herself around the shoulders of a little girl with a wounded leg who sobbed in fear and pain. "Jake, I'm going to have to cut away a lot of this crap around the wound here," Mark said carefully, pointing at pieces of infected flesh. "I'm going to need your help with that, but more importantly, I'm going to need you to help keep this beautiful little girl here calm," he said, his goatee-lined mouth smiling at the girl with sincere affection.

I hesitated. "Got any ideas on how to do that? I'm not quite sure I have your Mormon charm."

"Do what I do with my kid," he said, reaching for his iPhone. "Placate them with technology." Laughing, I grabbed the phone and pulled up the camera application. *Ok, then.* I took a picture of the girl's face—puffy and wet from a steady stream of tears—and flipped the phone around to show it to her. She giggled. *Promising.* I snapped another photo. Another hit. I repeated the game until she was fully laughing, begging for more. Her mother stroked her hair, grateful to have her little girl back.

Craig came over to help Mark with the wound. I saw Doc Griswell lying on the table, desperately trying to insert a catheter into the expectant woman I had just walked away from. Griswell's face contorted in concentration as he tried and failed. I stood and watched as he made another attempt. Drenched in sweat, he refused to give up. Slowly my heart filled with shame. How easily I had walked away from a woman suffering so horribly, dismissing her condition so callously as to call her *expectant. What a word*, I thought. *Expectant.* Probably chosen by military psychologists so it wouldn't further trigger soldiers on the battlefield. It's much easier to refer to your friend as expectant and continue fighting. If you used real words, like *bleeding to death*, you might break down and become a casualty yourself. The military had deliberately wired us to fight and to win, and that's a good thing. But everything has a cost, and part of the price was our capacity to feel. Or, as I was beginning to suspect, the ability to choose not to feel.

"How you doin', Jake?" Brother Jim asked, standing at my side and watching the same scene unfold two tables away.

"I'm good, Jim. Just trying to keep this little cutie from crying her heart out." I reached out and put a hand on her shoulder. But Jim was no fool and trusted his sixth sense: something was going on in my head.

"You look like you could use some water. Why don't you take this and go get some fresh air. I can handle this little heartbreaker." Jim held out a bottle. I grabbed it and walked into the blinding sun. I moved to the corner of the wall and squatted down, getting as low as possible to stay in the shade. The concrete felt almost cool. I sat there, eyes closed, trying to ignore the constant hum of flies buzzing around the piles of filth just a few feet away.

"Wood?"

I opened a single eye. "What's up?" McNulty was standing over me.

"I've got good news and I've got bad news."

"Hit me with the good news."

"Your dad got through to me about an hour ago. He said people are going crazy over our blog posts and photos, and donations are pouring in." We were making a real effort to share a raw, first-person perspective of the challenges and suffering on the ground, something that would become a hallmark of Team Rubicon in later years.

"That's definitely good news—we can pay for that second team to come down now. What's the bad news?" I asked suspiciously.

"Well, that's not all the good news. He said that because of the money, some lawyer in Minnesota, who was a Marine, called him up out of the blue and said we needed to incorporate so we're protected." William paused to see if I was tracking. I raised my eyebrows, signaling that I had no idea what to expect next. "So this guy, Pat something, incorporated us as a 501(c)(3) nonprofit."

Caught completely off guard, I furrowed my brow and asked, "A 501-c-3 what?"

"It's like a charity, it gives us nonprofit status. You're the president."

I reached up and rubbed my temples, nursing what was beginning to feel like a bad hangover. "Nonprofit . . . President . . . 501 . . . what the hell?" It all seemed too much to handle. The only things my mind had the capacity to process were security and logistics and operations. The idea of throwing tax liability and corporate responsibility in the mix was overloading my system. "This is horrible news," I said, laughing nervously.

William squatted. "Jake, we're on to something. Team Rubicon is on to something. This is special—just look at what we've done the last couple of days. Using veterans for disasters? This could be a game changer."

My mind foggy, I decided I needed to table the discussion for later in the evening. "I'm scared to ask, but what's the bad news?"

"Who's Clay Hunt?"

Oh no. "Clay? We served together. Same infantry platoon in Iraq, same sniper section in Afghanistan. He's like a brother from another mother. Why?"

"Well, your dad said Clay called Indra in the middle of the night saying that he was hopping the next flight to come down here and link up with us. I guess Indra's pissed. She told your dad she thought you were dead when Clay called."

I jumped up. "What? Are you serious? Tell me my dad told him to stay put in LA." I felt white hot. The situation on the ground was crazy. I couldn't possibly bear the responsibility of Clay wandering around the Dominican Republic and Haiti by himself, looking for us in the midst of the most horrific humanitarian disaster in modern history.

"I think he's already left. He told Indra that he had a GPS coordinate from one of our earlier posts."

"That stupid mother . . . I swear to God I'm going to kill him. Give me your phone—I'm going to call my dad and have him tell Clay to get on the first plane back to California."

"Phones are down, calls aren't going out. Plus, he's already in the air."

"Son of a bitch. He's going to get his ass killed and I'm going to have to tell his mother that her son was an idiot." I kicked a pile of trash in frustration, sending waste flying. Over my shoulder I shouted out, "If you get ahold of my dad, you tell him to have Clay turn around the moment he gets to the Dominican."

Near nightfall we returned to the novitiate and repeated our ritual from the night before, each member of the team recounting the moment from their day that would forever change their life. Recounting the story of how Doc Griswell's compassion had sparked soul-searching within me, I kept my gaze locked on the bottle of beer in my hand, embarrassed by my own callousness. Brother Jim smiled warmly at me from across the circle. He'd witnessed my moment.

The team gradually dispersed to their tents. I saw McNulty's face faintly illuminated by his BlackBerry. He was sending photographs from the hospital and some of Mark Hayward's writing back to my sister Sarah in Iowa, who was uploading it all onto a hastily built website.

"Any updates on Clay?" I asked. He shook his head. I imagined all the things that could go horribly wrong. "I'm going to rack out." He nodded.

Ten hours later we were back at the hospital, but this time the chaos was magnified tenfold. We'd awoken that morning to a massive after-shock. The earth beneath our sleeping bags pitched back and forth so violently that we struggled to escape them. When we finally scrambled out, we saw that the main building of the novitiate had sustained addi-tional damage, deep cracks appearing down the facade. Knowing that the hospital was also vulnerable, we raced to get back.

I stood in the center of the hospital's courtyard, now filled with gur-neys, makeshift beds, and tables. We spent all morning evacuating the patients from the interior rooms, fearful that another violent aftershock could bring the entire hospital down on our heads. Unfortunately, that meant that all these patients—many of them near death—were lying in the unforgiving Caribbean sun. Medicine, food, and water were all at critically low levels. The situation was dire.

Kneeling on the ground, I began cutting bedsheets in order to create makeshift sunshades for the patients. After a couple cuts someone behind me blocked the sun, their shadow stretching out beyond me.

"You look like you could use a hand, Marine."

"You son of a bitch!" I said. Clay's unmistakable laugh played behind me. Rising, I turned and embraced him. Every angry word I wanted to say disappeared as I pulled his head into my shoulder. "I'm glad you're here, brother."

"You didn't really think I was going to leave you down here by your-self, did you?" Clay glanced around and processed the situation. He slipped off his backpack and placed it on the ground. "What can I do to help?" he asked. There was no time for a protracted reunion. This was a mission.

"Take these," I said, scooping up the sheets, "and hang them up to create shade for these people."

Clay reached into his pack and pulled out a spool of paracord. "Where do I begin?"

I pointed behind him, to a gurney near a power pole. On the gurney lay the old woman from the previous day. She'd willed herself to survive another night. "Over there with that woman."

●　●　●

In the decade after returning from Port-au-Prince, I would often reflect on these moments. I didn't immediately appreciate the impact they would have on my life's arc—or how other moments on other missions would deeply change the lives of other veterans and volunteers.

I think of the boy whose leg I treated and hope that he found his way into a good primary school and sits today on the verge of graduating from high school. I imagine that he's selected a career that puts him at the intersection of making a living and rebuilding his country and helping his fellow Haitians. And, selfishly, I hope that he remembers the team of volunteers that came to help him in his darkest hour.

The old woman, whose name I never had the privilege of learning, brought something obscure within me into the light. She died later that afternoon. To some, she became merely a statistic, but Dr. Griswell had done his best to make her feel like a human being.

And as for Clay, people often write about the bonds forged in combat. Veterans will speak about the platoon mate they haven't seen in twenty years, but if they called them in need would show up without question to help. Clay would tell people that he got out of bed in the middle of the night and drove to the airport without a ticket because he wanted to help the Haitians. Of course that was true. But on a deeper level, Clay hopped on that plane because he couldn't bear the thought of me in a dangerous situation without him.

There are two types of friends in this world. Those who would run through a barrage of machine gun fire to come and get you when you're wounded, and those who wouldn't.

CHAPTER 10

WHEN THE BAGPIPES END

The phone vibrated on the kitchen table. It was Arguello. *That's odd*, I thought. Arguello and I had not really stayed in contact since getting out of the Marines, but he was a brother nonetheless. "Hey, Archie," I said, lifting the phone to my ear.

"Wood, what's going on?" he asked before continuing. "Hey, I'm calling because Audrey called me. Clay didn't show up for Taylor's violin recital this afternoon. She's worried about him." Audrey was Blake Howey's mother, and Taylor his sister. Clay had become close with both since Blake's death in Iraq.

"What do you mean?" I asked.

"I don't know. He was supposed to show up but didn't. Audrey is scared."

"Let me see what I can do." I thanked Arguello and hung up the phone. Clay had become increasingly depressed over the previous year. He was struggling in his relationships and with navigating the future. He'd returned from Haiti high on life, but the practical realities of the world soon smacked him in the face. Inspired by Mark Hayward, he considered switching his academic studies to become a physician assistant, but that didn't last. The local VA was struggling to treat his post-traumatic stress diagnosis, leaving Clay to feel like he was treading water in a chemical cocktail. Clay was not alone. Veterans coming back from Iraq and Afghanistan were having an increasingly hard time reacclimating to civilian life. Compared with their nonveteran peers, they were more likely to be homeless, jobless, and suffer from a variety of trauma-related issues.* Of course, not all veterans suffered these fates, and plenty returned home to leverage their training and experience to start businesses, enter politics, and become pillars in their communities. The difference between the two groups often came down to support systems. Those who had effective ones—whether family, the church, a local VA or veterans group—often thrived, while their brothers and sisters who floundered often found themselves alone. Clay had a supportive family, but they were fifteen hundred miles away in Houston.

I found Clay's number and dialed it. Voicemail. *Beep.* "Clay, it's Wood. I got a call from Arguello. He said you skipped out on Taylor's recital. You've got Audrey worried. Stop being an idiot and give me a call."

I looked at my computer screen. An unfinished business plan for Team Rubicon stared back at me. In the eleven months since Haiti, William and I had taken the lead on shaping Team Rubicon into a real orga-

---

* Carly Evans and Lawrence J. Korb, "Remembering America's Veterans in 2016," Center for American Progress, November 10, 2016, www.americanprogress.org/issues/security/news/2016/11/10/292211/remembering-americas-veterans-in-2016/.

nization dedicated to disaster response. We envisioned a small, elite group of military veterans and doctors who waited on standby for major international crises. Nothing too formal, just a loose network glued together by a shared spirit for action. There would be no employees, so we could keep costs to a minimum.

The group had done some interesting things since Port-au-Prince. I'd led a small response team down to Chile after an earthquake and tsunami there. We sent a small team into Burma to train medics. And William led a team into Pakistan following devastating floods in the Punjab river valley. We learned something new with each deployment. For me, this included a sneaking suspicion that we were narrowly averting catastrophe each time we sent people out and that our fundraising assumptions were proving inaccurate. Each mission launched since Haiti had failed to raise enough funding to cover its expenses. Now, with a mission to South Sudan on the horizon, I was struggling to figure out how Team Rubicon could shape itself for the future.

Ding. A text message appeared on my phone's screen. It was from Clay. *I'm okay, dude. Just figuring some things out.*

I shook my head. Clay's ups and downs frustrated me. Why couldn't he just leave the Marine Corps and Iraq and Afghanistan behind? He had his whole future in front of him, but he seemed to be actively tying himself back to the wars like a boat to an anchor. It was clearly dragging him down. Of course, Clay had gotten in the habit of telling me that I was compartmentalizing. That by not processing my time in war I was simply shoving my feelings into a little box and placing them on a high shelf in a closet deep in my soul. Sometimes I thought he was right.

Dinner smells drifted over. Indra was chopping an onion as cloves of garlic sizzled in a pan. I walked over and wrapped my arm around her waist. "Something going on with Clay?" she asked.

"Ehhh . . ." I debated not telling her. If she knew my friends were struggling, she'd try to shine a light on that little box I had packed deep inside. I took too long to answer, and her eyebrow twitched. "Well, he was supposed to show up with Audrey to Taylor's recital, but he didn't."

Indra nodded, giving me space. As we ate, the doorbell chimed. Indra looked at me quizzically. It was rare for us to get visitors. I walked down the stairs and opened the front door. Clay stood on the doorstep, the hood of his sweatshirt pulled low over his red and puffy eyes.

"Clay, what's up, brother?"

He closed his eyes and grimaced. Lifting a six-pack of beer, he opened his eyes and looked into mine. "I could use some company tonight. You up for it?"

I gestured into the hallway. Clay walked up the stairs, and as I followed him, I saw Indra appear on the landing. "Clay, so good to see you," she said, giving him a warm hug. Then she grabbed my hand and whispered in my ear. "I'll head to the bedroom and leave you two alone."

Clay sat at the kitchen table and pulled out two bottles of beer. He tried to twist the caps off, but soon realized they required an opener. I removed the steel bracelet from my wrist, snapping off the tops. We clinked our bottles together and took a long pull. Clay's posture was closed off, but he sat content. On the wall a clock ticked.

I decided to wait him out. *Tick. Tock.* Minutes passed, each of us drinking our beer as if alone.

"Sorry about today," Clay finally mumbled. I held my tongue. More silence. "I probably could have handled it better." I raised my eyebrows and grabbed another beer, popping it open and drinking.

"Clay, you don't need to apologize to me. But you should probably apologize to Audrey, and you sure as hell should apologize to Taylor. I think you broke her heart today, and Lord knows she's had enough

heartbreak." It was obvious Clay was hurting, thinking about the conse-
quences of his actions.

"I know," he managed to get out.

"Tell me what's going on," I said. And with that, Clay poured out a
war's worth of emotion. He spoke of the anxiety he suffered as a result of
being shot. How he'd close his eyes and imagine that bullet whizzing
right past his chin and through his wrist, mere inches away from turning
his brain into a pink mist. He talked about having to listen on the radio
the night that Blake was killed, and the gut-wrenching fear that my
name would come across the radio as another casualty. Watching Windsor bleed to death on the road outside the market while he sat helpless
behind the steering wheel of a Humvee, unable to fight. Clay grew angry
talking about the mission, about the lack of objectives or measurable
progress. Most of all, Clay looked at the country he returned to and was
saddened by his fellow Americans, each mired in petty bullshit, unable
to imagine the real cost of their security.

"Jake, how do you do it? How do you just march on like none of it
happened?"

I paused. Clay always ascribed to me more strength than I deserved.
The reality was, I too was grappling with the war. Sometimes for reasons
similar to Clay's. Other times I found myself inexplicably yearning for
combat. Part of me missed war. But whenever I felt that rising impulse, I
would try to stifle it. I would shove it down, ashamed.

Clay leaned forward and I noticed the paracord lanyard around his
neck. It was his Hog's Tooth. A few months back I'd taken mine off, no
longer feeling the need to wear a talisman to ward off an imaginary enemy's bullets. Though, if I was being honest with myself, I often reached
up to touch it in tougher times, only to discover my bare chest.

"I, uh, I guess I just focus on the future. What's done is done, you know?" I knew I wasn't being entirely truthful, but I didn't know why. I decided to deflect. "Clay, what do you enjoy? What makes you happy?"

"Honestly? The only time I've been happy and fulfilled this past year has been with Team Rubicon. Haiti changed me, dude." Clay's expression visibly brightened. Clay had actually returned to Haiti twice to continue with relief efforts. He leaned forward onto the table. He grew more upbeat as he talked about Mark Hayward and Brother Jim, two men Clay had grown to idolize. Like Marines in a foxhole, we recounted stories of our time in Haiti and Chile, shaking our heads at the sad moments and slapping our knees at the funny ones.

Clay took a moment and gathered his thoughts. "I'll tell you what it is. It's purpose. That's all it is, Jake. When I'm doing TR stuff, I have purpose, just like in the Marines. When I look in the mirror, I'm proud of the person looking back at me. And, honestly, if not for the people I've met in TR, I'm not sure I'd ever imagine finding friends as close as we had in Iraq and Afghanistan."

The words hung. "So how do we bottle that for you, Clay?" I eventually asked. We both knew that Team Rubicon was too small to provide those things consistently.

"I don't know," he said wistfully. Silence returned. I brought more beer from the fridge.

"Clay, what if we took TR's remaining funds and just sent you to Haiti? There's enough work down there for a decade. Brother Jim is still on the ground. You could help him rebuild the novitiate. It would be money well spent."

He thought about the offer. Clay knew that Team Rubicon didn't have much money left. It was hard to build a nonprofit in the shadow of the Great Recession, and, frankly, I wasn't sure that I really wanted to try. Finally, he shook his head. "No, Jake. This isn't about me. Team Rubicon is bigger than me. You and William need to build this. Don't worry about me."

Tick. Tock. "But I am."

Clay and I spent the next hour working on a plan to get him to a better place. We agreed that he would leave Los Angeles and move back to Houston to be near his family. Of course, Clay managed to convince me it was a good idea for him to detour to Colorado first so he could sleep on a friend's couch and ski for a month. When it was finally time to go to bed, I convinced Clay to spend the night on our couch. Before walking up the stairs, I embraced him in a long hug. "I love you, brother," he managed to say as I tousled his hair.

I crawled under the sheets and stared at the ceiling. Clay needed a tribe, a group that gave meaning to a sometimes meaningless world. There had to be a better way. I didn't have the answer.

MARCH 30, 2011

Click. BANG.

MARCH 31, 2011

My teeth sank into a burrito. "So, how do you guys think the announcement went?" I asked between chews. The previous day Team Rubicon had sent out an email announcing the launch of a new program. It was called TR-Transition, designed with veterans like Clay in mind. The goal was to raise enough money to send a platoon-sized element of transitioning military veterans to Haiti alongside a handful of civilian trade specialists like carpenters, masons, and electricians. For a year they would live and work there, rebuilding a single community and learning valuable employment skills along the way.

McNulty wiped his mouth and shrugged his shoulders. "Has a good open rate so far. Can't say the money is pouring in, though."

Money was increasingly an issue. It seemed like such a materialistic thing to worry about considering our line of work was trying to save people's lives. But everything cost money. Earlier in the year a man in North Carolina had pledged Team Rubicon a hundred thousand dollars. It was an enormous sum for a startup organization. With it, William and I finally made the decision to hire someone full-time to manage program development for Team Rubicon and had brought on board Joanne Dennis. We were introduced to Joanne by Clay, who knew her from his time at Loyola Marymount University.

Unfortunately, just three weeks earlier the would-be donor had rescinded his pledge and William and I were forced to sit Joanne down and tell her that, only two weeks into her job, we weren't sure how long we could pay her. That was why we were having lunch in Huntington Beach. We were on our way down to San Diego for a small fundraiser we'd organized, a celebration of the work our teams had just accomplished on a mission in South Sudan.

My phone vibrated on the table. Glancing down, I realized it was the same unknown number that had called twice over the last ten minutes. I reached down to send it to voicemail but hesitated. *Who do I know from a 713 area code? Where is 713?* I stood and picked up the phone.

"Hello?" I asked suspiciously as I stepped outside. There was a pause on the other end.

Finally, a voice responded. "Hello, is this Jake Wood?" a woman asked. It sounded like the beginning of a telemarketing scam.

"Yes, this is Jake Wood," I said, already preparing to hang up.

"Please hold for Stacy Hunt."

I flinched. Why was Clay's dad calling me? I walked away from the doorway and toward the corner of the building.

"Uh, hello, Jake?" Stacy's Texas twang was thick with emotion. It sounded like grief.

My body went very still. He didn't have to say anything: I knew Clay was dead.

"Yes, Stacy?"

"Well, uh, gee, Jake . . ." Stacy became short of breath, his lungs seizing fifteen hundred miles away from where I stood. "We lost him, Jake, my golly we lost him."

I screamed an expletive and insisted it wasn't true. My fist slammed into a street sign once, and then twice, and then a third time. Eventually I lay on the ground, face in my hands. Between muffled sobs I heard Stacy's voice from my phone lying on the concrete two feet away. Strangers sidestepped me on the sidewalk, no doubt whispering among themselves about the crazy man screaming, "No."

• • •

APRIL 4, 2011

The sun rose that morning in Houston at its scheduled time, an unwelcome wake-up for the dozens of Marines strewn about the beds of the cheap motel. One by one, they stumbled toward the restroom, kicking empty beer cans along the way. Eventually they rinsed off the night's armor, a cloak of beer and whiskey. Some went back to the coolers and opened another bottle, unwilling to face the day with sobriety's sense of nakedness.

Mark Hayward, never much of a drinker, moved through the rooms, checking in on everyone. He'd been a steady presence ever since receiving my note about Clay, flying down to Houston and serving as a driver as Marines from across the country flew in for the memorial service. Turns out the community Clay had sought was there all along. My father, whom I'd called and asked to meet me in Houston, strode up and down the walkway on the second floor of the motel. Without being told to, he was acting as a conductor, ensuring we would get to the church on time.

In my room, I sat on the edge of the bed and stared at a piece of paper. The outline of a eulogy danced around the page, my eyes finding it difficult to focus. No words seemed sufficient. Jeff Muir walked over and sat next to me, wrapping an arm around my shoulders.

"How's it coming, big guy?" he asked.

I just shook my head. I crumpled up the paper and threw it into the corner of the room. Outside, a voice drifted up from the parking lot. "Time to go! We have to get to the church. Everyone mount up!" Muir and I dutifully rose, facing each other. We examined each other's ties and jackets, no differently than if we were checking gear prior to a combat patrol.

Rolling into the church's parking lot, our convoy was greeted with the throaty growl of dozens of Harley-Davidson motorcycles. Clay's death had made headlines, with media eager to cover the tragic story of the hero Marine from a good family turned disaster responder and outspoken veteran advocate. Clay had appeared in a television commercial with the group Iraq and Afghanistan Veterans of America urging his fellow veterans to seek help for PTSD. He had even gone to Washington, D.C., to lobby Congress for disability pension reform with the same group. The bikes lined the long driveway up toward the sanctuary, the grey beards of their riders dancing in the wind. I saw quite a few Vietnam Veterans of America patches emblazoned on their leather vests, and all had "Patriot Guard" across their shoulders. After Westboro Baptist Church began picketing the funerals of men and women killed in the war, the Patriot Guard had sprung up to physically block them from the family of the fallen's view and drown their hateful chants with their motorcycles.

We gathered in the parking lot. The circle was no longer the battle-hardened platoon Clay had served with overseas. Muir, Bullard, Wherry, Rosenberger, Axelrod, and Butcher were there from our Iraq platoon. Shawn, Tim, and Thenn, from Afghanistan, were also there. Most of them were now civilians, many of them noticeably heavier and poorly shaven. Haircuts were out of regulation and suits were ill-fitting. A few, like Bullard and Rosenberger, wore their dress blues, belts and buttons noticeably taut across their waists. All of them had bloodshot eyes. All of them would have still run into machine gun fire for Clay.

Finally, the call came to move into the church sanctuary. The Patriot Guard lined the walkway, each rider holding an American flag that hung hapless in the still morning. As we walked past, they muttered words of encouragement. "Semper Fi, Marines" or "I'm sorry for your loss" or "Thank you for your service." Coming from Vietnam veterans, the words held meaning and lacked the hollow ring that the phrases often carried.

We took our seats. Each Marine reverted to his training, sitting forward, spine rigid and straight, hands on knees. A photo of Clay sat on an easel and stared at me. A boyish smile masked the torment I knew he'd felt. Across the aisle sat Susan, Clay's mother. Her eyes were hollow, their normal sparkle suffocated by grief. Richard, her husband, gently held her hand.

The numbness that came over me on the sidewalk when I learned of Clay's death had not left, but I could feel the pew's coolness seep into my legs and back. I welcomed it. I didn't want to feel warm. I hated myself, and that was fine by me. Clay died alone in a nondescript Houston apartment, three empty cans of beer on the table in front of him, his phone likely within reach. For some reason, he had reached for his gun instead of the phone. For some reason, he didn't think I could help him. I was not there for Clay, my sniper partner, the Marine I'd practically been tethered to in sniper school, never allowed to move beyond arm's length. The Marine who'd looked me in the eyes before every mission and asked me to make sure we came back alive.

I reached up and touched my Hog's Tooth, now returned to its place around my neck. Only three months prior I'd tried to convince Clay to take his off. To take his past from around his neck and put it in a box on a shelf, just like I did. Turns out Clay had needed to keep the bullet meant for him in plain sight. My head hung, the weight of guilt and shame too heavy.

The service began, white noise to the torment inside me. I stood when told. Sat when told. Sang when told, and said amen when told.

"And now we will hear a eulogy from Clay's friend and brother in arms, Jake Wood," the pastor said up front. The sound of people shifting in their pews to look at me was discomforting. I took in a breath and glanced at Shawn. Muir's hand squeezed my shoulder. "Time to go," he whispered.

I buttoned my suit jacket and shuffled out of the row. The hard soles of my dress shoes rapped the floor. When I turned to face the crowd, I saw that every row was filled, and dozens more people were standing in the back. I found my father in the crowd. His imperceptible nod gave me strength. My gaze wandered toward the front and made contact with Stacy Hunt, Clay's dad, whose life would obviously never be the same.

Susan's eyes captured mine and pulled them in close. Something happened. Susan's gaze seemed to wash me in warmth. This woman, burying her son, was silently praying that my own hurt would go away. I closed my eyes, afraid I would become a whimpering mess.

"Clay was . . ." I began, my voice cracking. The eulogy went as eulogies go. An accounting of a man's life that left us too early, hanging hypotheticals of what might have been. It spoke of the size of his heart and his foolish belief that the world around him could be better. Finally, it lamented a government that had failed its warriors. Disposed of them after their war like retired planes and tanks sent to an Arizona boneyard. The VA had failed Clay when he needed it most, and I swore to the crowd that we'd work toward never allowing that to happen again.

At some point, I stopped talking and returned to my seat next to Muir, unsure of what I had actually said. I hoped I hadn't said any curse words in front of all these nice churchgoing people.

"And now, Clay's brothers in arms will come forward to present the flag."

The Marines wearing their dress blues, led by Sergeant Rosenberger, rose from their pews and sharply turned toward the aisle and marched out. They approached Clay's flag-draped casket and posted at each of its four corners. Muir and I stood and made our way off to their side.

With an abrupt nod from Sergeant Rosenberger, the Marines thrust their hands forward and grabbed the flag. After a single count they lifted it in unison. It reached its pinnacle and tightened with an audible snap, its final waves rendered motionless. The Marines' jaws were clenched, with stares more apt for the battlefield than a Methodist church. Silently and with Marine Corps precision, the flag detail folded the Stars and Stripes along its long edge. With each fold, Sergeant Rosenberger took his white-gloved hands and solemnly smoothed out the wrinkles. Finally, it became a triangle.

With his back to the sanctuary, Sergeant Rosenberger lowered his head as he brought the flag in tight to his chest. A few seconds passed in absolute silence. Then he executed a crisp about-face and spun to face me. Standing in my dark civilian suit, I brought my heels together and stood at attention for the first time since I'd left the Marines. He strode forward and stopped an arm's length away. Rosenberger extended the flag and I reached out to take possession, pulling it to my chest. Slowly, Sergeant Rosenberger's right hand rose from his hip. His balled fist became a knife-edged hand, coming to rest several moments later against his temple in a salute. It paused there for a moment, rendering Clay's flag a painful farewell, before returning slowly back to his hip.

Once he finished, I took a deep breath and forced my racing heart to slow. I swallowed the lump in my throat and executed an about-face. Spinning 180 degrees and snapping my heels back together, I came face-to-face with Clay's mother, Susan. Leaning forward at the waist, I presented her with the flag. "On behalf of the President of the United States, the Commandant of the Marine Corps, and a grateful nation—" I stopped, unable in that moment to continue. *Be strong.* My mind encouraged my body to find strength where it had none. "—please accept this flag as a symbol of our appreciation for your loved one's honorable and faithful service."

Susan accepted the flag gingerly, hugging it into her chest as if Clay's soul might be wrapped inside. She looked up and with a hoarse whisper said, "Thank you, Jake. I know y'all are going to make Clay proud. We love y'all so much."

Self-pity drained out of me, replaced with commitment and resolve. As I sat, the unmistakable bass drone of a lone bagpipe filled the cavernous church. The low tone was cut by a shrill wail as a familiar melody emerged. Behind me, members of the church sang along in low tones. For them, "Amazing Grace" was a beautiful song of redemption. For the veterans in the front pews, however, "Amazing Grace" was an anthem of death.

Muir choked back tears and squeezed the bridge of his nose between thumb and index finger. Draping my arm around his shoulders, I leaned in close. "Be strong, brother," I whispered.

With a grimace he nodded rapidly. "I just hate those fucking bagpipes, man."

I squeezed him in closer. "It's what we do when the bagpipes end that matters."

CHAPTER II

ROLL TIDE

William's apartment—if you could call it that—was grungy. It was actually a detached garage squatting behind a larger home in Santa Monica. He'd moved into it a couple months prior when he relocated from Washington, D.C. The musty smell was most likely due to the saltwater riding in on the air from the beach only a few blocks away. Both of us were flirting with Team Rubicon, trying to figure out what to do with it. Up to this point, William was mostly focused on producing a film based on the life of a former Marine and CIA operative he'd come to know, while I had dropped out of UCLA's MBA program to work at a local startup. Neither of us had really considered doing Team Rubicon full-time.

But then the organization hit a crossroads. So many Team Rubicon volunteers had shown up for Clay's funeral. Some of them had never even met Clay, but nevertheless they wanted to honor his life of service. There was something else they came for: hope. Hope that Clay's tragic death would not be the end of what he had helped start. Hope that they also would be given the chance to find their own mission. Team Rubicon had given them a taste of hope, but deep down I knew that hope without a plan is just a dream. We wanted to honor Clay's legacy and build something that would last for the next hundred years. But how could we do TR full-time if we could only scrape together the funds to pay Joanne for the next few weeks? And barely at that.

The bagpipes had long since stopped playing, but the resolve that came in the silence after their final note had weakened.

"What are you thinking about?" William asked.

I shrugged my shoulders as I lay back into the deep couch. "How much I hate Clay," I said. William's head bobbed up and down. I shifted my weight and sat up on the couch's edge. A bottle of beer hung from my hand. As usual, my anger with Clay flamed out quickly and was replaced with sorrow.

A text from Joanne interrupted the silence. She wasn't really the excitable type, so the excessive use of exclamation points in her message caught my eye. "She says she has something important to tell us."

Her voice drifted in through the screen a few minutes later. "Hey, guys. Can you open the door? My hands are full." Outside, Joanne was holding two canvas shopping bags overflowing with envelopes. Her face was flushed with excitement.

"Guys, guys, you'll never believe this," she began as she made her way to the countertop in the middle of the room. "So, I went to our P.O. box to check on our mail, and the guy at the counter said he had entire bins of letters for us. I didn't believe him, but then he returned from the back room and dropped the first one on the counter!" She lifted her arms up to emphasize the hundreds of pieces of mail stuffed in the bags. "I opened up three or four of the cards and they're all for Clay!"

William and I mumbled about how special and thoughtful those gestures were. Joanne's face scrunched and she shook her head. "No, you're not getting it. They have checks in them! People saw Clay's story and they're sending Team Rubicon money to honor him!"

My jaw dropped. I reached out and grabbed a handful of envelopes. Under a dim lightbulb I tore open the first letter. Unfolding the paper revealed beautiful cursive prose.

Dear Team Rubicon,

I read the story of your friend's tragic death. It saddens me that our nation's warriors are returning home from war, only to continue to fight their wars here. Clay deserved better.

I was inspired by his work with your organization and would like to support it so the work can continue. Please use this money to further your efforts.

Sincerely,
Jacqueline

Slowly, I shuffled the check from behind the letter to the front. My eyes widened. "It's a thousand dollars," I said, looking up at William and Joanne.

"I know!" Joanne shrieked. "There's more. Guys . . . we're gonna survive. TR is going to survive!"

I opened a second letter and read a note from another generous and thoughtful citizen. A hundred dollars. And another. Twenty-five dollars. On and on it went as we read through hundreds of letters and cards. We tallied the total along the way, and gradually I gained Joanne's confidence. Team Rubicon would indeed survive.

I leaned back on the stool and looked at the mess. Torn envelopes were strewn about the floor, while piles of letters and checks dotted the countertop. I closed my eyes and thought of Clay. I would trade every single check for just one more day on earth with him, for one chance to pick up the phone and convince him not to pull the trigger. But that wasn't possible. The only choice now was to continue the mission.

"Clay, you son of a bitch," I whispered.

• • •

APRIL 27, 2011

Hope you had a wonderful birthday, son! the text message read. Indra and I had celebrated my twenty-eighth birthday the day prior the only way we knew how: a quiet dinner by ourselves. I was still getting reaccustomed to birthdays. Anyone who spends a couple of them overseas in a combat zone quickly learns the folly of looking forward to them. I'd witnessed too many birthday dreams get snuffed out.

Grabbing my phone, I tapped out a response to my mother. She'd returned home to Iowa with my father and sister Meghan just a few days before. The three of them had flown out to Los Angeles to surprise me. There was no doubt that Indra, worried about me in the weeks after Clay's death, had secretly prompted them. She wasn't one to sit and watch a problem fester. It didn't bother me; I was just glad to see them.

I turned back to the computer. A blank PowerPoint presentation stared back. The day before Clay's death, Team Rubicon had announced TR-Transition. Clay's death had revealed so many flaws in its logic. What good would it have done Clay to further isolate him by sending him to Haiti for a year? That wasn't transition; that was stagnation. Of course, for a few weeks we weren't sure any of it would matter, as the organiza-

146

tion's financial health had hung in the balance. All of that changed when donations began pouring in to honor Clay. In total, Team Rubicon received just over $40,000, effectively tripling the organization's cash. It wasn't enough for William and me to begin paying ourselves a salary, but we could continue to pay Joanne.

The funding also prompted us to completely reimagine what TR-Transition could become. We knew we wanted to continue to capitalize on what made Team Rubicon unique: leveraging the skills and experience of military veterans to help people after crises. Deployments in Haiti, Chile, Pakistan, Burma, and South Sudan, while a small sample size, had begun to prove the approach's effectiveness. Our teams could operate effectively in austere environments and uncertain conditions. But there was something else we wanted to tap into. Time and again, the volunteers who returned from these missions said the same thing: "I never thought I'd feel this way again."

"This way" meant something different to every veteran who said it. For some, like our special operations medics, it was the satisfaction that came from utilizing their truly unique medical training to heal those in need. For others, it was rediscovering a community—a band of brothers—akin to the tribe they'd left behind in the military. Some, like Clay, had gained a new identity through service. They finally looked in the mirror and were proud of the man or woman they saw staring back at them. At the core was this sense of purpose. The nobility of a life in service to others. Our mission was to help others, but there was no doubt these veterans found that service was helping themselves too.

The problem, of course, was: how could we sustain and grow? Time and again, potential funders told us our model was neat but wouldn't last. They said we'd caught lightning in a bottle with Haiti, but a broader underlying business model didn't exist.

The blank PowerPoint slide was leading me to believe they were right. Five months earlier we had been given the opportunity to pitch the CEO and executive team of a major global commercial real estate firm. We spent weeks crafting the pitch and felt good after delivering it. The company opted not to fund us. Clay's death may have miraculously provided us with enough oxygen to survive, but it didn't change whether people wanted to invest in our strategic vision.

My cell phone buzzed beside my computer. It was Zach Smith, a volunteer leader in charge of operations. "What's up, Zach?" I asked, expecting it to be about the follow-up mission we were planning to Burma.

"Tuscaloosa just got hit with a massive tornado. Turn on the TV," Zach said hurriedly. Sure enough, every channel was breaking with the news of a devastating tornado in Alabama. Initial pans of the destruction revealed a community leveled. Dozens were feared dead.

"Do we deploy a medical team?" I asked.

"Like we've talked about, there's no way we get approval to do that domestically," replied Zach, who was also a firefighter and paramedic in his day job. At this point, Team Rubicon saw its mission as providing elite mobile medical teams in the developing world. As far as we knew, America's robust medical and emergency services infrastructure didn't require those services.

I continued watching the footage. The cities, Tuscaloosa and Birmingham, looked just like my hometown in Iowa. Unassuming skylines and quaint neighborhoods, all filled with salt-of-the-earth Americans. In fact, my cousin Amanda had graduated from the University of Alabama just a few years earlier and now called Birmingham home.

"Zach, get the team on a conference call. We need to do something."

Several hours later I punched in an access code and joined William, Joanne, and Zach on the call. A ding indicated Matt Pelak had joined from New York. Zach led the call with a situational overview, briefing out the high-level statistics about damage and casualty counts. "Jake, over to you," he finished.

"Okay, team," I started. My voice came through crisply—the growing crisis had awoken the confident Marine that had been hiding somewhere inside me since Clay's funeral. "The situation in Alabama is still unfolding, but there's no doubt assistance will be needed. Now, obviously we have never responded to a disaster here at home, but that doesn't mean we don't try."

"But, Jake, what's the mission set? Clearly not medical," a voice interrupted.

"To be honest, I don't know. But we didn't have a clear mission when we went to Haiti either, and just like then, I feel like inaction is not an option." A debate ensued. Good arguments for and against were made on all sides, but the truth was that my mind was already made up. We would deploy.

"Listen, guys, this isn't that hard. It's U.S. soil. Let's send twenty people down there and figure it out." Pelak's voice rose above the others.

"Pelak is right. We're going. Matt, start assembling a team. I'll join you on the ground."

• ● •

TWO DAYS LATER

The rain beat softly against the metal roof, like someone impatiently tapping their fingers. People milled around, occasionally hopping into cars or taxis as they pulled up to the curb. I saw a familiar grey car cutting across terminal traffic. Behind the wheel sat Shawn, sun-faded baseball cap perched on top of his head. His car pulled up and I hastily opened the rear door and shoved my pack inside before settling in the front seat. "You have a habit of being late? I about started walking," I said grumpily, staring out the windshield.

"Traffic," Shawn replied matter-of-factly.

No longer capable of busting his balls, I broke into a wide smile. "Good to see you, brother."

"Good to see you too."

It had been four weeks since Shawn and I had seen each other at Clay's memorial. Normally we would happily fill any void with conversation and storytelling, but this afternoon we were content to listen to the sound of his tires on wet Tennessee pavement. The silence was comforting, in many ways reminding me of lying in a sniper hide alongside him. In a hide, there was so much implicit communication and understanding that verbal communication was almost lazy. Conversation was also dangerous, because the enemy might hear the noise. We rode in peace.

Four hours later we pulled into a gas station near the intersection of two country roads. A group of trucks sat haphazardly parked. I recognized Pelak and motioned for Shawn to pull forward.

"Wood, you made it!" Pelak exclaimed as I unfolded myself from the cramped passenger seat. Matt was tall, trim, and handsome. He'd spent a dozen years in the Army National Guard working in one of their long-range reconnaissance units. In his day job he was a firefighter and paramedic. I embraced Matt in a big hug. I could feel the dampness of his shirt as I wrapped my arms around him. Stepping back, I could see his arms were covered in sawdust and scratches from a day spent hauling away debris. It was clear the team had been hard at work. Looking over his shoulder, I saw Nicole Green, another familiar face.

"Hi, Jake," she said with a shy smile. I made my way over to Nicole and gave her a warm embrace. Clay and I had met Nicole the year prior while lobbying Congress in Washington, D.C. Nicole was a former Air Force intelligence officer currently feeling her life drain away as a consultant. Clay and Nicole had quickly developed a special bond, and at the funeral it was evident that she was hurting deeply.

Pelak put his arm around my shoulder and walked me around to some of the other vehicles. He introduced me to Levi, another Marine veteran, and JC, who'd been in the Army. Finally, I noticed a car idling a few feet away. As I approached, the engine shut off and both doors opened wide. Two of my cousins, who lived nearby, exited the vehicle. We quickly caught up on family. Eventually Pelak shouted for everyone to begin loading up.

Our caravan drove a few miles down the highway before exiting onto a nondescript backcountry road, the trees slowly encroaching on the roadway until the canopy came close to smothering out the sky. After a few miles and a couple of unmarked intersections, it was clear why Pelak didn't want to try to find our destination in the dark. Shawn parked his car in front of a low-slung cabin.

I threw my pack on an empty bunk and returned outside, where the cabin's owners appeared. I thanked them for their generosity. They brushed off the gratitude and handed me a hot dog. I sat next to Pelak to learn about how the mission was unfolding on the ground. Todd Bowers, a Marine veteran, worked on the firepit, stacking wood like every man on the planet who believes he has the secret to starting the perfect fire. Eventually a warm blaze illuminated the circle.

Headlights from a truck suddenly lit up like searchlights. My muscles twitched when I saw two silhouettes walk into the beams, each holding an unmistakable object: an AR-15 rifle. I looked with concern at Pelak and Shawn. Matt smiled.

"They like to hunt," he said with a hint of disbelief. Despite being an infantryman, Matt was a New Yorker through and through, and the gun and hunt culture of the South amazed him. I glanced at my watch; it was a few minutes before ten p.m. "Don't ask, man," Matt said. "I don't get it either."

One of the them approached, a young college-age kid. "Y'all wanna go shoot some hogs?" he asked, presenting his loaded rifle as if it were a base-ball bat at a batting cage. Heads around the campfire shook back and forth.

The boy shrugged and trudged away. With a few hoots the truck spun its wheels and disappeared. I grabbed two cans of beer and sat next to Shawn. *Tsk. Tsk.* We each cracked open our cans and feigned a toast. "Thanks again for picking me up today," I said. "Means a lot to have you out here."

"Anytime," Shawn mumbled, content to stare into the fire. It's hard to say how much time passed. Perhaps two or three logs' worth.

Gunfire erupted in the distance. Shawn and I jumped, hands reach-ing for weapons long since returned to armories. More gunfire joined, our ears easily making out a different caliber. *Woohooo,* the exclaim drifted in on a breeze. Realizing it was the hunters, our trigger fingers—now used for nothing more violent than pointing—relaxed.

The next morning, as the convoy drew closer to Tuscaloosa's out-skirts, the signs of the storm began to appear. Trees were downed and signs for local businesses had been ripped off and flung away. "Just wait," Pelak warned me. "This is nothing."

He took a couple of turns, eventually cresting a hill. I looked down into a shallow valley and for the first time saw the scale of destruction. "Holy shit," I muttered, fumbling to lower my passenger-side window.

Not a single structure remained standing, and all the contents of all the lives of the people hit were on display. Off to the right, a bike frame, pink tassels still attached to the handles, sat bent at ninety degrees

While living in Austria in 1989, my family and I visited Mauthausen, which had served as a Nazi concentration camp. It was this moment that first inspired me to want to serve in the military.

As a senior in high school, I was a highly recruited football player. Rather than join the military, I took a scholarship to play for the Wisconsin Badgers. I earned two varsity letters for the Badgers but had an otherwise disappointing career. As my senior year was set to begin, former NFL star Pat Tillman was killed in Afghanistan. That week I committed to joining the military after playing my final game.

My parents were huge influences in my life, and I was lucky to have them join me in San Diego at my graduation from boot camp. My next stop was the School of Infantry, and then on to the fleet. In the back of everyone's mind was the inevitable—a deployment to Iraq or Afghanistan.

My unit, 2-7, was sent to Iraq in 2007 as part of the surge strategy. For seven months my platoon conducted counterinsurgency patrols in an area known as the Triangle of Death, during what would be the bloodiest year of the war. Left to right: Joe Piram, Mateo Arguello, Jake, and Kevin Colbert in Anbar Province after a patrol

My unit would conduct counterinsurgency patrols on foot daily. During some weeks we would have contact with the enemy, and at all times we would ensure our patrols were disbursed fifteen meters apart so that if one Marine stepped on an IED it would only kill him and no one else. The persistent proximity of death became normal.

Occasionally we would visit with Iraqi families that welcomed our presence. We visited this young boy several times over a period of weeks, and he developed an infatuation with the tall Marine that would come to speak with his father. Here he dons my flak jacket and poses for a photo.

ABOVE LEFT: After Iraq I passed the selection for a Marine scout-sniper platoon. After ten grueling weeks at sniper school I graduated at the top of my class and deployed to Afghanistan's Helmand Valley in 2008. Our team's mission was to hunt Taliban and insurgent forces. Our battalion would take more casualties than any other Marine unit that year.

ABOVE RIGHT: Our team would often run its missions at night, sneaking through fields and villages with our faces painted, hoping to find the enemy planting an IED or moving weapons. Some nights the roles were reversed and we knew the enemy was hunting us.

ABOVE LEFT: I came back from the wars physically unscathed, but different. Not wanting my life to be defined by war, I made the toughest decision of my life—to get out of the Marine Corps.

ABOVE RIGHT: My best friend, Clay Hunt, endured sniper school alongside me. While in Afghanistan he became critical of the war—questioning whether our efforts would lead to progress. Wounded in action on our Iraq tour, Clay would later succumb to the war and take his own life in March 2011.

We crossed the border into Haiti four days after the earthquake, piled high atop our gear in the backs of trucks. When we entered the capital city, it looked like a war zone.

Clay Hunt, my closest friend from the Marines, watched Team Rubicon's first couple of days unfold on social media. Unable to stay on the sidelines, Clay bought a ticket in the middle of the night and flew to the Dominican Republic, intent on finding his way to us on the ground. Twenty-four hours later he linked up with us at the general hospital.

After a long day of work, few things are as relaxing as an ice-cold beer, a warm campfire, and good company. Team Rubicon's "campfire culture" builds bonds that some volunteers say rival their military friendships.

Mark Hayward, a former special forces medic, was a clear example of how Team Rubicon could repurpose the skills of highly trained veterans for disaster response.

In 2013, TR responded to a typhoon in the Philippines. The mission was a return to the organization's expeditionary roots and demonstrated its knack for getting to tough places fast.

Memorial Day is sacred for veterans. In 2013, Top Washington addressed Team Rubicon's veteran volunteers about his son's sacrifice in Afghanistan.

TR's volunteers may get the credit, but it's ultimately about the people we serve. Here a Greyshirt hugs a survivor of Hurricane Harvey.

After my friend Clay's death in 2011, Team Rubicon pivoted to focus on domestic disasters. When Hurricane Sandy hit a year later, it catapulted the organization to a new level.

As the organization grew, my responsibilities became more corporate. But I still took opportunities to join the team in the field. Here I'm riding toward a jobsite in the back of a truck in Moore, Oklahoma.

In 2017, Hurricane Harvey devastated the Texas coast. As Team Rubicon assisted local authorities with rescues, I couldn't help but imagine a future when all of Houston's more than one hundred thousand military veterans were organized as an auxiliary disaster response force.

With Harvey's overwhelming destruction, Team Rubicon knew it had to launch an operation larger than anything it had ever done. Partnering with American Airlines and Southwest Airlines, Team Rubicon deployed nearly two thousand Greyshirts to Houston on chartered airplanes. Here I greet new arrivals on the airfield.

The work our volunteers take can be backbreaking, but our Greyshirts love the challenge. Here they help Pateros, Washington, recover after a wildfire.

One of the defining moments of my postwar experience was bringing Indra to a Syrian and Iraqi refugee camp that Team Rubicon was operating. The conversations there helped bring closure to me and my wartime experiences. Here I am playing basketball with an Iraqi man, who begrudgingly befriended me, and his son. In the second photo, Indra carries his daughter on our way to saying goodbye.

In 2018, Indra and I welcomed our first child into the world, a daughter. For her middle name we chose one of the English language's most powerful words: Hope

After Hurricane Harvey, Team Rubicon had the opportunity to help Clay Hunt's mother recover from the storm. The experience helped me feel like I could finally free myself of the guilt I carried from Clay's death.

At a time when America lacks unity, Team Rubicon can bring together communities through service and help restore the America we love.

After our initial response operation in Houston, Team Rubicon launched a home-rebuilding program that taught transitioning veterans construction skills while getting residents back into suitable housing. It was implemented under the Clay Hunt Fellows Program.

around the corner of a cinder-block wall. Near one of its tires, a crumpled crimson Alabama football jersey lay soiled. Ahead, a driverless rusty blue sedan was flipped upside down, the jagged edge of a tree trunk piercing through its roof like a medieval pike. Next to it a high school yearbook lay open, its pages flipping in the wind, in search of its alumni. Everything everywhere was an artifact of someone's past. For some, their most prized possessions; for others, the secrets they kept behind closed doors or locked in drawers. A box truck with a Red Cross logo rolled down the street. Its back gate was open, and a volunteer sat on the ledge handing out bottles of water. Crawling over the piles of debris were rescuers from an Alabama task force.

Our convoy snaked through the rubble. Finally, Pelak pulled up in front of a house. "Here we go," he said, easing the truck to a stop in front of the yard. "We saw this house yesterday. A neighbor said the old lady is still living inside but can't get her car out of her driveway. He was concerned because he knows she needs to get her medication."

I looked out over the property. Two fallen trees, a giant maple and a smaller oak, blocked all access to her driveway. The maple's root ball had been ripped out of the soil, leaving a gaping hole the size of a small swimming pool in her yard. I shuddered as I imagined the force required to rip that root system out of the ground. Behind me, truck doors opened and slammed shut as the rest of the team dismounted and gathered around the bed of my truck. I grabbed Pelak. "Hey, why don't you go knock on the door and ask her if it's okay that we start working." He nodded.

I turned to the rest of the team. Each of them wore Team Rubicon's new uniform, a simple grey T-shirt with the organization's logo emblazoned across the front. My sister Sarah had designed the logo, a cross on its side with a river—the Rubicon River—running through the middle of it, upon our return from Haiti. Years later we would come to refer to

Team Rubicon's volunteers as Greyshirts because of the uniform. It became a term of endearment, a title that for some held as much meaning as being called "Marine." When designing the shirts, we'd chosen to put a broad white bar across the chest under the logo. This both made them more visible and provided the wearer the chance to scrawl their name across it. Seeing several new faces, I was glad for that added touch.

"Alright, team, gather round," I said. "Who here knows how to run a chain saw?" Ten arms shot up enthusiastically. "Of course, you all do. If you can run a machine gun, you can run a saw, right?" The group chuckled. "Seriously, be safe."

Saws, axes, ropes, and chains were meticulously laid out on the lawn as if for inspection by a commanding officer. The volunteers moved among the tools and selected what they needed. *Brum. Brum. Brum. Brahhhhhhhh.* The first chain saw roared to life.

They got to work like well-trained ants, sawing and dragging components of the tree from the driveway to the roadway. Soon the grey shirts clung tight to sweat-soaked backs.

I approached a volunteer. "Here, drink this," I said, uncapping a bottle of water and handing it to him. The volunteer wiped the sweat from his brow and took a long swig of water. Standing on the edge of the hole left by the tree's root system, he pointed down into the freshly turned dirt. "I watched an insurgent blow himself up in a car overseas," he said evenly. "It was a big-ass blast. My ears were bleeding. Left a hole in the ground about this size." We sat and stared in silence. He turned from the hole. "Well, time to get back to work."

We called it a day in the late afternoon after completing a few jobs. A certain liturgy was emerging in the evening hours after an operation. After showering under garden hoses and wolfing down dinner, a cooler of beer was dragged toward the firepit.

A scavenger hunt commenced as each person went in search of logs and kindling. The smell of fresh pine softened the ripe odor clinging to each of us. One by one, the members of the team grabbed lawn chairs and buckets and anything else that could be fashioned into a seat and formed a ring around the prior night's ashes. Finally, after depositing a heavy moss-covered log onto the pile, I took a seat next to Shawn.

To my left, Todd entertained the group with the story of the time he was wounded in Fallujah, when an enemy sniper's round pierced his scope and significantly damaged his eye. As only Todd could, he managed to turn the terrifying ordeal into a story that had the group laughing uncontrollably. Across the fire, Pelak was engaged in a more hushed conversation with JC, the contents of it indiscernible. I tossed rocks into the fire, content to listen.

It's amazing what happens when humans eliminate man-made distractions and sit around a primitive fire. The petty trappings and false urgency of life disappear, and the only thing that is important is the person on your right or left. It's one of the reasons that soldiers love war. Phones and televisions and computers are left behind. Complicated romances are placed on hold and dysfunctional families spend Thanksgiving without you. All that's left is the mission and the people. It is a purifying process.

I noticed Pelak pull his cell phone out and look at it quizzically. There was virtually no cellular signal at the cabin, so it was a surprise to see a call coming through. He raised it to his head, covering the opposite ear with his free hand to reduce the noise. "Hello?" I heard him ask. "Wait, what? Say that again?" His demeanor changed dramatically. With widened eyes, his jaw stammered silently. "You're sure?" he asked forcefully. "Okay, I'll let everyone know." He ended the call and brought the phone to his lap. Pelak gathered himself and cleared his throat.

"Everyone, listen up!" he said, but the group was too immersed to pay him any attention. "Everyone, shut up!" he screamed, the sergeant inside him emerging. The conversations ceased, and the fire ominously illuminated Pelak's face as he stood.

"I just got a phone call from Ford Sypher, who is trying to drive in and meet us." He paused. "He told me that we just killed Osama bin Laden."

A log popped loudly and embers drifted into the sky, sailing on the wind until they faded into the night like old soldiers. The group remained silent and still, each person processing the news. I looked at Pelak through the flames. There was an emotion in his eyes that was difficult to place. Not zeal. Not anger. Neither excitement nor indifference. Simply . . . closure.

JC popped up. "I'm going to turn on the radio in my car." We followed him over as he tuned in to a satellite radio station.

"Crowds have gathered outside the White House, where we expect the president to address the nation soon," a reporter said. Our group huddled in tight with arms wrapped around one another's shoulders. *"Here is the president of the United States now, walking up to the podium."* There was a brief pause.

"Good evening," Barack Obama's unmistakable voice emerged from inside the car. *"Tonight, I can report to the American people and to the world that the United States has conducted an operation that killed Osama bin Laden, the leader of al-Qaeda, and a terrorist who's responsible for the murder of thousands of innocent men, women, and children."** Obama continued, and when he was finished there was just the sound of the fire.

"Fuck yeah," someone to my right broke the silence. "Hell yeah," a different voice answered. A lump formed in my throat, born of years of

---

* Jonathan Mahler, "What Do We Really Know About Osama bin Laden's Death," *New York Times*, October 15, 2015, www.nytimes.com/2015/10/18/magazine/what-do-we-really-know-about-osama-bin-ladens-death.html.

sacrifice made necessary by the man now pronounced dead. We had gone to war because of Osama bin Laden. I'd spent every moment of every mission hoping that we'd miraculously be the group that stumbled upon him and brought him to justice. It was a foolish hope, but foolish hopes are often the only thing that can keep someone going in trying times. Now he was dead. A victory we could all claim, though we were still counting the costs.

Shawn put both hands behind my head and brought my forehead in to touch his. "All that bullshit. All that sacrifice. Now maybe it means something." For maybe the first time in my life I could hear emotion in Shawn's voice.

I closed my eyes and thought of Clay. And of Howey and Windsor and Washington. And the dozens of other men that our battalion had lost on our tours. *Rest easy, brothers.*

• ● •

In the weeks following that mission in Alabama, dubbed Operation Roll Tide, I couldn't shake a nagging thought: *What if Team Rubicon's destiny wasn't to be a boutique international response organization? What if we could be a transformational force here at home?*

I ran the numbers. Three million veterans had served since 9/11, but our current international model only targeted the small sliver with medical and special ops backgrounds. Academic research suggested that most veterans wanted to serve their communities but couldn't find organizations that were the right fit.* Meanwhile, the FEMA numbers were

---

* Derrick Kranke, Alicia R. Gable, Eugenia L. Weiss, and Aram Dobalian, "'I'm in a Good Place Now': A Case Study of Empowerment of a Combat Veteran Engaged in Peer-Led Disaster Relief," *Social Work in Mental Health* 15, no. 6, 2017, pp. 663–676.

terrifying. Disasters kept increasing in frequency and cost and were getting worse due to climate change. A thought struck me: If Team Rubicon pivoted to focus on domestic disasters, we could help more communities, engage more veterans, and at less cost. It was a win-win-win.

One day about a month later, Indra came home from her work at the station. "Good news," she said. "The higher-ups just approved my vacation time to fly to Dallas tomorrow and link up with those tornado chasers I worked with two years ago. Why don't you buy a ticket and come along?"

For two days we crisscrossed Kansas and Oklahoma in a convoy of SUVs and armored chaser vehicles that looked like they'd rolled off the *Mad Max* set. Indra and her colleagues would track storm cells with special equipment and on their iPads and try to predict the next funnel cloud. They got it right once or twice—an awe-inspiring sight.

On the second night I received a Team Rubicon alert. A twister had just leveled Joplin, Missouri—160 people dead. Indra's phone buzzed and dinged. Her crew was already preparing to chase that same system farther across the state. She made a quick phone call and confirmed that she could get a seat in another chaser's vehicle, then tossed me the keys to our rental car.

"Be safe," she said as I stuffed a grey shirt into a pack.

CHAPTER 12

HURRICANE SANDY

An airplane's engine screamed overhead as it descended into Los Angeles International Airport. Dipali, Team Rubicon's finance director, frantically manipulated the keyboard in front of her, toggling between Excel spreadsheets and charts. My shirt clung to my back in the un-air-conditioned room. We'd moved into this, our first office, earlier in the year. It was all we could afford. It sat underneath the airport's flight path, right in the middle of Inglewood. The windows had bars on them, which was good since we had to keep all the windows wide open. Foreign workers ran a machine shop next door, their indecipherable conversations wafting through the thin walls along with the smell of their cheap cigarettes. It wasn't much, but it was Team Rubicon's first home. And we were proud of it.

I stared past Dipali as she spoke. It's not that I wasn't paying attention to her. It was that I didn't like what she was telling me.

"Jake, are you listening to me?"

"Yes, of course. We're running out of money, and at our current burn rate we'll be insolvent by Christmas."

Since Tuscaloosa and Joplin eighteen months prior, the organization had grown like crazy. When the dust had settled from those two operations, I had sat down with the rest of the leadership team. We determined that William and I would finally come onto the payroll and that the organization would begin focusing on building a domestic response capability. Our new assumption was that domestic disasters—which were happening more and more frequently—would cost less and allow us to help more people and engage more volunteers. Since that time we'd hired a staff of nine. Still small, but able to leverage a team of a hundred volunteer leaders throughout the U.S., who in turn helped deploy our fifteen hundred volunteers. We believed responding domestically would help us build muscle memory and establish a reputation upon which we could scale. Early successes led us to believe that we could transform how the disaster response industry perceived volunteers and the value they could bring.

The problem was that we couldn't convince funders to pay for it. When the Home Depot Foundation and the Bob Woodruff Foundation came in earlier in the year with a combined $250,000 in grants, we thought that our sleepless nights were close to an end. We were wrong. From other funders we heard a constant refrain.

This idea won't scale.

This idea won't sustain.

With Dipali pointing at our most recent financial statements, I realized that the numbers agreed. Cash was dwindling. We'd responded to over a dozen disasters so far in 2012, but the general public simply wasn't donating money to fund those efforts. It turns out it's hard to get Americans to care about people they've never met in communities they've never heard of.

"So, what do we do?" I asked Dipali.

"I think we should start talking about what bills we will and won't pay if this doesn't turn around in the next couple of months."

I sighed. This wasn't the entrepreneurial dream I'd expected. For the next ten minutes I went over the list of accounts payable with Dip, putting little checkmarks next to the ones we could delay payment on. There was one big line item without a check: payroll. There were people counting on me to figure this out.

Finished, Dipali stood up and walked out of the office. Watching her go, I leaned back and stared at the ceiling. The uncertainty was gnawing at me, literally causing my health to deteriorate. A few months prior I had been so stressed that I ground my teeth until two of my molars cracked in half. *I need stability,* I thought.

I pulled the top drawer of my desk out and looked down. There it was, the little box I had been hiding for three weeks. I picked it up and discreetly pulled it into my lap. I turned it over in my hands, snapping the lid open and shut. Finally, I cracked open the lid and brought it up to my face. The diamond sparkled, even in the room's depressing light.

Yep, tonight's the night. I closed the lid and stuffed the ring in my pocket.

"I'll see you all tomorrow."

Andrew, our operations director, looked up from his monitor. "Cool, Wood. Just so you know, there are a couple hurricanes spinning way out in the Atlantic. That season is really just ramping up, so I'm getting our teams prepped for the next few weeks."

I nodded and walked toward the door, reviewing my plan for the evening. Asking Indra to marry me marked a personal turning point. Immediately after Clay's death, I'd pushed her away. I felt insufferable guilt that I had let Clay down, and I grappled with whether I wanted to be in a position to fail someone I cared so deeply for ever again. It caused me to repel Indra's love for several miserable months. Indra, for her part, was equal parts patient and clear that she would not suffer the presence of a self-wallowing man.

Tonight's clarity was not spur of the moment. It was the result of months of soul-searching and, truth be told, late nights at a therapist's office trying to work through Clay's suicide. I finally came to realize that I was carrying Clay's lifeless body with me through life, no differently than if I had slung him over my shoulder on the battlefield. I sought the weight because the weight brought pain. I wanted the pain because pain was the price I needed to pay for letting him down.

Indra, being a source of joy in my life, had threatened my self-imposed sentence. It was only when I'd forgiven myself for Clay's death that I was able to love her, or anyone, again.

• • •

OCTOBER 31, 2012

I walked through the heavy door of Team Rubicon's office before dawn. "Good morning, Maurice," I said to our office manager. The clock on the wall read six a.m. I recalled leaving the office less than six hours before, after midnight. It wasn't the team's normal work schedule, but this was an extraordinary circumstance. Two days prior, Hurricane Sandy had made landfall in New York and New Jersey, wreaking havoc on the nation's most densely populated metropolitan area. Nearly one hundred thousand residences on Long Island were damaged or destroyed. Meanwhile, underground tunnels and subways were rendered inoperable for weeks, and in some cases months, grinding public transportation to a halt. When it was all over, Sandy would become the second costliest hurricane in U.S. history. In 2013, a year after the storm, FEMA records showed that fewer than half of residents who'd requested relief assistance from the agency had qualified for it, while thirty thousand residents of New Jersey and New York still remained displaced. Team Rubicon had activated teams from Washington, D.C., all the way through Boston who were now on the ground helping communities clear roads with chain saws. A palpable energy cut through the stale air.

The news media was covering the disaster around the clock. Nearly eight million people were without power, many of them almost unreachable. We had only sporadic communication with our team on the ground in New York City, led by Matt Pelak, but he needed more people. He needed more supplies. He needed help.

My computer screen fired up and I reached forward to tap a username and password into the website portal. There it was, Team Rubicon's checking account information. The situation had not changed since Dipali had raised it with me several weeks prior. In fact, our cash had only dwindled further. Twelve hours earlier we had discussed deploying every volunteer who would answer the call to NYC. We knew the need was there. Our only limiting factor was money, and it was a big factor. Would this be it? The moment that would make or break Team Rubicon?

Andrew popped his head into the office. "Some lady from Goldman Sachs just called. She wants you to call her back immediately." He handed me a piece of scrap paper with a phone number scribbled on it.

"Did she say anything? What did she want?"

"She just wants to speak with you," he said.

Goldman Sachs was a behemoth. Exactly the type of company that Team Rubicon needed to convince of its merits. It was also the only company in lower Manhattan that had power at the moment, the result of effective emergency planning by its leadership. I picked up the phone and punched in the numbers. Anxiety filled my belly as the phone rang. *I really need to get a cup of coffee,* I thought. Four hours of sleep was not cutting it. A woman's voice answered on the other end.

"Hello, this is Anne Black."

"Hi, Anne. This is Jake Wood from Team Rubicon returning your call."

"Oh, Jake, hello. Would you hold for a quick moment?" The line clicked. *Please be good. Please be good. Please be good,* my mind chanted, willing the universe to bend to our needs. "Jake, are you there? I'm now joined by Dina Powell. Together we run corporate social responsibility and the Goldman Sachs Foundation. How are you?" We briefly exchanged niceties before Dina got down to business, a sense of urgency in her voice.

"Jake, obviously this city—our city—is crippled. We keep calling around to figure out who is on the ground and doing good work, and Team Rubicon's name keeps popping up. The problem is, we've never heard of you."

I chuckled before responding. "Well, I've never heard of you either!" The playful retort didn't land as well as I'd hoped. There was an awkward silence.

"Jake, can you explain to us what you're doing on the ground?"

I proceeded to explain that Team Rubicon was working throughout New Jersey, New York, and Connecticut, helping to clear roadways and access to homes. That in the coming days we would begin working to muck out and gut the homes that had been impacted by the storm surge, helping to organize community volunteers along the way. And that what made Team Rubicon different was its use of military veterans. They found that last part intriguing.

"Jake, that's amazing. By everything we're hearing, nobody else is out there doing this right now. What do you need to scale?"

This was it. The moment. The next words out of my mouth had the potential to define the organization. I mustered all the confidence I could find before answering. "Listen, Team Rubicon has the best volunteers, the necessary equipment, and the right system." Part of that was bluster, but I was truthful when I said, "What we don't have is capital, and I suspect you have plenty of that."

The silence on the other end of the line was deafening. The pulse in my temples became audible. *Maybe I came on too strong?* Finally, Dina broke the silence.

"What could Team Rubicon do if we funded your operation?"

"Ma'am, we will deploy a thousand veterans and volunteers into New York City." I had no idea if we could pull off such a feat. That would be twenty times more volunteers than we'd ever deployed on a mission. But fortune favors the bold. Goldman Sachs was not going to be interested in funding the mundane.

"Here's what we'd like to do. Goldman Sachs is going to wire you $250,000 today to get you started. In the coming week we will see how you're doing and consider additional funding." We didn't know it at the time, but the firm would make similar calls to Team Rubicon after many future disasters, donating millions of dollars over the years.

My jaw dropped. The variables governing our situation had just changed dramatically. I offered effusive thanks. Then I ran into the main room. "Everyone, gather round!" I shouted into every corner of the office.

One by one, the small team entered. Mike and Kirk from the marketing team; William and Joanne, Andrew and Cal from the operations team. Maurice swung around in his chair and leaned back.

"Listen up. I just got off the phone with Goldman Sachs. They're wiring in two hundred fifty thousand dollars today, with more potentially to come. I want us to put the word out to every volunteer in the system that this is a nationwide mobilization. Every volunteer that can get to New York in the next four weeks needs to deploy." William nodded, fully bought in. Others in the room had incredulous looks on their faces. "We need to get a thousand boots on the ground." Eyes grew even wider. The team knew that target was insane.

"Jake, that's not enough to pay for a thousand deployments," one of them challenged.

"Yeah, and we can't even house the team we have on the ground now!" another offered.

I nodded. What they were saying was true. The situation was still littered with unknowns. "Team, this is our moment. You know it. There are dozens of critical things we need to figure out on the ground in order to pull this off. That's why we are all flying to New York City tomorrow. We are shutting this office down and relocating it east for the foreseeable future."

"What about Nicole?" someone asked. I'd forgotten that we had just hired Nicole Green, one of the volunteers from Tuscaloosa, convincing her to leave her cushy job at Deloitte to join our scrappy startup. Her first day was Monday, and she had just started the drive across the country with a car full of belongings. She was probably somewhere in Tennessee.

"Tell her to turn around and drive back east. We'll meet her on the ground."

• • •

VETERANS DAY, NOVEMBER 11, 2012
BROOKLYN, NEW YORK

The warehouse was cavernous. Forty-foot ceilings and tens of thousands of square feet of cement floors and corrugated metal walls. Half of the fluorescent bulbs overhead flickered; the other half didn't work at all. At night, when the lights were turned off at ten p.m., you could hear the rats scurrying along the walls. The row of porta-potties brought in earlier in the week emitted an indescribable smell, part human waste, part chemical disinfectant. Amid all of it, hundreds of cots dropped off by the Red Cross were set up in rows, their edges aligned with military precision. Sitting atop the cots were rucksacks and sleeping bags, many of them olive drab or camouflage.

It was our home, and it was amazing.

New York's mid-November chill meant you could see the breath of several hundred volunteers milling about the area. Earlier in the day we had arranged a day of service for various veteran organizations in the Far Rockaways, the neighborhood in Queens that Team Rubicon had descended upon to assist in the recovery. Our pitch was simple. Rather than spending the day marching in parades, veterans should instead join Team Rubicon in service to their community. It had been a success, and veterans from The Mission Continues, Team Red White and Blue, the Pat Tillman Foundation, the Headstrong Project, and Student Veterans of America had come out in support.

I walked among the cots, introducing myself to volunteers and catching up with old friends. Each one of them was filthy, cold, and sore.

Walking up to a cot, I reached out and shook the hand of a volunteer I had not met. "Hi there. I'm Jake." He took my hand and shook it firmly. I noticed an Eagle, Globe, and Anchor tattoo on his forearm. "You a Marine?" I asked.

"Yes, sir, I am."

"Same here. Semper Fi," I said, before adding, "Happy belated birthday." The Marine Corps birthday is on November 10, the day before Veterans Day. Marines love their birthday.

"Yeah, hey, man. I just came in from the New Jersey operation," the volunteer said. We had recently made the decision to consolidate the New Jersey efforts into our New York one in order to streamline logistics. He continued, "We actually had a birthday ceremony last night. Yeah, some old Marine—a retired master sergeant, I think—led it."

"That's great," I responded.

"Yeah, he lost his son in Iraq. Or maybe Afghanistan—I can't remember for sure. Anyways, it was awesome. His story was powerful. I think he grabbed a bunk over there." He pointed around the corner toward a section of the warehouse that wasn't visible.

I thanked the Marine for being there and moved on, eager to meet this other Marine. But first I collided with two old friends, Paul and Ryan, who'd served in my battalion and been involved with Team Rubicon for several months. We hugged.

One of the most special moments in a war zone is reuniting with friends separated by time and space. Your paths will cross at some large forward operating base (FOB) and for a moment you can let your guard down knowing that your friend is alive and in one piece. You embrace and catch up on all the close calls and unabashedly say how much you love each other. After Clay's death, several other suicides from our unit followed. In fact, over the next decade our battalion would have its war-fighting legacy eclipsed by its suicide legacy, as we lost more men to their own hands than any other unit in the military. Every time I received a phone call from a Marine friend, my first thought was to wonder who'd killed themselves. The result was that any reunion among combat veterans felt as though we were still on the battlefield, because so many of us were still dying. That's why embracing Paul and Ryan was so special.

"Wood, you'll never guess who's here," Ryan said.

"Who?"

He motioned to a cot in the center of the room. An older gentleman was sitting on it, unpacking his socks. His dark scalp was clean-shaven. Beneath it a weathered face was framed by a square jaw. There was no mistaking the man. It was Top Washington. Top was the father of Mike Washington, the friend I'd lost in Afghanistan.

"Top!" I bellowed.

Top, a common nickname for a Marine master sergeant, looked up from the cot and smiled. "Wood," his deep baritone echoed off the walls. "How you doin', Devil Dog?" He rose from the cot as I strode forward, wrapping me in his arms and pulling me in so tight it squeezed the air out of my lungs. We swayed back and forth, neither of us anxious to let go.

"Top, it's so good to see you. What are you doing here?"

He released his grip and stepped back. His chin tilted upward. "I saw the call go out. I'm sick of feeling sorry for myself, so I came here to serve. For Mike." He looked over my shoulder at Paul and Ryan, and then behind himself, a twinkle in his eye. "And to keep these knuckleheads out of trouble." I looked past Top and saw several more Marines we'd served with.

"So you're the Marine who held the birthday ceremony out in New Jersey?"

"Oh, hell yeah. You know Top don't pass up a chance to toast the

Marine Corps and tell sea stories." He pulled out his phone and pulled up a video. He pressed "play" and soon the low, rhythmic chant of the Marine Corps hymn could be heard. The Marines in the frame were gathered in a low-slung, dimly lit bar, pints of beer swinging back and forth to the tune. In the middle of it all was Top, singing his heart out.

I spent the evening sitting around the cots with Top and the rest of the Marines from 2-7, catching up on each other's lives and reliving tales of battlefield glory, some true, some just how we wanted to remember them. We rarely drew a distinction between the two. When the lights went out at ten p.m., I left them and retreated to the office, where I joined the rest of the team to plan the next day's work.

The next morning we arrived at our FOB, which was located in a parking lot in the Far Rockaways and donated to us by two brothers who were Army veterans. The parking lot had been transformed, with tents, trailers, and a green bus nicknamed Large Marge sitting behind a chain-link fence. By eight o'clock in the morning the FOB was bustling, with Greyshirts scrambling to assemble tools and get their work assignments for the day. Outside the fence, hundreds of volunteers from the local community would line up, eager to be put to work. A week earlier, Team Rubicon had realized that its teams of veterans were more useful if they were broken up and assigned to lead groups of local volunteers, who were often wandering about looking to help but unsure how. Our volunteers, many of them former squad and platoon leaders, were eager to lead, and the soccer teams and youth groups showing up were willing to follow.

With militaristic discipline, Team Rubicon's men and women would shout instructions to those joining the effort, quickly processing them through the necessary paperwork and just-in-time training before assigning them to team leaders and shuttling them to work sites. It was chaos conquered.

Pacing across the compound, I checked in on various groups. The planning team was hard at work learning a new software system, called Palantir, that was transforming the way we were collecting data and directing work. Damage assessment teams were crisscrossing neighborhoods with Palantir-enabled smartphones, evaluating every home's damage and insurance levels and uploading the information into the cloud. Large Marge was full of nerds sitting in front of computers, eyes squinted at screens streaming with maps and the mountains of data coming in from those teams. The logistics section was frenzied as ever, never in possession of enough tools or supplies, but always finding ways to improvise and overcome. The registration team was processing volunteers with exuberant enthusiasm, their smiles and gratitude assuring locals that they'd come to the right place to assist.

Looking over, I saw Top finalizing a wheelbarrow of gear. A sheen of sweat had formed on his bare head despite the brisk day. I walked over. "Good morning, Top."

"Morning, Jake. Just getting ready to take a team down the street. Got a work order for an elderly couple. Storm surge deposited a foot of sand in their basement, and the waterline is at twenty-seven inches on the main floor." That was approaching catastrophic damage for a home, especially if it had not been gutted by now.

"Mind if I walk with you?"

"Not at all." I followed Top as he made his way over to his team. He was joined by three others from Team Rubicon and a half dozen volunteers from a local synagogue. "Alright, listen up!" Top shouted, his posture reflecting that of a Marine who'd spent a life of service in the Corps.

"My name is Top Washington, and I will be your team leader for today," he began, before communicating the day's work plan and safety brief. "But, before we begin, I want to tell you why I'm here." Top proceeded to tell the story of his service, his decades in the Marines and the Seattle Fire Department, and his son Mike's sacrifice. "I'm here because I know Mike would be here, and it's my honor to take his place. You're all here for different reasons, but the goal is the same. To help someone." With that, Top grabbed the handles of the wheelbarrow and began walking down the street. "Alright, let's roll," he yelled rearward. As we departed the FOB, I noticed a spray-painted sign: *Welcome to FOB Hope,* it read.

All around, Sandy's wrath was on display. Street signs were toppled, cars were swept into yards, some homes were even knocked off their foundations. Everywhere you looked were huge deposits of sand, swept onto the narrow barrier island from the beach and ocean floor. Near some homes you could already smell mold setting in.

Meanwhile, Team Rubicon was an omnipresent swarm. Greyshirts could be seen on doorsteps and in yards, through windows and standing at the top of cellar stairs. I watched as two volunteers gingerly peeled decades-old black-and-white photographs out of a wedding album and clipped them to a clothesline to dry. It was the type of effort that would make a world of difference to the elderly couple watching from the porch.

Our gamble was paying off. In the two weeks since the Goldman Sachs call, dozens of other companies had come forward to support Team Rubicon. Media outlets were doing live shots from the FOB almost daily, telling the story of the veterans bringing order to chaos. Most importantly, the emergency management apparatus was taking note, inviting the organization to its planning meetings for updates. FEMA's deputy administrator even came to the FOB to see Team Rubicon in action. For the first time ever we had a seat at the table.

Team Rubicon didn't come close to deploying the thousand volunteers I had promised, but several thousand veterans across the country signed up over those weeks so they could deploy on future missions. The roughly four hundred volunteers who did deploy helped hundreds of homeowners and led over ten thousand local volunteers. The work was so impactful that I still get stopped on the streets of New York by someone noticing my Team Rubicon shirt so they can tell me the story of how we helped someone they knew in Sandy's aftermath.

Perhaps most important, Team Rubicon had proven on the world's biggest stage that its model worked: military veterans, with their training and experience, were the 9-1-1 force that the country needed.

CHAPTER 13

TORNADO ALLEY

MARCH 2013
LOS ANGELES

The coffee was bad. Not Iraq bad, but bad. The kind you get when you sign a cut-rate deal to host a small conference at an off-brand hotel near LAX. And yet it was my fourth cup.

This was a big moment. Team Rubicon's response to Hurricane Sandy had put us on the map. A gut decision to fly in a group of engineers from a little-known Silicon Valley startup resulted in a total transformation of how Team Rubicon managed data collection and intelligence generation in the field. The on-the-fly innovations, combined with our volunteers' uncanny ability to manage the chaos of thousands of unaffiliated volunteers, had led to our inclusion in the planning at the emergency operations center in Brooklyn. Team Rubicon's financial situation had also changed dramatically, as the organization raised five times more money in the final two months of the year than it had the entire first ten months combined. On top of it all, President Obama had invited us to the Oval Office to thank us for the work we did after the storm. I still remember the sense of awe I had when the door to the Oval Office opened behind me and President Obama boomed, "Team Rubicon—get in here!"

All of that had led to this moment. Four months after operations in New York ended, I called a meeting of all our staff and volunteer leaders from across the country. Now they sat waiting in a bleak conference room, choking on instant eggs. All were wondering why I'd called the meeting and handed them a shirt emblazoned across the front with *Burn the Boat.*

By now, I'd delivered the commencement address at the University of Wisconsin and testified before a Senate committee, but I'd never been more nervous. Finally, after one last run-through of my deck, I walked to the front of the room and tapped the microphone three times. It didn't work. Of course it didn't work. Nothing in this hotel worked. "Hey! Quiet down—time to get started!" I hollered. Finally, the din died down and a hundred eyes trained on me. "You're probably all wondering why I flew you in here this week." There was some head nodding and off-color jokes.

I proceeded to thank them for their service and recount for them the impact our work had on people in New York. They saw charts and graphs and bullet points that indicated the organization was growing as fast as any venture-backed startup. Chins tilted higher and chests puffed with pride.

"And, unfortunately, that is why you are all fired from your current roles."

Eyebrows shot up. Brows furrowed. Furtive glances darted back and forth. A few people squirmed uncomfortably in their seats. "Listen, Sandy revealed for us the potential this organization has to scale its impact.

But we aren't going to do that if we keep doing things business as usual. We have to fundamentally change. Every system, every process, and every role must evolve to meet the needs of tomorrow."

I returned to the slides and began walking them through the coming changes. We would have to professionalize and begin adopting industry standards, which meant that we would be moving to FEMA's Incident Command System (ICS)—a modular, scalable system for command, control, and coordination—to manage all operations. As expected, half the volunteer leaders threw their hands in the air. Moving to FEMA's system was seen by some as becoming the bureaucracy we loathed. "ICS doesn't mean we have to move slower. In fact, if we perfect it, ICS should allow us to move faster and with more consistency," I said with confidence. Deep inside I hoped I was right.

Training and safety equipment would become the norm. The cowboy mentality would have to fade . . . somewhat. I assured them we would remain committed to our culture, that we would maintain our bias for action, and that we would never allow bureaucracy to slow us down. If those present were on board with these changes, they could reapply for new positions in two weeks and help us build the best disaster response organization in the world.

Clicking to the final slide, I ended with a story. "Everyone, look at your shirts. Does anyone know what this phrase means?" I waited to see if a hand would shoot up. "There's a legend about the general who leads his army across the open seas. Upon reaching the enemy's shores the general orders his men to burn all their boats on the beach. Why?"

"So that there's no going back," replied Carol, a volunteer leader from Kansas.

"Right! So that the only option is to press forward and achieve victory. There's no option for retreat. Team Rubicon is at that moment right now. We must make a choice. Are we ready to build the best disaster relief organization in the world? If so, it's time to let go of the old way of doing things. It's time to burn the boats."

I'm not sure I realized it at the time, but this moment was one of the most consequential in Team Rubicon's history. We lost a lot of volunteers that week in Los Angeles, volunteers whose vision for the organization diverged from ours. I can't remember any animosity, but I do recall one thing—coming to the realization that entrepreneurs aren't in the business of making friends.

* ● *

MAY 31, 2013
MOORE, OKLAHOMA

The airplane shook like a raft entering rapids on a raging river. Overhead, a luggage bin popped open. The pilot's voice came over the intercom. "Well, as you can see we are hitting some turbulence on our way into Oklahoma City. I've turned the 'Fasten Seat Belt' sign on. Please remain seated until we learn more." It always amazed me how cool, calm, and collected pilots could be. In Iraq, our squad was once ambushed from two sides while patrolling down a road. Pinned down, our radio operator called for air support. Two fighter planes and two helicopters were diverted in our direction. I can still hear the pilots' voices: "Hey there, Golf-Three-Charlie, this is Hellraiser Two-Six, heard you boys were in a bit of a scuffle . . . We are supersonic en route to your location now . . . Happy to help any way we can." Meanwhile, as we hugged the earth, the volume of machine gun fire coming in above was literally snapping stalks of tall ditch weed above.

I was on a flight to Moore, Oklahoma, which a few days prior had been hit by a massive EF-5 tornado. Team Rubicon was already on the ground conducting operations, and the early indications were that this would soon eclipse Hurricane Sandy, only six months prior, for the largest mission in our history. It was also our first large-scale rollout of ICS, and I was eager to see it in action.

Ding. "Ladies and gentlemen, there are confirmed tornadoes on the ground in Oklahoma City. Air traffic control has diverted us to Dallas–Fort Worth, where we'll await further instructions upon landing."

Shit. I opened CNN and Twitter in my browser, anxiously scanning the updates. Multiple tornado cells were being tracked around the city. One caught my eye—it was right next to Moore. The airplane began its descent into DFW, and soon the flight attendant was instructing the passengers to put away all electronics. I folded my tray table and pulled my computer onto my lap, waiting for the flight attendant to pass before continuing to scan the updates. My people were in harm's way.

When the airplane landed, I was met with grim news. A funnel cloud was on the ground, tracking directly toward the high school that our teams were using as a FOB. A Twitter user shared a shaky cell phone video. I tapped to open it up. It showed a ferocious vortex indiscriminately destroying anything in its path, moving across a field near a major highway. Nearly two hundred Greyshirts were sitting in its path a few miles away.

My heart raced. I rushed to call the office in Los Angeles. The phone was picked up without a greeting. "Jake, we know, we are tracking it. We were just on the phone with our team leader on the ground. He was rushing everyone into the school's locker rooms, but our call was cut off. We haven't been able to reach him again."

I stood in the airplane's aisle with my bag, patience wearing thin with the passengers ahead of me taking their time to disembark. The televisions around the waiting area were all tuned in to CNN or Fox News, each showing live updates of the situation near Moore. I stood in front of a television, helpless. *Am I about to witness this tornado kill hundreds of my people?*

My phone buzzed. Looking down, I saw a text message from Indra. *Please tell me you're not in Oklahoma yet?!?!* Ironically, Indra had taken a job as a meteorologist with CNN in New York City just two weeks prior. Her career was taking off, and that meant that we spent the first couple years of our marriage twenty-five hundred miles apart. She wasn't just watching what was going on; she was reporting on it around the clock from CNN's studio. I called her.

"Hey, hun. I'm not in Oklahoma. We got diverted to Dallas." Indra's relief was audible. In the background I heard the gate attendant make an announcement on the intercom. Our flight would be canceled until the following morning. Indra must have heard it too.

"Jake, I know what you're thinking. There is no way you are renting a car and driving into a tornado cell. I'm not going to be widowed less than a month after getting married." Indra rarely minced words. And she was right. Our wedding was so recent that my ring still didn't feel like a natural extension of my finger. I looked at the ring and back at the television. The funnel cloud was beginning to track away from the school. Team Rubicon's volunteers appeared to be safe, at least for the moment.

"Indra, I promise you I will be safe."

"Does that mean you're staying in Dallas tonight?"

"It means I will be safe." I glanced at my watch. It was getting late in New York, and I knew Indra would have to go to bed soon to get rest before her shift on the morning show. Time was on my side. "Listen, I know you have to get to bed. I'm safe now, and I'll be safe when you wake up. I promise."

She bid me a begrudging good night, and I speedwalked to pick up a rental car. I thought back to three years earlier when Team Rubicon had responded to the earthquake and tsunami in Chile. Before leaving, Indra had made me promise that we would not sleep inside any buildings, as aftershocks were still roiling the country. But by day three we were so exhausted that we collapsed onto gurneys in a hospital and fell asleep. Naturally, an earthquake that registered 6.6 on the Richter scale literally shook us out of bed that night, and we rushed out of the building fearing it would collapse. Indra was pissed, a fact she often reminded me of.

When the woman at the counter asked if I wanted to insure the car against damage, I scrolled down the options until I found the highest coverage possible and scribbled my initials. No point in taking unnecessary risks, I figured.

Besides a few roads washed out from flash floods and a highway patrolman turning me around at a bridge that had water lapping over its edges, the drive was uneventful. Eventually, as the risk of tornadoes faded, I turned the volume down on the radio and rode in silence. It was not often that I got to enjoy mindless nothingness. Just me, my thoughts, and I.

Memorial Day had been four days earlier. Top Washington, hooked on Team Rubicon since his deployment to Hurricane Sandy, had been with our troops in Moore. He shared the gut-wrenching story of his son's sacrifice in front of hundreds of Greyshirts. Over the course of the weekend, we asked each of them to share on video who they were serving in honor of on this Memorial Day. For some the list was long. People on work sites would stare into the camera, beads of sweat on their brow, and rattle off names and dates. The list was committed to memory, every bit as personally identifiable to them as their social security number or birthday or mother's maiden name. The combination and sequence of loss their own unique fingerprint of war.

I'd chosen not to deploy to Moore for Memorial Day. The year prior I'd spent Memorial Day at a gravesite with a case of beer. I sat on the grass with Bullard, Wiley, Robles, Trejo, and Blake Howey's mom, Audrey. We clinked our bottles and toasted Blake. We thanked him for his sacrifice. We apologized for his sacrifice. We told him what we were up to, where our lives were and where they were going. We swapped war stories, some funny, some tragic. Occasionally there would be a pause, and we would draw on our beer and look at nothing in particular. In those moments we privately missed war, but that didn't make sense, so we'd quickly move to fill the void.

Eventually I found myself telling Blake's mom the full story of how he died. I told her how our patrol had gotten lost. How Arguello and I had almost been put at the front of the convoy because we knew the road to turn down. I shared Sergeant Rosenberger's grit as he coordinated our evacuation despite his wounds and assured her Blake's death was not his fault. I told her how Latcher and Payne reached into the burning Humvee to pull Blake out. I told her it was all too late, but she already knew that.

This year I chose to be alone on Memorial Day. It was simply too painful to be around others.

Finally, I arrived in Moore. Opening the car door, I was met with the songs of thousands of crickets. Three volunteers huddled outside smoking cigarettes, the red embers gently illuminating their faces. They were engaged in a serious conversation and paid me no mind as I moved toward the door and into the gymnasium.

I navigated through the gym's annex, piled high with supplies donated by locals. In the soft light I could faintly see hundreds of chests rising and falling. The room was full of souls from across America, each inspired to serve. To drop everything to help a community they'd never been to and people they'd never met.

There was Steve from Boise, a Navy Corpsman and firefighter. A towering figure and compassionate leader. Sue was an Army veteran from Hawaii, who between her battles with cancer chose to battle tornadoes. She was a Vietnamese refugee, marooned by another American conflict. A self-avowed Bubba and Marine veteran from Arkansas, Chad was the loudmouth whose rough exterior was softened by a gentle heart. He loved America dearly and was called to serve due in equal parts to patriotism and the Good Book.

Robert, from out east, served to escape a deteriorating life at home. "I don't know how many more times I can walk through the front door and be told by my wife that I'm a deadbeat," he would say dejectedly. Service gave him purpose where he otherwise had none. We'd first met Nicholas as a young volunteer from Tennessee who'd been involved in the pseudo-military Civil Air Patrol. He'd proven to be a whiz with our tech systems. Two years later, when Nicholas grew his hair out and asked us to begin calling him Samantha, there were no questions, and her worth was only measured by her desire to serve.

Stacy, not an inch over five feet tall, saw the world simply. There were three kinds of people in the world, she liked to quip: wolves, sheep, and sheepdogs. She was in Moore because she was a sheepdog. Albeit one built more like a Yorkie.

"My brother would love Team Rubicon," Maggie would often say, before explaining that her brother had been killed in Afghanistan. She was here for him. In the quiet by the campfire, Tom and Cindy would hold hands and wish their daughter would join. "She came back from

Iraq a different person," Cindy would say softly. Tom and Cindy were there to try to better understand their daughter's experiences. They would listen as other veterans shared their stories, eager for whatever insight they might glean.

Jon was in Moore because there were no wars when he was in the Corps, and his shoulders sagged with the burden of wondering if he'd done enough. "I'm here because I feel I carry a debt to my brothers and sisters who actually fought," he'd say, hiding behind a beard. When told his debt was folly, he'd hear none of it. The burden was real, at least to him.

Kelly was in search of a tribe. The cutthroat sales team she worked on now was nothing like the one-team, one-fight aircraft she flew on in the Air Force. Team Rubicon gave her the opportunity to look out for others, not just herself.

Some yearned for adventure, while others showed up simply to help survivors. For one or two it might have been an escape, but for most it was, in some way or another, an attempt to write the next chapter of their story. Alongside them were dozens of Greyshirts who had never served in the military, yet many found themselves in search of those same things.

Democrats and Republicans. Coasties and Midwesterners. Teachers, firefighters, bankers, and down-on-their-luckers. Rich and poor. All races, religions, and creeds. Bound together by a universal call to serve. This was the lifeblood of Team Rubicon. I stood still and watched them sleep.

When I reached my cot, canvas stretched taut across an aluminum frame, I found a note on top. "Welcome to the Four Seasons, boss." Exhausted, I dropped my pack and pulled off my boots. I ripped off my sweatshirt and rolled it into a pillow. Lying down, I closed my eyes and became one of the two hundred Greyshirts in search of something.

Five hours later, the lights in the gymnasium flipped on. Canvas squeaked as volunteers rubbed their eyes and sat up. "Morning brief is in thirty minutes!" a voice bellowed from the gym's corner. Outside, large buses idled as they waited to take us the thirty miles to our work sites. After final orders and checks were made, the teams boarded the buses and began the journey. Some leaned against the window and slept, no longer accustomed to waking up before dawn. Others sat sideways into the aisle, eager to get to know their new friends from around the country. The bus soon filled with the hum of kinship. The dull roar continued uninterrupted until suddenly it died. Solemn faces looked through the windows on the right side. "What's going on?" I asked. "That's the school that got hit. The one where all the kids died." I turned and saw what had been an ordinary elementary school leveled, as if stepped on by a giant's boot. The chain-link fence surrounding the school was adorned with flowers and signs of mourning.

We arrived at the Home Depot parking lot that served as our FOB to retrieve equipment and supplies. Our relationship with Home Depot had deepened, and we'd frequently establish our responses near their stores, where they'd let volunteers grab supplies and equipment charged to a master credit account that the company's foundation funded. Before long, my team was riding in the back of a pickup packed full of saws, shovels, and water.

We turned off the main road and entered a neighborhood. The road before us was clear, likely scraped clean by a massive road grader after the storm. As in Tuscaloosa, the tornado that had hit Moore indiscrimi- nately destroyed everything in its path. Survivors milled about, returning for the second or third or fourth time to the place they called home, hop- ing that on this next attempt they'd discover it was all just a bad dream.

Our truck pulled up to a home that had sustained substantial damage. Entire sections of roof had been ripped away, possibly the shingle-adorned plywood we'd passed two lots back. The gaping holes that remained looked like lesions on a leper. The off-white siding was pockmarked from flying debris, similar to the chips and dimples that adorned the mud-brick walls of Iraqi or Afghan homes that had endured the fury of a 7.62mm machine gun. A man stood in the driveway, hands on his hips. I watched our team leader approach him. Behind me Grace and Jose began unloading equipment.

"Good morning, sir. I'm with Team Rubicon. We are here to work on your home." The man slowly shifted his focus from the house to the volunteer. He looked the team leader up and down, noticing the Navy fatigues tucked into desert-colored combat boots.

"Are you a vet?" he asked.

"Yes, sir, I am. Navy."

"So am I," the man replied, before adding, "Desert Storm." He pointed to the back of a pickup truck parked in the lawn. There was an Air Force sticker in the window. "Didn't think anybody would come and help." It was evident the man was still trying to process what had happened.

"We're here to help, sir." He stepped forward and extended a clipboard with a stack of papers, all the documents that we needed to have signed to begin work. The man took it and began to read. After a few seconds he simply shook his head and signed the documents. We got to work.

Hours later, after a lunch of sun-warmed ham sandwiches, I wandered back into the house. Shattered glass crunched under my feet. A layer of grime covered everything in the home, and my fingers traced lines on the kitchen counter. Turning a corner, I saw the man in a hallway, his back toward me, softly illuminated by sun filtering in through an unseen hole. The rays caught the dust floating in the air, and it almost looked like fog. Getting closer, I could hear him sniffle as he turned to look at me, revealing what he was holding. The picture frame had speckles of mud on it, but the photo of his family was unmistakable. Unsure what to do, I asked if I could hold it. "You have a beautiful family," I said, wiping away the smudges with my thumb.

He pointed past me into a bathroom. It was the source of light, its ceiling ripped away in the storm. "That's where we rode out the storm," he said. I looked at him in disbelief. He nodded his head to confirm. "We didn't have much time. I put my two kids into that bathtub and threw my wife on top of them. Then I wrapped my arms around the base of that toilet right there and . . ." He drifted off, shaking his head. "It sounded like a freight train," he choked out.

I felt like I was invading his privacy. I stayed silent and looked at the photograph, silently tracing its frame with my fingers.

"When the roof ripped off, you could hear the trusses snapping. And then all of a sudden it was like a giant vacuum cleaner just trying to suck us up into the sky. I just screamed and screamed and screamed." We both looked up through the roof. Lazy white clouds floated across the blue sky, a vivid contrast to what he would have seen that day. "I'm supposed to protect my family. That's my job. But all I could do was hug that toilet and scream."

Finally, I understood. He wasn't struggling because of what had happened. He was struggling because he felt he had failed to be the man his wife and kids needed. It was, of course, irrational. But our minds often fail to process these kinds of moments rationally. It was no different than how so many veterans assign themselves fault for things entirely beyond their control. Like not keeping your friend from killing himself.

I looked over at him. "Actually, your family survived because you acted quickly and threw them in the safest place in the house." He didn't make eye contact. "You know what your family cares about? That you rebuild this house. That you start over and move on." The sound of equipment being picked up drifted in from outside.

The man, still not looking in my direction, responded, "Thank y'all for coming. I really didn't think anyone would come to help."

PART III

CHAPTER 14

TYPHOON HAIYAN

NOVEMBER 10, 2013

After Hurricane Sandy and the Moore tornado, we outgrew the Inglewood office and graduated to an office in a building that had suitable power, heating, and ventilation. The floors were polished concrete, framed out by tall walls. We painted many of them deep red, Team Rubicon's primary color, and adorned them with photographs of our missions. Above the reception desk was a custom-cut Team Rubicon logo. It was actually starting to feel like we were a real company.

It was a Sunday evening and Team Rubicon's office was humming with activity. It was November 10, a full year since Top Washington had led Team Rubicon's Marines in a celebration of the Corps' birthday out in New York. Over the previous forty-eight hours, Typhoon Haiyan, the strongest typhoon ever recorded, had raked over the Philippines. The death toll would eventually surpass six thousand. The Philippines is composed of thousands of islands that differed widely in terms of their level of development and preparedness for something like this. Fifteen-foot storm surges had damaged or destroyed hundreds of villages, towns, and cities along the eastern coasts of the islands of the southern provinces, shutting down air and seaports. It was chaos incarnate.

While Team Rubicon had spent the previous two years focused on growing domestically, dealing with this disaster would require a return to Team Rubicon's expeditionary roots. Deploying a search-and-rescue team into the Philippines with only the supplies on their backs was massively more complicated than rolling into an American town, where Walmart was never far away. We were assembling a team of our best volunteers and staff, preparing to send them onto a far-flung island with limited food, water, and information. Many of the faces were familiar. JC and Pelak were both longtime volunteer leaders. Lourdes had been a manager on an Air Force critical-care transport team; she was Filipina and spoke the native language, Tagalog. Bob was a tested field leader for us, a former Navy Corpsman and chief in a Florida fire department. Wharton and Valverde were both veterans and seasoned deployers. Kirk, camera in hand, would travel along to document the team's experience. Ken Harbaugh was my new chief operating officer, brought on to help me navigate Team Rubicon's explosive growth. He approached me as we began assembling the roster. "Jake, I would like to go with the team," he said, indicating he felt it would help him establish credibility internally. I hesitated before nodding approval. Brian, Kate, Kristen, Ron, Chris, Elana, and Breaux rounded out the manifest, each deeply skilled in search and rescue, technology systems, or austere medicine.

Tonight, on the eve of Veterans Day, all lined the hallway, sitting on the floor, the contents of their go-bags splayed out between their legs. They traced their fingers down a list of gear, marking each item as accounted for. They checked and rechecked batteries for headlamps and radios and GPS devices. They rolled their clothes and waterproofed them, tucking each article neatly into its designated nook. Various staff members passed out mission planning documents and gave quick refresher classes on satellite communications equipment. JC, chosen to lead the team, picked his way down the hall, bending over to inspect his team's gear. If the overhead lights had been a soft red or some sand blew in, one could have mistaken the group for a platoon making ready for a mission in Iraq or Afghanistan.

I followed behind JC, kneeling by each deployer and shaking their hands, thanking them for being there. This mission would be hard and dangerous, I told them, looking them in the eye. It would require grit and tenacity. We would have to take chances and challenge conventions. And, I added, we would take those chances because the stakes warranted it. The survivors in Tacloban, the coastal city toward which we were directing our efforts, desperately needed help.

As I made my way down the line, my stomach filled with an unpleasant feeling. Dread. I was sending men and women into harm's way. Putting them on a plane bound for calamity while I stayed behind in Los Angeles. Truthfully, I had floated the idea of leading this team myself. In the early hours of mission planning, our team worked through a list of possible candidates, but each of them had uncertain availability to deploy. Eager to jump back into the action, I suggested that I could do it. The awkward pause that followed was all I needed to hear. The reality was that the organization had by now outgrown having its CEO jump into disaster zones and lead small teams. My role had changed. I didn't lead teams into danger; I ordered them into it. I was a colonel, not a sergeant. I wasn't sure I liked the shift.

I moved into the emergency operations center, a large bullpen in the center of the office. A bank of television screens mounted on the wall showed Team Rubicon's various planning documents and latest intel. "Everyone, gather round!" I shouted. The team shuffled in, joined by all the staff and volunteers flooding the office to support the mission from the States.

"Alright, team. Thank you for being here." I moved my eyes from left to right, making a point to lock them with each individual in the room. Establishing personal connections was essential in moments like this. "In twenty-one minutes, we will be loading up vans and taking you to the airport. In two hours and twenty-seven minutes, you will be on a plane bound for Manila. And in approximately three hours, the clock will strike midnight and it will be November 11—Veterans Day. Don't for a moment let the significance of that escape you. Tomorrow is a day our nation has set aside to honor your service in uniform, and instead of spending it stuffing your face with hot dogs, you'll be flying to a foreign land to continue your service." I paused, wanting that point to sink in. "Make no mistake: this will be the highest-stakes mission we've run since Haiti. You're the tip of the spear. We don't have a plan to get you from Manila to Tacloban. You're carrying your shelter on your backs. We don't know when we'll be able to resupply your food, water, and other supplies. Timeline for reinforcements is uncertain." Heads nodded. "Embrace the suck and get shit done. Take these final moments to recheck equipment. Vans will load up in twenty."

There's something oddly meditative about moments spent preparing for chaos. I can remember sitting in dusty buildings on sweat-stained cots, inspecting rifle magazines and tightening straps on my gear, feeling oddly calm moments before a nighttime raid or sniper mission. It took me a full tour to learn how to cultivate this peaceful stillness. In Iraq, our platoon would blast heavy metal on speakers during those times. Somehow Metallica felt like the appropriate soundtrack for combat. So many songs started slow and melancholy, guitar strings building. Then the crash, the frantic percussion of drums, the distorted guitars. Afghanistan was a different soundtrack. There I would put headphones on and play Jack Johnson. By then a seasoned veteran of combat, I didn't need to artificially amp myself up. Combat, I'd learned, wasn't about rage. It was about calm. Poise under pressure. Lyrics about rainy days and banana pancakes kept me calm—even as I turned over a claymore mine in my hands or straightened the pins on a grenade so they would be easier to pull.

"Hey, all the Marines in the office, gather round!" David Burke shouted. David was a new addition to the team. A former Marine captain and logistics officer, he'd applied for an open logistics job at Team Rubicon and was turned down. He then did the only natural thing—he drove from D.C. to Los Angeles and asked us to give him an internship. As the Marines shuffled into the room, a small cake emerged. Someone had bought it at the grocery store around the corner and begged the baker to write a message on it: *Happy Birthday, Marines*. "I know you're all about to load up into vans, but traditions are traditions. In every clime and place, you know," David added.

The group tightened into a circle. David looked at me and nodded, handing over responsibility for the ceremony. "Alright, oldest Marine present?" I asked.

The group exchanged glances and two hands tentatively rose. Their owners exchanged birthdays and Liane spoke up. "Looks like I have the honor," she said, not enthused.

"And youngest?"

David sheepishly raised his hand.

"OK, then," I said. I reached behind me and grasped my noncommissioned officer's sword, given to me by my father when I was promoted to corporal. I handed the sword to Johnny Crespo and pulled out a piece of paper from my pocket. Lifting the paper, I began reading General John A. Lejeune's birthday message, first authored and delivered in 1921. The message was short but full of references to the Corps' prestige in combat, and the legacy that it built protecting America. "*. . . So long as that spirit continues to flourish Marines will be found equal to every emergency in the future as they have been in the past, and the men of our Nation will regard us as worthy successors to the long line of illustrious men who have served as 'Soldiers of the Sea' since the founding of the Corps. Major General John A. Lejeune, Commandant of the Marine Corps.*" I looked at the gathering. "Happy birthday, Marines."

Johnny Crespo, on cue, stepped forward and drew the sword. With one hand to guide the blade, he sliced through the cake once and then twice. He pulled the piece onto a flimsy floral paper plate and handed it to Liane. She in turn passed the plate to David. These traditions, from the cake cutting by sword to the plate handing from oldest to youngest— traditions familiar to all Marines—symbolize the passing of knowledge and responsibility from one generation to the next. David shoveled a forkful of cake into his mouth.

"Gents, do right by the Marine Corps out there," I said.

• ● •

The next ninety-six hours were a blur. The rescue team landed in Manila and secured transportation down to Tacloban via a Philippine Air Force plane. When they landed, they were faced with near total destruction. Throngs of Filipinos huddled, wet, on the airport's tarmac, the terminal behind them a twisted heap of metal. The team quickly set up an encampment on the airfield and began running missions into Tacloban and surrounding villages.

Meanwhile, back in Los Angeles, we were scrambling to establish both resupply mechanisms and a viable follow-on mission. Caffeine-fueled marathons ensued. The Philippines was fifteen hours ahead of Los Angeles, forcing our ops team to stay awake until the middle of the night to receive the rescue team's end-of-day report. Quickly, our highly coordinated communication schedule, with predesignated communication windows, fell apart. Twice-daily check-ins became sporadic, unstructured updates. *"Team safe. Split between Tac and [garbled village name]. Red on food and water. Resupply crit—"* No dialogue, no chance for clarifying questions. Murphy's Law had taken root, and we were left to trust their training.

In Manila, bone-crushing bureaucracy was setting in. The Philippine government was allowing archaic customs procedures to grind the inflow of critical supplies to a halt. There were few indications that special provisions would be established for humanitarian aid. Multinational agencies were dutifully doing their best to manage the chaos, but at what cost? Soon our team, one of only two foreign humanitarian teams on the ground in Tacloban, was forbidden from using military flights because they'd failed to file the appropriate registrations. Never mind that there was no one to file with when they'd arrived in Tacloban.

A Marine Corps Expeditionary Unit arrived from Japan with helicopters and cargo planes, but another administrative fumble put them just out of reach of our highly skilled teams. And the local government's insistence on logjamming humanitarian supplies into its customs quagmire meant that mounting a meaningful response was limited to what our teams could mule in their checked bags on commercial flights.

"David, Nicole, how do we solve these problems?" I asked. I secretly hoped that David, as a former logistics officer, would pull out some camo-covered manual and flip to a page that had a simple solution. And Nicole was always willing to pitch crazy ideas.

Nicole pursed her lips and looked at the ceiling while David grabbed a dry-erase marker and moved to the whiteboard. For the next thirty minutes we mapped out the situation and discussed possible courses of action. None of them worked. Finally, I threw up my hands and said, "We should just charter our own jet and fill it with volunteers. That way we can fill the entire underbelly with everything we need and have our volunteers bring it through as personal baggage." It would all still go through customs but would be treated as if it were luggage filled with Hawaiian shirts.

"It's not the worst idea I've heard you come up with," David allowed.

Chartering a jumbo jet would be the boldest decision we'd ever made. The cost would be astronomical, but the impact could save lives. I made the call. "We're getting an airplane. David, call International Medical Corps and every humanitarian org on the West Coast to see if they want seats on board. Nicole, find me an airplane." I may as well have asked her to find me a unicorn.

I'd been in meetings for several hours when my phone rang. It was Arguello. My heart sank. I hadn't spoken to Arguello in a year, and it seemed I only received calls from old Marine friends when someone was dead. I excused myself.

"Arguello, what's up, brother?"

"Jake, how's it going? Hey, listen. I just moved back to Colorado from Ecuador. Long story. Anyway, I saw what you guys are doing in the Philippines. If you'll have me, I would love to go and help. I think I could use it."

I needed people I could trust. People who could stay calm under pressure and solve problems. Arguello, for all his quirks and oddities, was a Marine I'd seen rise to the occasion in action. A man I'd literally run across fields with under machine gun fire. "We'll book you the next flight from Denver to Los Angeles—you better be able to pack within the hour."

"I'm already packed."

I laughed. As Arguello and I spent a few minutes catching up, there was a thump on the window next to my office door. Nicole's palm was pressing a piece of scratch paper against the glass. *I HAVE A PLANE,* it read.

"Arguello, I have to go," I said.

Twenty-four hours later, I was loading up another team into vans for transportation to the airport. Despite having found a plane—and a donor willing to give a half million dollars to fund its flight—we were opting to continue to steadily send in waves on commercial flights. I would be joining this wave.

I walked back into the operations center to give final instructions and to transition authority to someone. I looked around at the staff members present, all highly capable, some with several years' experience with me. My gut told me who the right person was, though the decision wouldn't be popular. A sign on the wall caught my eye. It read *MAKE BOLD DECISIONS*. I'd hung the sign up around the office in the first hours after the typhoon. I wanted to set a tone that would nudge people toward making the hard choices.

"Team, while I'm out, David will be in charge of Stateside operations. I expect you all to follow his lead." Half the group's eyebrows cocked upward in surprise; they were wondering why David, the intern with less than sixty days at Team Rubicon, was being left in charge. But other heads nodded. David had demonstrated a knack for managing all the functions and their inputs, and I wasn't going to let management norms or people's feelings get in the way of the right decision.

• ● •

MARCH 2007
AL-ANBAR PROVINCE, IRAQ

Arguello and I had been on post for only an hour. I sighed and leaned forward onto the sandbags. Through the opening to my front, this part of al-Anbar Province slept dutifully under our watch. The palms and the sand and the trash all lay still, as if aware of the two grieving Marines on post.

"What time is it?" Arguello asked.

"Just turned three. Still got five hours." I was worried about Arguello. Howey and Windsor had been his only good friends in the platoon. Now both had been shipped home in flag-draped coffins, and Arguello had changed. Always a little quirky, he was now withdrawn and solemn. His normally quizzical eyes were muted with the pain of loss and loneliness. I thought about the weekends Arguello had gone out with Howey and Windsor back in the States just two short months prior to this evening. To Arguello, those weekends were two lives ago.

"What are you thinking about, Corporal Wood?" Arguello said.

"The ambush."

"Yeah, I figured."

"How 'bout you, Archie? How are you doing with everything?"

Arguello shifted his weight uncomfortably. "I don't know. I just don't know. I mean, Howey had become my best friend, and now he's dead.

And now Windsor is dead too." Arguello took a deep breath. "I feel like I don't have anyone left to talk to. I mean, I have friends, but they aren't really friends, you know? It's just not the same, you know? And if all my friends have died, how long until I'm next?"

I let the words sink in. "I know, buddy. I know." But I didn't know. Closing my eyes, I thought about my sisters, Erin, Sarah, and Meghan. About the pain and anguish I would cause them if I didn't make it home.

I thought back to a cool spring night in Madison, Wisconsin. I was on the verge of graduating from the university and had made the final decision to join. Sarah, Meghan, and I had been out all night partying. The night ended with us sitting outside a pizza parlor. That's when I blurted, "I'm joining the Marines." Their bewildered looks seemed to stop time. Meghan sobbed and begged me not to go, telling me she didn't want to lose her older brother. She called me an asshole and stupid and selfish. I put my arm around her and told her with false bravado that of course I'd make it back.

Now, standing next to Arguello, I feared I might be made a liar.

I thought about the ambush that killed Windsor, and the men firing at me from behind the white car. My mind struggled with the concept that someone wanted to kill me. On the surface it was obvious. I was the Marine; they were the insurgent. But the obvious did little to settle my mind. What had I done to make them wish me harm? I was a Marine, a liberator, a hero deserving of a ticker-tape parade. I went to church and said my prayers. Most of the time, anyway. They were illiterate, woman-beating, ignorant freedom haters. At least that was what we'd been told. They had no right to want to kill me. Right? *Right??*

I wondered where they came from. What were they before they were terrorists? Had there ever been a time when they didn't hate us? When they were growing up, in Baghdad or Kirkuk or Mosul, and they played soccer, did they dream about playing for the Iraqi national team? Did they look up at the stars and imagine becoming astronauts? Did they read books and think they could be heroes? I had.

"What are we going to do if we find them?" Arguello's voice startled me.

"Find who?"

"Them. The guys who got Howey and Windsor. Like, say we find a guy next week, and his house is full of explosives and wires, or he's got a sniper rifle. What are we gonna do?" I cracked my knuckles and pondered the scenario. I imagined finding him standing amid a pile of evidence that proved his culpability. Blood on his hands. A sniper rifle leaning against a wall under a picture of Saddam Hussein. Wires and bombs and radios strewn across an old wooden table.

"I don't know, Archie. I can't say what we'll do. How would we know he's guilty? That he's the one?"

"I don't know, but just assume we find him and there's no doubt. What are we going to do?"

I closed my eyes and pictured it, cycling through the feelings of rage and retribution. "If we knew—" I hesitated before continuing. "And I mean, if we *knew*, we would drag his ass to the nearest canal, put him on his knees, press a muzzle to the back of his head, and blow his fucking brains out." I knew it was a lie, that we would never carry out an extrajudicial killing, no matter how guilty. But Archie needed something to live for.

"I was hoping you'd say that," Arguello said. "Can I pull the trigger?" he asked, jaw clenched and eyes fixed toward the front.

I knew the right thing was to end the conversation and bury the impulse. But . . . "Yes."

"Promise?"

"I promise," I said.

• ● •

MANILA, PHILIPPINES

Three days after we spoke on the phone, Arguello and I leaned against the team's packs and equipment staged near the tarmac. We hadn't spoken much about Iraq. I'm not even sure he would have remembered the conversation where I promised him he could pull the trigger.

For my part, knowing Howey's and Windsor's killers were likely still alive when we left Iraq had gnawed at me for years. Having put away my uniform and my weapons a final time, I still sought peace by killing them in my dreams. Not that it would have been healing to actually do it. With time those fantasies faded. I no longer cared about those men or their fate. It was liberating.

I glanced over at Arguello, his nose buried in a book, and hoped he'd also moved on. If he hadn't, then I knew his heart was heavy, and I hoped that perhaps he'd find in Tacloban what he'd lost in Anbar.

For the past eight hours we'd played a game of hurry up and wait, familiar to most military veterans. The team was waiting for space on a Marine Corps C-130 airplane to take us from Manila to Tacloban, but various agencies kept scratching Team Rubicon from the flights, despite there being space on the aircraft.

I thought I'd solved the problem two days earlier. I'd tried accessing the Marine operations center to ask the brigadier general in charge of the military response for help moving our teams on his aircraft, but was denied access by a captain who had no interest in my pleas. Knowing I would have to get creative, I noticed that all the Marines inside had to come out to use portable toilets lined up along the road. *Well, even generals need to take a piss,* I thought as I sat down next to the foul-smelling porta-potty. Several hours later, a man with grey hair and stars on his shoulder emerged from the ops center. I intercepted him. After I'd explained Team Rubicon, our mission, and our problem, the general turned to his staff and directed them to get us on the flights. For two days our teams regained access to seats on the aircraft and moved freely about the island. Unfortunately, on humanitarian missions, generals don't control who gets to take rides, and forty-eight hours later we were back to square one.

"I'm going to go check on the flights," I announced to no one in particular. Standing up, I stretched out my back, stiff from sleeping on the floor of a Manila warehouse. "Hey, Chad, you got any tobacco? I've got an idea." Without even opening his eyes, Chad reached into a cargo pocket and extracted a can of Copenhagen. I grabbed it and went in search of a lance corporal.

Marine lance corporals are a legendary bunch. Low in rank and high in mischief, they are notorious for their willingness to skirt rules to accomplish tasks and often flout regulations they dismiss as asinine. If a brigadier general couldn't solve my problem, my next strategy would be to tap the lance corporal underground.

Near the hangar, I found three junior Marines sitting around a pallet of supplies. They paid me little mind until I was close enough to extend a Marine Corps greeting. Rising, they asked me what I was looking for. I explained what I was doing in Manila and what Team Rubicon was, taking extra time to recount the story of nagging their general while he was trying to take a piss. They found that one particularly hilarious, cementing my credentials as a former enlisted Marine. I dug the tin of tobacco out of my pocket.

"Hey, listen up, gents. If you guys could point me toward the Marine around here who can actually make something happen for me, there'd be this tin of Copenhagen in it for you." I whapped the tin with my finger, just like I'd seen countless lance corporals do in the field.

"Man, that'd be Gunny Jones. He's right over there—" One of the Marines pointed across the parking lot to a Marine standing near a folding table. With a shaved head and mustache, he could only be a gunnery sergeant.

"Thanks, fellas," I said, tossing the tin toward the Marine and wishing them luck with the rest of the mission. I made my way over to Gunny Jones, making sure to greet him as if I were still in uniform. "Good evening, Gunnery Sergeant."

• ● •

Two hours later I watched as our team leader checked and rechecked everyone's gear near the flight line. Earlier, Gunny Jones had listened to my plea and, after glancing around to ensure nobody could notice our conspiracy, agreed to load us onto the next aircraft headed to Tacloban. Their time for departure was nearing, the low rumble of C-130 engines their cue. Headlamps and orange ChemLight sticks faintly illuminated the Greyshirts' faces, and I easily picked out Arguello's.

At first I didn't hear my name called out from behind. "Wood! Wood, is that you?" *Shit, I got caught,* I thought, cursing my luck. Turning around, I saw a trim Marine standing twenty feet away, just beyond the Chem-Lights' reach. There was something odd about his uniform. He wore his camouflage top tucked into trousers and his pant legs were both unbloused around his boots. Both were out of regulation for a Marine's uniform but were common practice in sniper platoons.

The Marine stepped forward. "Wood, never imagined I would see *you* here," he said. The voice was familiar, and soon his face was illuminated.

"Solum? Staff Sergeant Solum??" I exclaimed in disbelief. I had not seen Solum since Afghanistan, when he served as our sniper platoon's top enlisted Marine. It had been almost exactly five years since the last time we were in a gun battle together. "What are you doing here?"

Behind Solum sat three Marines watching our reunion with vague interest as they packed long rifles into hard-sided waterproof cases. "I'm the sniper detachment commander for the expeditionary unit. I'm taking one of my teams down to Tacloban to provide security at the airport. What are *you* doing down here?"

Solum was familiar with Team Rubicon, so I filled him in on the team's mission over the prior week in and around Tacloban. His laughter carried across the tarmac when I told him about the Copenhagen bribe. Soon we were talking as if huddled under a tent flapping in the Afghan wind. Solum began telling me about a second deployment he had done to Afghanistan in 2012, four years after our notoriously bloody tour in 2008. The stories of battles and bureaucracy and ineptitude were too familiar. Listening to him, I could feel my shoulders droop slightly. Eventually Solum noticed. "Wood, what is it?"

I paused. "I—I—I guess I'm just sad to hear you talk about being back on the ground in Afghanistan. I mean, we left that place five years ago with twenty fewer men than we took there, and for what? Did any of us leave thinking that we made America any safer? What the hell are we still doing there today?"

The indignant look that flashed across Solum's face was not born of anger. "I'd like to think that we did. I'd rather fight them in Sangin than in San Antonio."

"Yeah, but when does it end?" I asked. "Can it end? Or will our children be fighting this war in twenty years?"

"I'll fight it as long as there are bad people that need killing," Solum said. His last comment hung between us. As snipers, it was the frame of mind we'd been taught. We'd been fashioned into lethal hammers, and all the world's problems were nails. The Marine Corps makes Marines—warriors made to believe we can kill our way to peace and security. But as I'd grown older, I wondered how effective that had been. If Solum and I had a crystal ball that evening, we would have seen that Sangin would fall back into the hands of the Taliban by 2017, evaporating the sacrifice of hundreds of American, British, and Afghan lives, including many of our friends. Had we known that and set out to prevent it, I wonder if we would have advocated killing more bad guys, or empowering more good ones. I also knew that the question was an absurd oversimplification.

"When are you finally going to get out of the Marines? What will you do next?" I asked, breaking the silence.

"Wood, I'm not gonna lie. I don't know what the hell I'll do when I get out." He paused. It's amazing that our nation's most fearsome warriors can be paralyzed by the fear brought on by separating from the military. For some it's economic uncertainty. For others it's fear their skills won't translate. For many, however, it's a lingering doubt that they'll ever again be the warrior they once were.

"I mean, this is the only job I've ever had. Being a Marine. It's all I ever wanted to do. Sure, I have to put up with a lot of bullshit. But nothing on the outside will give me the opportunity to be who I am."

A whistle cut through the air. I saw Gunny Jones directing the Greyshirts toward the back of the idling C-130. Solum and I stood for a final embrace. "You'll always be a warrior, brother. And you don't need to carry a gun for the rest of your life to prove it. Good luck on your mission."

"Same to you, Wood. Two-Seven is proud of what you're doing." With that, he turned around and began barking orders at his Marines. I smiled. Solum really was made to be a Marine.

I walked back over to Team Rubicon, now preparing to move onto the tarmac and board the cargo plane. One by one I shook their hands and offered words of encouragement or last-minute reminders. They would be forward deployed for at least ten days, and the conditions were austere. Tens of thousands of volunteers and donors back in the U.S. were looking to them to make the organization proud.

Finally, I reached Arguello bouncing his ruck up and down on his back while cinching and uncinching the straps. I smacked him on his shoulder. "Do I need to check your equipment for you, Lance Corporal Arguello?"

He rolled his eyes. "You're not my NCO anymore, Wood."

"Lucky you." I squeezed his shoulder one last time and moved on. Fifty feet away, the Marine security team moved out with their gear and filed into the airplane's belly. Solum boarded last after checking the final Marine. Walking up the ramp, he turned and gave me a faint salute before disappearing.

Moments after the final Greyshirt boarded, the plane spun around and taxied to the end of the runway.

Watching the plane barrel into the night sky, I thought about the Marine Corps saying: "Once a Marine, Always a Marine." It reflects the Corps' transformative impact on young men and women and its ability to forever encode itself into their DNA. War did the same thing. It forever changed us. Some of those changes were for the worse. Certainly no one reflects fondly on their trauma or warmly embraces their survivor's guilt and moral injury. And we cannot unbury our dead or breathe life back into any innocent people we may have killed. But, for many of us, we emerged from the wars stronger, more capable. We can view the world through a lens most will never see, lending a perspective that others don't know exists. Yes, warriors are forever changed by war.

Solum and Arguello would always be warriors. Only their missions might just change.

CHAPTER 15

SIGNATURE WOUNDS

I have a recurring dream. You know, the type of dream people sometimes ask me if I have.

I don't remember the last time I had it, but I always hope that each time is the last. Sometimes I sense it coming, so I snap my eyes open and fight off sleep. Mostly it comes at night. In the darkness.

I'm riding in a car. Not just any car, a big black sedan. I don't know why it's black, but it always is. It is very comfortable. I ride in the backseat and I run my hands over the smooth leather.

Someone else is always driving the car. I can see the side of the driver's face from my seat in the back. He is a handsome man, greying at the edges of his hairline. He looks stern and somber, as if driving this car is the worst job in the world. There is a second man in the seat in front of me. He spends the entire trip with his elbow resting on the window ledge, his right hand rubbing his temple. It always surprises me when I notice that both men are wearing crisp green Marine Corps uniforms. Their jackets are flawlessly pressed, their rank insignia shine brightly. I usually struggle to catch their reflection in the rearview mirror. I want to see their ribbons and medals and see if they've been to the war, to see if they're heroes. Eventually I look down at my own clothes and see that I'm wearing dress blues, with rows of shiny medals adorning my chest. I am surprised because I have a Purple Heart, but I don't remember ever earning a Purple Heart. When I listen closely, I can hear the medals clink as the car drives down the road. The clinking makes me proud because the clinking sounds like valor.

I always try to talk to them. I ask them what their names are and what we are doing and where we are going. They never answer my questions. They just drive and rub their temples. Sometimes I persist. I ask them what unit they are with and if they've been to Iraq or Afghanistan. I look at my own chest and see that I've been there. None of it matters; they continue to ignore me.

The Marines' indifference always annoys me, so I settle deeper into the seat and stare out the window. The scenery is always the same. We are driving down a two-lane highway, rolling up and down gentle hills. On our left is a mighty river. It flows along with us, languidly trying to keep pace with our black sedan. On the right, the landscape is painted green. Green as far as the eye can see. Green until green meets blue and blue becomes dotted with billows of white. Tall stalks of corn sway in the wind, an ocean of green ebbing and flowing like the sea. The fields are planted in strict rows, one stalk behind the other, obedient to the order and discipline of their planter. The rows of corn race by as we race onward, but I am still unaware of our destination.

I want to roll down my window and breathe the cool country breeze, but my window never works. I will ask the driver if he can roll down my window, but he just stares straight ahead and continues to drive. I just stare at the corn and think about what those big, juicy yellow ears must taste like with a little salt and a lot of butter. I imagine running through the rows and letting the stalks brush by my face and arms and hearing the wind gently rustle them.

I sit there and I stare, and I want to be out of the car. I think about the cornfield until the car finally reaches a town. The town is simple and small, and I sense that I've been there before. The road is busy. We pass car after car and I continue to stare. Through their windows I see mothers and babies and teenagers and old people and husbands and delivery boys. We pass an ice cream parlor and the sign says *Homemade*. I ask if we can stop, and again they say nothing. The driver always looks grimmer after passing the ice cream parlor. I don't understand the driver's mood because the ice cream parlor looks like a happy place to me. He checks a small piece of paper. It has something written on it I cannot see, and then he begins looking for something I do not know. It's never long before he turns right into a quiet little neighborhood.

The neighborhood is boring. By boring I mean perfect. The houses sit proudly off the street, front doors gazing smugly over manicured lawns. Trees and flowers and dogs abound. Children are walking home from school, laughing and playing and not caring about a thing. We drive past home after home and I stare at the bricks and the siding and the stucco. I think to myself, this is the neighborhood I want to raise my family in.

The men in front of me mumble something to each other. I cannot hear what they say but the car begins to slow down. The men glance out of their windows on both sides of the street, searching for something. Finally, the Marine in front of me taps the driver on the shoulder and points to our right. The sedan rolls to a stop.

The driver turns to the other Marine and asks him if he's ready. He replies by asking if there's ever such a thing. "Ready for what?!" I beg. They never answer. The Marine pulls out a briefcase and extracts a letter stamped with a fancy gold-foil seal. He hands it to the driver and says that it's his turn. The driver nods his head and takes the letter. They get out.

I reach for my door handle and pull, but it never opens. I slap the window with my palm and yell at the Marines as they walk up the grassy lawn. In time, I give up and settle for watching them. They step up onto the porch and turn to face each other. They quickly brush each other's jackets and straighten each other's ribbons. Then they turn and face the door. The driver reaches out and touches the doorbell. He presses it once and lets his arm fall crisply to his side. Both men stand at rigid attention.

Through the window I can hear a dog bark. The bark is muffled but the beast sounds old. I can sense him as he runs from a rear room to the front, barking the entire way. The Marines wait like statues. The door opens. The Marines reach up and remove their caps. The woman in the doorway is bent at the waist holding on to the collar of a golden retriever. She looks up at the men in surprise. Her lips move as she greets the two sharply dressed Marines. Her face is tender and her eyes glimmer with God. At this moment I will recognize her. She is my mother. I press my hands and face against the window and call out for her, but she does not hear me. The dog lunges forward to sniff the legs of the men. The driver brandishes the fancy letter while telling her something I cannot hear. My mother clutches her chest with both arms and stumbles backward. My father appears behind her and catches her. He looks at the men, unsure whether to hate them. My mother and father seem to pull each other to the floor, and my father holds her head in his hand. I watch as he absorbs her sobs and I pound harder on the glass and scream.

I again tear at the door handle, but to no avail. I am trapped. I pound the glass with my fists until my knuckles bleed. Calling for my mother and father, I try to tell them to stop crying, that I am right there in the car. Eventually I give up. I bury my face in my hands and weep. Finally, the Marines return to the sedan and start the engine. I open my eyes and see mangled legs. They are mine. I am no longer wearing dress blues. I am wearing desert camouflage trousers, and they've been soiled with piss and shit. The tibia of my right leg is exposed, gleaming white in the afternoon sun pouring in through the window. Nothing is attached to the end of it—no ankle, no foot, no toes. My left leg is charred and twisted at an impossible angle. My boot lies limply on the floor, attached only by two stubborn ligaments that refuse to let go. The dog tag in the laces catches a ray of light and shines. It tells me the leg is mine.

I scream but hear no sound.

The car turns around and heads back down the road. I twist rearward just in time to see my father, still holding my mother in his arms, reach up and close the oak door of my childhood home. The door clicks shut as the sun melts downward toward the horizon.

This is when I wake up and wait for the sun to rise.

* * *

"Do you have PTSD?" It's an absurd question that I'm sometimes asked by people who pretend they know what PTSD is. If it were a foreign film, the subtitle would read, "Are you crazy? Am I sitting with a crazy person?"

The truth is, I don't know, and I'm not sure I care. I know what my medical records say. They say I don't have PTSD, at least as far as can be determined. When I was out-processing from the Marines, the doctor doing my medical examination looked at my record and made a face like a crossword puzzle clue had just confounded him. "You were with 2-7 in Iraq and Afghanistan?" he asked, though he knew the answer because the medical records told him so. "I'd like for you to go see a psychologist before I sign off on this." At the time, I was assigned to the 1st Marine

Division's headquarters battalion, working as a sniper instructor. Most of the battalion consisted of noncombat personnel, so I assumed this was the doctor's standard move when confronted with a Marine who had just endured grueling back-to-back deployments. I took possession of my record and walked down the hallway and awaited my appointment with the crazy doctor like a good Marine.

The psychologist asked me a battery of questions, only feigning interest. The questions were tone-deaf. "Have you ever seen someone killed?" "Did you or your unit kill anyone?" "Have you ever been forced to do something that contradicted a value or deeply held belief from childhood?"

I may have snorted audibly, despite her rank. "Listen, I don't know what the point of these questions is. The answer is yes. Yes to everything you've asked and probably everything you're going to ask. Want to hear about the time we called in a JDAM on a house full of insurgents? When the bomb hit, the guy on the roof flipped up thirty feet into the air. We cheered and laughed. How about the time I was tending to a Marine hit by an IED, both his legs shredded, and I had to reach down and scoop his testicles off the ground and put them on his stomach so he wouldn't lose them? Want me to go on?"

She stared patiently. I wasn't the first petulant Marine to project onto her. "Do any memories haunt you?"

I thought about the gunshot echoing off the canyon walls and the screams of terrified children. I thought about the dream in the car. "No," I said. That was a lie.

"Do you have suicidal thoughts?"

"No." That was the truth.

She scribbled something down. Five minutes and three questions later she signed my paperwork, and I walked off base for the last time a few weeks later with a clean bill of health.

Of course, there have been times that I've wondered. A decade since my last ambush I can't walk into a room without assessing the danger points and likely approaches for a vehicle-borne IED. Walking through crowds or festivals sometimes makes the hair on the back of my neck rise. Sights and sounds get cataloged by a mind now searching for signs of danger, not joy.

Is that PTSD? I don't know. I do know that when I watch massacres on television, like the country music festival in Las Vegas or the movie theater in Aurora, I silently value my hypervigilance.

Most often, when I think about it, I get dismissive. PTSD or not, I can function at a high level. I wake up every morning ready to tackle challenges, and I usually go to bed fulfilled. In between I have the capacity to love those around me.

But it's not perfect. There are moments when a deep sadness overcomes me. It can be a story on the news of some stranger's suffering. Or a date on the calendar that reminds me of a moment of loss. Sometimes it will simply be in the car, mindlessly driving to work. My chest will tighten and my nose will itch and my eyes will water. I'll stop at a light and I'll swallow the grief, hoping it will pass before the light turns green. I can't explain those moments.

After Clay blew his brains out, Indra convinced me to see a shrink. She was understandably worried. I fought her at first, but she put her foot down. Every other week for a few months I would sit in his nondescript office, the scratchy fabric of his couch never quite letting me get comfortable. The shrink would sit in his chair with his legs crossed, a notepad in his lap. He was a nice enough guy. We'd talk about killing, about death and life. He'd probe the recesses of my mind, looking for clues. Often I would find my gaze fixed on the potted plant near the window by his desk. I suspected it was fake and would wonder whether he had the courage to try to keep a real plant alive. This educated, well-intentioned man wanted to talk to me about life and death, but he lacked the accountability to maintain the survival of a palm frond. One night I finally asked him, "So, Doc, what do I have?"

He placed his pen down and looked at me kindly. "Well, Jake, I don't think you have PTSD. I just think you are grieving. You're grieving not only the loss of your friends, you're grieving the loss of who you once were." That made sense. Too bad I couldn't kill grief.

Nor does it help when I see the progress of my wars fade. The Islamic State's blitzkrieg of al-Anbar Province wiped away any advances we bled for there, and it was made worse knowing that many of those ISIS fighters were at one time allied with us during the Sunni Awakening, when the Sunni tribes we were fighting tacitly joined our side to fight our common al-Qaeda enemy. Or in Afghanistan, when I watched the Taliban retake Sangin and heard our generals and politicians state matter-of-factly that Sangin had no strategic importance, and thus the loss was inconsequential. In other words, nearly a dozen of my brothers died for an Afghan city of no consequence. If our blood watered the tree of progress in either of those countries, the fruit now hung rotting, black flies swarming around it in the summer heat.

If I have learned anything in the decade since I left the Marines, it is this: coming home from war is a lifelong process. Sometimes we try to fool ourselves into thinking that we've made it back, but that's never the case. So when people ask me if I have PTSD, I simply tell them that I'm different from the person who went to war. I think I can live with that.

• • •

The wars in Iraq and Afghanistan, like all wars, can be defined by the signature weapons or tactics introduced and the unique wounds they created. World War I saw the advent of the machine gun and armored tank, which led to trench warfare. Trench warfare led to bacterial diseases such as trench foot, but also precipitated the use of chemical weapons, exposing hundreds of thousands to things like mustard gas. World War II will forever be defined by the atom bomb, when the world first saw the horrors of nuclear warfare. Devious land mines in Vietnam robbed thousands of men of their limbs, and Agent Orange has haunted that entire generation with deadly cancers.

Most people would probably say that improvised explosive devices, or IEDs, were the signature enemy weapon or tactic that arose in Iraq and Afghanistan. They would be correct. Shortly after the invasions of both countries, a smart and determined insurgency took root. With plenty of unexploded ordnance lying around, and technical assistance from al-Qaeda and later Iran, insurgents became so adept at building and planting bombs that they nearly paralyzed the most powerful military in the world. A well-placed IED could evaporate a Humvee and everyone inside. Howey learned that. As did Washington and three Marines in his truck.

Every time we defeated an IED tactic, the insurgents evolved. We defeated pressure plates by putting heavy rollers extending fifteen feet in front of our trucks, so they moved to detonating the bombs with cell phone signals. Then we developed Chameleon devices that jammed cell phones, so they laid copper wire and detonated them that way. Every once in a while, they'd take matters into their own hands, literally, and strap an IED to their chest and deliver it themselves. We never developed a good countertactic for that, except that we began pointing our weapons at every local we saw, expecting we might have to shoot them in the face. That's an interesting way to walk down a street and make friends.

And the terror wasn't just reserved for the roads. IEDs would be placed on footpaths and in markets. Just ask Garret, one of Arguello's friends, who stepped on a booby-trapped artillery shell that launched him ten feet in the air and reduced his left leg to a red mist. The insurgents filmed the entire thing and put it on the internet. I suppose that should be considered a tactic as well. To avoid more Garrets, we began to embed engineers carrying metal detectors with our squads. Unfortunately, the insurgents understood how metal detectors worked and evolved to using homemade explosives (HMEs) packed in plastic PVC pipes. They were effectively invisible. Just ask our engineer Henagir, who stepped on one after his metal detector convinced him the ground underneath his feet was safe.

It was never safe. We knew that. It's why every time we closed our eyes we imagined the boom.

What most people don't understand is that the wars in Iraq and Afghanistan shouldn't simply be characterized by the weapons or tactics implemented, but also by the lifesaving medical training every soldier received and the network of trauma centers established on bases throughout both countries. Early in the wars, the Department of Defense adopted a "Golden Hour" policy that instituted a standard: any critically wounded soldier should be capable of being evacuated and in surgery within sixty minutes. Survival rates shot through the roof, a tremendous achievement. It also meant that men and women with extremely complex wounds, who previously would have died on the battlefield, were coming home to a society that had yet to figure out how to accommodate their injuries.

When Henagir stepped on that HME-packed PVC pipe, the explosion ripped off both of his legs and half of his left arm. His lungs collapsed. He had forty-five seconds to live. Maybe sixty if he could stay conscious and fight. But we all carried tourniquets and knew how to shove needles through a rib cage to decompress a lung. We stopped the hemorrhaging and reinflated his lung. Our doc carried morphine, just enough to reduce his wails to a whimper. We dug our knuckles into his sternum to keep him conscious while we awaited the helicopter. While waiting, we walked in growing concentric circles until we found one of his legs and his mangled rifle. Neither would serve as a trophy for the insurgents. We placed them on his litter and then carried the litter onto the Blackhawk. Henagir took off. To be honest, we thought he was dead. Toast, we'd say. We'd be sad, but then we'd move on. To dwell was to die.

Two weeks later we learned that Henagir had survived. Saved by the Golden Hour. Today, with only one and a half arms, Henagir plays on the U.S. Paralympic ice hockey team, pulling himself around the rink on a custom sled. He is a miracle. In some ways it's Henagir's survival that defines the wars.

Of course, post-traumatic stress disorder, or PTSD, became the topic du jour. For some reason, Americans naively thought that Iraq and Afghanistan were the first wars that returned their sons and daughters home with mental wounds. That couldn't be further from the truth. In prior wars it was known as shell shock or battle fatigue. Men had a "thousand-yard stare" and we celebrated that because we thought it meant they were battle-hardened. It really just meant they were fucked up. It just so happens that in this war we decided to put a clinical name on it.

PTSD is real, and it is clinical. Most believe that it results from physical adaptations that occur in the brain following prolonged exposure to heightened levels of stress hormones like adrenaline. The body rewires to accommodate a new normal, but when the soldier returns to what is *actually* normal, their brain still functions as though in a combat zone. People suffering PTSD experience a host of symptoms, including hypervigilance, anxiety in public or in crowds, loss of pleasure in things that used to bring joy, or the inability of the brain to process short-term memory effectively. Of course, there are other symptoms.

Clay had PTSD. He was diagnosed with it following our tour in Iraq, right after he was shot through the wrist by that insurgent sniper. I'd probably have PTSD too if my wrist had been shot while my chin rested on it. That's about as close to toast as you can get. Less than a year later the Marines let Clay deploy to Afghanistan as a sniper, despite his diagnosis. That was probably a mistake. When Staff Sergeant Solum came to me and asked me if I would vouch for Clay, I said that he'd be fine. What was I supposed to say?

Of course, PTSD, for all the advances made in understanding it over the last two decades, is still generally misunderstood and misdiagnosed. First, most of the public assumes that it's just a military thing and everyone who went to war develops it. Second, that having PTSD means you're crazy. Therefore, we're all crazy. The majority of combat veterans do not develop PTSD, and most of those who do are able to manage it and lead normal lives. PTSD does not have to be debilitating, and it does not have to define our warriors who develop it. We fought an invisible enemy overseas and we can fight this invisible wound here at home. PTSD is treatable, and each year we're developing better techniques to do so, while doing a better job of reducing the stigma associated with it.

As a nation, we owe our men and women a better understanding of post-traumatic stress and better solutions. For a tragic few, it can be fatal. Clay's death, if not caused by PTSD, was certainly hastened by it, and the ineptitude of certain Veterans Affairs policies and procedures did nothing but exacerbate the issue. At the time of this writing, an estimated twenty veterans a day are dying by suicide.* Two-Seven, Clay's and my unit from Iraq and Afghanistan, has lost more men to their own hands than we did to the enemy across two tours at the height of the war. Things have to change. Complex issues like mental health never have simple solutions. They require steady, incremental change and progress—backed by data and research. Unfortunately, too often our society has neither the patience nor the commitment to make meaningful progress. But not always. In early 2015 Congress chose to demonstrate both.

• • •

FEBRUARY 12, 2015
WASHINGTON, D.C.

Nervous, I walked up to the podium and stared across the East Wing. Hundreds of people sat in rows facing me, many of them veterans of an older generation, wearing service caps with their organization's post number on them. Giving speeches had become a normal part of my job, but this moment—providing brief introductory remarks for the day's events—had nervous energy coursing through my body.

I glanced at the front row and found Susan Selke seated among

---

* "VA Releases National Suicide Data Report," U.S. Department of Veterans Affairs, June 18, 2018, www.va.gov/opa/pressrel/pressrelease.cfm?id=4074.

powerful and recognizable senators and representatives. Susan and I had grown close following Clay's death. In fact, her husband, Richard, had married Indra and me two years earlier. Just as we had four years earlier, at Clay's funeral, we locked eyes and shared a moment. There was less pain this time. Or perhaps pain's sharp edges had dulled. There were also new emotions: excitement and hope. Next to Susan sat Paul Rieck-hoff, leader of Iraq and Afghanistan Veterans of America, who was a driving force behind the day's event. Sensing the world's most powerful man on my right, I realized it was time to begin. Clearing my throat, I grabbed the podium on both sides and leaned into the microphone.

"Ladies and gentlemen, today marks an historic event for the veteran community.

"I first met Clay in the Marine Corps. I saw embodied in him the ideal that men and women don't fight for politics, but rather for one another. At one point, in Afghanistan on our second tour, Clay was voicing his frustration with the mission. I asked him, 'Why are you even here, then?'

"'I'm here for you, Jake.' That was the type of guy Clay was.

"Clay left the Marine Corps a decorated veteran proud of his time in uniform. After leaving the Marine Corps I went to Haiti with Team Rubicon to provide earthquake relief. Clay, seeing our efforts unfold on social media, took off by himself in the middle of the night to join us on the ground. When he arrived, he said it looked like we needed some help. Then he flashed his trademark sheepish grin."

I looked at Susan and she smiled broadly, both of us imagining Clay's embarrassment had he lived to see all the attention being focused on him.

"Nonetheless, Clay brought home with him the burden of war. He battled with post-traumatic stress; he struggled to find a job that would provide him with the same sense of purpose he had in uniform; and he longed for the days wherein he was surrounded by brothers in arms.

Amid his challenges, Clay believed it was the job of the VA to care for him and others, and he lobbied with Iraq and Afghanistan Veterans of America, nearly five years ago to the day, in this very town to ensure the VA had what it needed to take care of their job.

"That's why it is so fitting that we honor his memory with this legislative bill today.

"Ladies and gentlemen, please join me in welcoming the President of the United States, Barack Obama."

Stepping back, I turned and faced the man who was once my commander in chief. We shook hands and I exited the stage. The president gave his remarks and then I stood over his shoulder as he signed into law the Clay Hunt SAV Act, focused on mental health and suicide prevention reform at the VA.

The bill was not a silver bullet. But among other things, it provided the VA more funding to hire more mental health providers. It mandated third-party evaluations of VA services. And it incentivized collaboration between VA and nonprofit groups working in mental health. While Team Rubicon wasn't one of those nonprofit groups—PTSD treatment was not our mission—we were confident that the bill was a step in the right direction and would better prepare our fellow veterans who sought help to serve alongside us.

CHAPTER 16

FIVE-HUNDRED-YEAR FLOOD

2007
AL-ANBAR PROVINCE, IRAQ

An M-16 lay inert in my lap. I blew sharply into the ejection port, removing flecks of dust and grime. Little bits of Iraq. I picked up a wire-bristled bore brush and scrubbed. In and out. Around and around. Cleaning my rifle had become second nature. The sequence of disassembling and reassembling the pieces seemed more complicated than it really was. The M-16 is a simple weapon, a harmonious closed system of metal parts and mechanical theory whose only request is to be kept clean and oiled. In return, it kept you alive.

In and out. Twist and turn. I watched the bore brush enter and exit the chamber, maintaining a rhythm as my right hand worked like an oil derrick. Up and down, up and down. If kept clean and oiled, the M-16 fires straight and true. And then it fires again and again, running through its cycle of operations as fast as you can squeeze the trigger. Firing, unlocking, extracting, ejecting, cocking, feeding, chambering, locking.

Squeeze, squeeze, squeeze, *clickbang*. Firing, unlocking, extracting, ejecting, cocking, feeding, chambering, locking. Breathe. Repeat. Squeeze, squeeze, squeeze, *clickbang*. Firing, unlocking, extracting, ejecting, cocking, feeding, chambering, locking. Repeat. *Clickbang*.

In and out. Twist and turn.

The military teaches weapons maintenance for some obvious reasons. Rusty and dirty weapons are unreliable. Unreliable weapons don't fire. Weapons that don't fire can't kill the enemy, and their purpose is to kill the enemy. But weapons maintenance has other, subtler outcomes that can't be underestimated.

Weapons maintenance teaches discipline. When Marines return from a long patrol that stretches beyond meals, the commitment to readying your rifle before filling your belly creates a discipline that cascades through other actions. It teaches a mastery of priorities at the expense of personal comfort. It's the type of discipline that's elusive in most organizations.

Weapons maintenance teaches humility. Warriors—even the fiercest— come to understand that their success or failure on the battlefield can depend on the performance of an inanimate object. That no matter their proficiency in wielding that tool, if the tool fails, they fail. That self-awareness spreads to other areas of their psyche, helping them understand their reliance on their teammates in addition to their weapons, further intensifying the tribal nature of a platoon.

Weapons maintenance helps the warrior regain control and focus. Each time he steps outside the wire, the battlefield attempts to wrest control of his fate from him. To counter that, the warrior expands his focus to every possible input. Every sound, every glint of light, every smell.

The local population's patterns of life. Even silence can be a signal. Sometimes the most foreboding signal. Narrowing your focus to the sound of a wire brush rhythmically scraping a rifle's chamber is meditative.

I snapped the rifle's lower receiver into its upper and clicked the pins into place. Reaching over, I grabbed a component of Clay's rifle off the rag carefully laid in front of him and began to help him prepare for the next day's battle.

• • •

2015
WIMBERLEY, TEXAS

The parking lot was a beehive, Greyshirts crisscrossing in every direction. Rising above them was a fifty-three-foot trailer donated by Tyson Foods, Team Rubicon's logo emblazoned along its side. Inside, the mission's command staff diligently clicked away on their keyboards while looking at massive screens mounted on the wall. The screens projected digital maps layered with thousands of data points, ranging from social vulnerability indices to individual damage assessments and work orders produced by Team Rubicon's assessment teams. Aside from the uniforms, it was indistinguishable from a tactical operations center in Baghdad.

A high school sat across the parking lot. It was nondescript except for a minor geographic distinction: it sat on a gentle slope. That small distinction was the difference between the high school staying dry or succumbing to the devastating flood that had destroyed 350 homes and killed thirteen people only weeks earlier. Wimberley, located along the Blanco River in Texas Hill Country, had always suffered from flash floods.

But when the Blanco rose forty feet in a matter of hours, it was unprecedented. Experts called it a five-hundred-year flood, meaning its chances of happening are, statistically, only once every five hundred years.* Put another way, there's only a 0.2 percent chance of it happening in any given year. One can imagine the shock and despair in Wimberley when it was hit with two five-hundred-year and one three-hundred-year floods in a three-year span. Soon after, Houston would be hit with back-to-back thousand-year floods. The state of Texas appeared under assault. Politicians loved to argue about climate change. Was it man-made? Was it even real? The politics of the issue never dominated Team Rubicon's discussions, nor did it enter most of our minds. The facts spoke for themselves: disasters were increasing in frequency, strength, and damage. Others could tear each other apart arguing about the cause. Team Rubicon just had to deal with the effects.

Making matters worse, Americans didn't seem to care. Wimberley wasn't a major metropolitan area, and despite the magnitude of the flooding and the lives lost, the media moved on quickly. It was a pattern we'd grown accustomed to. These low-attention disasters caused billions of dollars of damage each year, but rarely received federal or state disaster declarations.†

This, however, was one of the things that Team Rubicon had been built for. Over its first five years of existence, Team Rubicon gradually built the infrastructure and systems that would enable it to deliver

---

* Dara Lind, "The '500-Year' Flood, Explained: Why Houston Was So Underprepared for Hurricane Harvey," *Vox*, August 28, 2017, www.vox.com/science-and-health/2017/8/28/16211392/100-500-year-flood-meaning.

† Nancy Beers, "Tackling the Midwest's Low Attention, High Cost Disasters," Center for Disaster Philanthropy, June 22, 2017, https://disasterphilanthropy.org/blog/tornadoes/tackling-midwests-low-attention-high-cost-disasters/.

quality services, consistently, to communities that would otherwise be left behind. The organization now had over thirty-five thousand volunteers registered across the country. Several hundred of them were selected to serve as volunteer leaders at a regional or state level, overseeing critical functions, from logistics to communications to operational planning. That meant that no community was ever too far from trained Greyshirts eager to assist. In 2015 alone, Team Rubicon responded to thirty-eight disasters, of which nearly all were in communities that received no federal or state declaration, effectively leaving them to manage the disaster on their own with no additional funding. These were communities that America was essentially ready to leave behind.

Seated in a circle on the grass in front of the school's entrance, a dozen volunteers were dutifully cleaning Stihl chain saws, wiping and scrubbing and blowing each piece before holding it up in the sunlight for inspection. Sawdust from Central Texas's legendary cypress trees could get into any crevice.

Walking around the circle, one of Team Rubicon's chain saw instructors commented on the day's mission. In true military fashion, each action was unpacked in search of lessons to be learned. Good enough simply wasn't good enough.

While the instructor discussed the virtues of a particular cutting technique, Mike sat and diligently sharpened the chain on his saw. At sixty-seven years old, he was one of the older Greyshirts on the mission. He was actually part of a growing trend: Vietnam veterans, many just now reaching retirement age, were joining up left and right. Mike took great pride in his fitness and made it a point to outhustle any younger veteran assigned to his team. Then he'd tell anyone within earshot that Marines of his generation were simply tougher than today's softies.

Mike slid his round file through each right-handed blade—first pass, second pass, third pass. Then he'd pull the chain forward an inch and repeat the process. When all the right-handed blades were sharpened, he'd move the file to his other hand and repeat the ritual with the left-handed blades. If he'd wanted to, he could have completed the whole chain in five or ten minutes, but this was Mike's favorite part of the day and he always wanted it to last. It reminded him of something, but he couldn't quite place it.

"Remember to keep that file at thirty degrees when you're passing it through the teeth," the instructor said over Mike's shoulder. "Otherwise you're going to foul up the blades."

"Right, right. Got it, got it," Mike answered, carefully checking the angle of his file. There was a right way and a wrong way, and he wanted to make sure he was right.

On the opposite side of the circle, Katie, a former captain in a military police unit, spoke up. "Anyone else feel like they're back on the rifle range, cleaning weapons after a long day?" Mike nodded his head and returned to his chain. Perhaps Katie was right. Perhaps he enjoyed this part of Team Rubicon missions so much because it unconsciously reminded him how, nearly five decades earlier in and around Khe Sanh in Vietnam, he would maintain his M-60 machine gun.

Mike had never wanted to go to Vietnam. He thought the war was wasteful. But when his draft number was called, he knew that he would serve, because that was what his country was asking him to do. Rather than get drafted into the Army, Mike joined the Marines. "If I was gonna fight," he'd say, "I was gonna fight alongside fighters, not a bunch of guys forcibly drafted." He was a machine gunner in the war, part of a platoon that was in frequent contact with the enemy, NVA regulars. He was wounded twice. Once when a grenade peppered his legs with shrapnel. Not that bad, he would tell people—like a little pinch on your thigh. And again when a North Vietnamese regular shot him in the ass while trying to take some meaningless hill. That one, he'd say, hurt like hell.

With his file at thirty degrees, Mike continued sharpening the blade, but his mind was now on his beloved M-60. He'd taken great pride in his machine gun back in the war, knowing that a single spot of rust could mean the difference between life and death for himself or one of his friends. He liked to tell people that he carried two toothbrushes in the bush—one for his machine gun and one for his ammo. If he'd intended on killing any NVA with his teeth, he would have carried a third.

Finished with his chain, Mike noticed a newer Greyshirt, one who had just completed his two-day sawyer course earlier in the week, struggling to find a rhythm with his blade. "Here, try it like this," he said, taking the file. "We gotta get these things right. Mission calls for a lot of cuttin' tomorrow."

In the background, Team Rubicon continued its preparations for the following day. The logistics team had set up a pressure washing station, and Greyshirts were dutifully cleaning all their dirty tools. Beyond them, a hasty car wash was rinsing off trucks and vacuuming their interiors. A volunteer once asked why we bothered washing the trucks each day if we knew they were just going to get dirty the following day. Because discipline breeds discipline, and sloppiness is contagious, the Transportation Unit Leader replied. Three cars drove up the long roadway and parked in front of the school's entrance, near Mike and the sawyers. A half dozen people hopped out of the cars and smiled and waved at the Greyshirts nearby. Sue walked out of the high school and greeted them with arms wide open. A gay Asian American woman with tattoos down her arms, Sue was not the typical friend profile for the buttoned-up Methodist congregants showing up. But Sue had a way with people, and they embraced like it was the high school's twenty-five-year reunion. Soon the back hatches of the minivans popped open and the women ducked in, emerging moments later with aluminum trays of chow. It's a misconception that food availability is an issue for communities following disasters in America. Food insecurity is extremely rare. Part of that is due to well-developed infrastructure and robust corporate supply chains—if they're not moving product, they're not making money—but community organizations are a huge element as well. Throughout the United States, communities can often count on their faith-based organizations—their churches, temples, and mosques—to rise up and meet the need.

Word spread that dinner was ready. Saws were finished and reassembled, trucks were cleaned a little faster, and sidewalks swept without delay. Finally, the Greyshirts trickled into the school and assembled in the large cafeteria. Everyone waited patiently until the final volunteer arrived. Then they lined up to pile the food on their plates, Bob and the rest of the team leaders dutifully staying back. In Team Rubicon, leaders ate last. I eventually grabbed a plate and piled it high with barbeque and mac and cheese. I kept walking until I found an empty seat next to unfamiliar faces. I asked the group how their day had been. A volunteer named Steve wiped his mouth.

"My strike team has been working on the same work order for the past few days. Big muck-and-gut job. House sits up on this ridge overlooking the river. Nobody in their right mind would ever believe the river could have crested that high." He raised his arm above his head. "Sure enough, this nice old lady owns the home. She lost her husband a few years ago and you can tell money is tight. She didn't have flood insurance because her house isn't in a floodplain. You could tell she thought she was going to lose everything."

Other Greyshirts from Steve's team weighed in. The homeowner, Jane, was clearly suffering from emotional distress. She'd lived in the home for decades with her husband and seen the river rise dozens of times, but that week the rain just wouldn't stop. When the waters started lapping at her door, she knew she was in trouble and tried to call her son, who lived a few hours away in Dallas. But cell service was spotty in Hill Country, and she couldn't get through. She was terrified and alone. Soon the water seeped under the door and began rising inside the house. One inch. Two inches. Eventually its rise accelerated. It passed one foot and then three. Jane scrambled to salvage her treasures, grabbing photo albums and family heirlooms and shoving them onto shelves high inside closets. She grabbed the Bible she kept on her nightstand and hustled into the kitchen, putting a chair on the kitchen counter and climbing up to sit on it. There she sat, reading and praying and wishing her husband was still alive to protect her. At one point, the waters rushing by outside sent an entire tree through her living room window, like some medieval battering ram. She thought she was going to die, cold, wet, and alone.

Steve picked the story back up. "So, we get there a couple days ago and the waterline was at about forty inches and there was this layer of mud on *everything*. We had to call in a saw team to take care of the tree, and it took us a whole day just to get all the contents out of the house. Almost none of it was salvageable. But we found something really special." Steve scooted forward in his seat.

"So, Joe over here"—Steve nodded at one of the Greyshirts sitting near me—"finds this soaking-wet cardboard box. He opens it up, and inside sees this old Army uniform covered in mud. Turns out it was Jane's husband's, and you could tell it was probably in perfect condition before the flood. All of his rank and badges and ribbons were on there. So we sneak it out of the house without Jane seeing it, and a few nights ago we take it into town to a dry cleaner. We tell the owners the story and they say they know Jane from the Rotary Club here, so they agree to try to restore the uniform!" Steve's excitement was growing. "Well, today we go back to Jane's house and we have, like, three hours of work left to do. Jane's son from Dallas is there pitching in. At lunch, we ask Jane and her son to come outside. The rest of us"—he gestures at the volunteers seated at the table—"are standing near this flagpole in the driveway that ain't got no flag on it. When they walk up, Katie here presents Jane with her husband's uniform, perfectly restored." Katie blushed, clearly uncomfortable with the praise.

"And then Mike, one of the saw guys who helped with the tree—I think he's a Vietnam vet—presented her son with a Greyshirt that had their name, *McCLELLAN*, stenciled on it. He handed it to him, and then he and Jane just broke down. Mike said something like, 'As a fellow Vietnam veteran, I wish your husband could have lived long enough to wear this shirt and serve alongside me.'" Steve paused. "Man, I'm telling you it was the most powerful thing I've ever seen." He slapped his hands on the table.

After presenting Jane and her son with the honorary Greyshirt, the team presented them with a crisp new American flag for their flagpole. "We just felt like they deserved to know America has their backs, you know?" Katie said.

I was in the middle of asking them how the home looked by the end of the day when Bob, the incident commander, grabbed a microphone and called for the cafeteria's attention. "Ladies and gentlemen, we have two special guests here with us today. Team Rubicon's CEO, Jake Wood, and our COO, Ken Harbaugh, have joined us in Wimberley to work alongside our teams for the next couple of days. I'm going to ask them to come up here and share a few words."

Having no prepared remarks, I leaned against a stage at the front of the cafeteria and looked out over the crowd. Some of them knew me, others knew of me, plenty had no idea that the CEO of the organization they loved so much was so young.

I began as I always did when addressing Team Rubicon's volunteers: by thanking them for their service and singling out some of the great work from this particular op. After five or ten minutes, we opened it up to questions. "What keeps you up at night?" one man asked.

This was not a softball. By now the organization had twenty-five employees, $7 million or $8 million in donations annually, and was executing nearly forty disaster operations a year. There were plenty of things to stress about: making payroll, recruiting great talent, dialing in the right strategy, ensuring our volunteers had the right equipment and training to stay safe and effective in the field. I took my time and finally pulled the microphone to my lips. "One word: culture." I paused to let the word sink in. "Listen, we are scaling fast. People often ask me if I'm worried that the price of that growth will be our culture. And of course, I have to worry about that. But I believe that if we're to be successful, the opposite must be true. What I mean is that culture can either be the victim of rapid growth, or it can be the driver of it. I believe we're building something special. We know our values; we've empowered people to take ownership of them. We treat one another with trust and respect. We value our diversity. And at the end of the day, we are relentlessly committed to our mission and vision." Heads nodded enthusiastically. "You know, I spent a lot of time early on at TR trying to figure out if the culture we were creating was taking root. And then I saw someone with a Team Rubicon tattoo for the first time. That blew me away. And then I saw a second—though, don't get me wrong, that individual had about fifty tattoos, so I'm not sure it was a really well-thought-out decision . . . Actually, anyone in this room have one?" I asked. A chair skidded across the floor and a thirty-something volunteer stood, lifting his shirt. On his rib cage was Team Rubicon's logo. On the other side of the room someone else stood and turned, propping their leg on a chair to show a tattoo on their calf. Two or three more arms shot in the air, Team Rubicon's "X" inked in various locations along them.

You will often find evidence of a veteran's service tattooed on their bodies. It is not uncommon for freshly minted privates to walk straight to a tattoo parlor and ink their branch of service onto their skin, memorializing their newfound identity. They do it because being a Marine, soldier, sailor, or airman is a way of life, not a job. Seeing all of the Team Rubicon tattoos reinforced for me that we weren't just building a volunteer organization, but a tribe.

Ken and I took questions for another fifteen minutes. After the last question, I handed the microphone back to Bob, who brought it to his lips and uttered the words most of the Greyshirts anxiously awaited: "Team, the beer flag is up!"

Cheers erupted. Few things were as refreshing as an ice-cold beer after ten hours working in the Texas heat. I nursed mine while watching Greyshirts mill about. Eventually chairs were pulled up around a firepit, and the circle tightened. I heard something scrape in the dirt nearby and looked over to see Mike, the crusty Vietnam veteran, pulling up a chair alongside me. He extended a fresh beer my way.

After some small talk, Mike told me his story. It started in Vietnam. He told me about the wounds he'd received and how he thought he was the unluckiest guy on earth. Until, he said, an enemy mortar landed directly in his buddy's foxhole. Swiss cheese, he called it. Human Swiss cheese. Coming back at first was easy. Nobody was shooting. No lieutenants were barking orders. He worked some odds-and-ends jobs, settling in as a dockworker for a period of time. He got a girl pregnant, so he married her. It wasn't love, he said, though I'm not sure he was telling the truth. Eventually he realized he didn't like being around people, so he became a long-haul trucker. Spending weeks alone on the road helped him avoid people, but it also meant he wasn't home for his daughter. Eventually his wife left him. She told him that he was emotionless at best, an angry prick at worst. She took their daughter and moved to Ohio, where he lost contact. Mike felt abandoned. None of his buddies in Vietnam would have left him like that, he thought at the time.

Mike said that he proceeded through life angry and alone. He never felt like the war haunted him. He had flashbacks, though they never interfered with his ability to earn a living. But he felt that his country had sent him to war and discarded him. He was sent on a mission that didn't matter, and the whole time he was overseas he had the sense that no one cared if he came back in a box. Often, he said, he wished he hadn't come back. It wasn't until he reconnected with his daughter years later that he began to see the impact Vietnam had had on him. She convinced him to see a counselor and, eager to earn his way back into her life, he agreed. After months of counseling, Mike finally realized that he'd been failing to cope with the war, and those failures to cope and his bitterness had led to failures in his personal life.

A year or two later, Mike saw Team Rubicon on the news following the tornado in Moore, Oklahoma. He immediately signed up and jumped into the training locally. He deployed on a few smaller, local ops. It was like a drug, he said, service. He'd been sent to Vietnam without a choice, but Team Rubicon gave him the chance to choose. He had found a tribe that reminded him of the men he'd served with—the types of Americans he never thought he'd serve alongside again. His daughter noticed something too. His callous demeanor softened. He loved more readily and felt without fear. Situations like the one with Jane showed him that human suffering is universal and helped him find perspective for his own pain. Finally, Team Rubicon filled him with pride—an emotion he wasn't too familiar with. He even mentioned he'd put a Marine Corps sticker in his truck's back window for the first time in his life—right next to the Team Rubicon one.

Mike fell silent. Then he looked at me and put his hand on my forearm. "Jake, if you guys had been around when I came home in 1969, maybe I would have led a different life. You're fifty years late for me, but I think what you're doing will change the lives of these younger folks forever."

CHAPTER 17

BROKEN PROMISES

2007
AL-ANBAR PROVINCE, IRAQ

The night before, under the cover of darkness, our platoon had arrived at the house that would serve as our temporary base. We had entered the house and handed the patriarch a wad of cash and told him to go to a relative's house and not return for three days. We had been through the routine dozens of times before—show up, gather the family, let them pack some things, shuffle them out the door and into the night, and then begin transforming the house into a temporary fortress.

Now, six hours later, we were leaving the compound to conduct a patrol. That mostly meant walking from house to house and talking to the adult males. Men who hated us and told us, loved us and told us, hated us but told us they loved us, or refused to speak to us at all. We would ask them where the enemy was. They would respond, "Meestah, no al-Qaeda heeah. No, meestah." We would say, bullshit, we knew al-Qaeda was around because we had hit three roadside bombs on the way in. "No, meestah, I know nahthing." We would roll our eyes. I would tell them that we cared about their well-being and that we would never leave them until their neighborhood was secure, but I wasn't sure I cared and knew we would certainly leave.

I walked through the gate, staring at the backs of Arguello and Bullard. The column fell into a stagger. Archie walked down the right side of the dusty road, lazily scanning back and forth for an indication that he was about to die, Bullard offset to the left. The distance between us grew, ensuring that Arguello's or Ray Ray's unfortunate misstep on a land mine wouldn't kill anyone else.

I motioned for Arguello to take the patrol off the road and into a field. I hated the roads. The roads went boom. Off to our right, across the field, stood a nondescript cinder-block house. Outside, a woman in an ankle-length red dress and light blue scarf was carrying a basket of vegetables against her hip and walking toward the door. Her son, seeing us from the garden, dropped the weathered handle of a makeshift farm implement and rushed over to her. She turned and took in the scene.

Bullard sauntered up and took a knee at the far corner of the building, holding security. In broken Arabic, I asked the boy where his father was. He spoke rapidly and pointed toward the field opposite the house. I pointed to the field and then to the ground at my feet, attempting to say that I wanted his father here. The boy nodded and ran off.

"*Salaam alaykum.*" The greeting came from behind. I turned to see a thickly built man dressed in a grey dishdasha and a red-and-white-checkered headdress. His thick mustache glistened with sweat.

"*Alaykum salaam,*" I replied, touching my right hand to my heart in the customary manner. Williams approached.

I gestured for the man to move inside, and Williams and I followed him in. He motioned for us to sit on the mats, and, after removing our helmets and flak jackets, we obliged. We asked him the standard questions. What was his name? Which was his clan? Where was he from? What did he do? Where was his mosque? Had he seen al-Qaeda? He assured us that he was an honest man. That he was a simple farmer. That he prayed six times a day to Mecca, Allah be praised, that al-Qaeda was nowhere to be found, that the newly elected president of Iraq was a thief because he was a Shiite, that Marines and George Bush and America were all "veddy, veddy good, meestah." We suspected that he was lying. One of the pictures on the wall confirmed that he'd served in Saddam's army. You only displayed that photo if you were proud of the fact. This man was likely either an active participant or a supporter of the insurgency. During a lull in the conversation, which was beginning to turn into an interrogation, the son brought in a platter, upon which sat a kettle of steaming tea and little glass cups. "Chai?" asked the man, whose name was Mohammed. There was always chai.

"Yes, *shukran*," we replied. The boy distributed the cups and began lumping piles of granulated sugar into each, eventually pouring the scalding tea into the glassware.

"Tea veddy good," Mohammed said as he sipped his glass. He was putting on a good show, careful not to rouse the anger of the Marines sitting across from him. But the mutual distrust and disdain were palpable between our forced pleasantries.

"*Zien, zien,*" we assured him as the chai burned our tongues. Finishing his glass, Williams turned to me and asked, "You about ready to get out of here? I'm beginning to want to punch this guy in the face."

"Yeah, let's gear up and move on."

We left the house in much the same manner as we'd approached. Arguello spotted a house down the road and began moving the patrol in that direction. Smoke was rising from an unseen tandoor oven behind its gated wall. A thousand paces later I walked through the gate and caught the smell of freshly baked *khubz* bread. Bullard casually leaned against a blue car, eyeing the tandoor across the courtyard.

"That shit smells good," he said.

"Corporal Wood, the family's over here."

I walked past Bullard to where Arguello stood at the corner of the house and saw a large family spread out on a blanket around an ample dinner. An elderly man rose to his feet and smiled. "Welcome," he said. I blinked in astonishment. The man spoke with only the slightest accent.

"Hello, hajji. You speak English?"

"Yes, sir. Welcome to my home." The man gestured to the blanket and returned to his spot on the ground. I looked at the gathering. Seated on either side of the man were two thirty-something women. Neither wore head coverings, their dark hair falling down their shoulders in waves. They might not have been considered traditionally beautiful, but their confidence was magnetic. Four children hid shyly behind dirty palms, peeking at me through cracks in their little fingers. I smiled. They giggled. I smiled broader. They giggled and buried their faces in their mothers' laps.

"Chocolate?" I asked. Their eyes lit up. The old man laughed and shooed them forward. They approached me tentatively with outstretched palms. I turned toward the gate. "Colbert! Get your ass in here and get these kids some candy."

Colbert was our resident candy man. If we stayed in areas long enough, children learned to look for him among the patrols and would swarm around him begging for sweets. We knew it posed a security risk, but it brightened our days.

"Roger that, Corporal." Colbert produced a handful of colorfully wrapped candy. The women on the ground gasped in mock excitement and clapped their hands. The kids swarmed Colbert's hand. "Whoa, whoa. Not the Jolly Rancher, kids, that be mine."

"Arguello, Williams, get in here and have a seat." I moved to the opposite side of the blanket and leaned my rifle against a column, just within reach. General Jim Mattis's famous line echoed in my head: *Be polite, be professional, but have a plan to kill everyone you meet.* "Williams, this gentleman here speaks perfect English." I turned to the old man. "How did you learn English?" I asked.

"I studied for many years in Europe. I am a doctor. My daughters here speak English as well."

"Welcome," the woman on my right said as she leaned forward to pour a cup of chai. She lumped in a spoonful of sugar and passed it to me. I took the glass and glanced down at the little boy leaning against her lap. He had not stopped staring at me since I sat down.

"What's your name, little one?" The child buried his face deeper into his palm. "Do you have a name?"

"His name is Ali," his mother said as she reached down and patted him on the head.

"Nice to meet you, Ali." I extended my arm to shake hands, but he sought refuge in his mother's arms.

"He is very shy."

"We are very glad you are here. This place is very dangerous." The old man's face darkened. "There are bad men who control this area. We very much like that you have come."

"Of course, of course." I dropped my hand back onto my thigh and turned slightly to face the man. "We are here to help."

"Where are the bad guys?" Williams asked.

"I do not know where they live, but they drive up and down the streets all day watching us. They drive a black car. A Mercedes. Sometimes they will stop and talk to me because they know I speak English. They will ask if you have come and visit me."

I turned and looked at Arguello. "Archie, make sure you're writing this stuff down." For the first time in weeks it felt like we were speaking with a local who might actually be on our side. Looking back to the old man, I continued, "Are they from the area? Do you know who they are?"

"I do not know them. They are bad men. They are not from here."

"Do they threaten you?"

"No, they have not said this, but I know that they would."

"Are you afraid?"

The woman across from me threw up her hands. "We are always afraid, mister. Always."

"I know, I know. I am sorry." Nodding, I looked at the old man. "What do you need to be safe? What can we do to help?" Empathy jabbed at my heart for the first time in weeks.

"Nothing. We need the war to be gone. We need the Marines to leave, but if you leave they will hurt us. If you stay, they will hurt us." He smiled, knowing that he was asking too much of a simple soldier. "If there can be no more war, then we can be safe."

"Believe me, we want this war to end so we can go home to our fathers and mothers and children too." We contemplated a peaceful Iraq in silence while chewing mouth-watering bread.

Outside the wall, a car engine rumbled down the road past the house. As it drove by, it slowed. Small pebbles popped under the rubber tires. The man stiffened. I noticed the fear in his eyes. He didn't breathe until the car's engine faded down the road.

"That was them."

"Who?"

"The bad men. Al-Qaeda."

"How do you know?"

"The sound of the engine. That was the Mercedes." I glanced at Williams, neither of us sure what to do next.

"What do you think?"

"I don't know," I replied.

I didn't know. We couldn't get everyone geared up and running down the street after a Mercedes in time to catch it. On the other hand, sitting there drinking tea while terrorists drove laps around the neighborhood was emasculating. "Send it up?" Williams nodded and rose to his feet in search of a radio. I changed the subject. "Is this your home?"

"No, this is my son's home. We are living in it while he is gone."

"Where is your son?"

"He is in Belgium. He is a—how do you say? Engineer. I do not know where my other son is."

"What do you mean?"

The old man placed his hand on the knee of the woman on my left. "This is my son's wife. My other son is also a doctor. We have not seen him in three years. He left to go to Baghdad, he has never come back. We fear for him."

The woman across from me leaned forward with pleading eyes. "You are American. Can you find him? Perhaps Americans thought he was bad and put him in your jails. Perhaps he is in your jail and you could find him?"

I looked again at the old man. "He went to Baghdad to work in the hospitals?"

"Yes, he wanted to help his countrymen."

"Perhaps he is in your jails, or he is working in a hospital for Americans. Could you find him for me?" The woman's voice trembled. I looked at her and knew the truth. She looked at me and refused to accept it. Her husband was dead. Killed by whom, I couldn't know. But I knew that no man would walk away from this family and abandon it. If he was alive, he would have been back. He would have come back to see his beautiful children, to hold his wife, to take care of his father. I looked into her eyes and did what I had been told to do.

"Yes. We will help you find him." Hollow words. They did little to assuage her anguish. She forced a smile and nodded. "Why don't you leave and go to Belgium to live with your other son?"

"We are Iraqi," the man said. "We do not want to leave. He sends us money and we stay so he can one day come back." I admired his conviction. I saw glimpses of my own father in the way he spoke, so matter-of-factly. We talked for two more hours. Williams and I rotated different guys off the roof and onto the blanket so they too could interact and feel human. I played with the kids and helped them draw pictures in my notebook. I gave them my pen and they wrote my name for me in Arabic. When I looked down at my watch, the sun was pulling toward the horizon.

"What time is it, Wood?"

"Nineteen thirty," I replied.

"We should get going."

"I don't want to leave," I said.

"It is time for you to go? You can stay here at our house. Yes, please, you can stay here." The old man rose to his feet and motioned for us to follow him. "We have lots of space."

"We are sorry. We would love to stay, we really would. But we have to go."

"Allah keep you safe, my friend," the old man said as he shook my hand and draped his arm behind my neck. "You are very good men. You keep my family safe." I couldn't tell if it was a statement or a question.

I realized I did not know the man's name. "What is your name, hajji?"

"Ali."

"Like the child?"

Ali's face lit up. "Yes. Ali, like my grandson."

"Goodbye, Ali."

"Goodbye, *sadiqi*," he replied, using the Arabic word for "friend."

I joined the Marines preparing to exit through the gate. I spotted Williams. "We need to watch this house tonight, make sure they're safe," I told him. The family sat on the blanket, watching us.

"Yeah, but we're supposed to be back in twenty minutes."

"You think Second Squad is going to bitch if we delay them going out on patrol for an hour? I just want to make sure those muj don't roll up the second we leave here."

"Alright, let's move out three hundred meters and set up an observation post."

We moved out silently, our night vision goggles turning the landscape an eerie green. I motioned for Arguello to move off the road and into a thicket of bushes with a view of Ali's house. The squad set up a position. I settled in against a tree and faced back toward the house. I thought about the old man, Ali, his daughters and grandchildren, his sons, one alive, one almost certainly dead. I thought about the false promises I made, the promise to look for his son and keep his family safe. I thought about my family back home in Iowa, the sun rising on them just as it set on me.

The call came over the radio summoning us back to base. One by one, the squad rose. Stepping onto the road, I looked at the house one final time. Another promise broken. I turned and followed Arguello and Bullard and the rest, staggered and dispersed, so as not to get killed by someone's unfortunate misstep.

• ● •

By 2016, any progress made by the coalition in Iraq had unraveled, leaving the nation on the brink of collapsing into a failed state. Iraq was not alone. Across the region, the political fallout from the Arab Spring had sparked violent civil wars. Tunisia, Egypt, and Libya all saw their dictatorships crumble. In 2011 in Syria, what began as peaceful protests against President Bashar al-Assad turned bloody when progovernment forces began firing into crowds of demonstrators. All-out war followed, and Syria devolved into one of the bloodiest civil wars of the century.

Making matters worse, a new threat had emerged in Syria and spilled into Iraq. By 2013 the Islamic State of Iraq and the Levant, known as ISIS in most Western media, captured huge swaths of land in both nations, bringing it under a brutal interpretation of sharia law. ISIS quickly caught the world's attention with its unparalleled wickedness.

By 2014, ISIS had stormed through western Iraq, seizing the cities of Ramadi, Fallujah, and Mosul. The Iraqi army, trained over the previous decade by U.S. troops at the cost of billions of dollars, dropped their weapons and fled. Veterans of the Iraq War were forced to watch as ISIS unfurled its black flag above cities they'd fought street to street to clear of militants a decade prior. It hurt even more as it became clear that ISIS was the product of America's misguided policies and detention program, where ISIS ideology was born and spread among detainees and former Baath officials.

For those veterans who relied on the defeat of al-Qaeda in Iraq and a fledgling, if precarious, democracy in the country as a justification for the pain and suffering they'd endured, the rise of ISIS was a knife in their heart. They could no longer think of Johnny and say that he died to give Iraqis a future of peace and liberty. The rise of ISIS tore open the emotional wounds of the war and infected them.

Later, in 2015, the image of a three-year-old Syrian boy named Alan Kurdi lying dead on a Turkish beach rocketed around the globe. The photograph showed the boy's lifeless body, legs slightly tucked, arms straight along his sides. If not for the waves gently lapping against his face, one could have imagined him sleeping peacefully in his crib. He may as well have been young Ali.

• • •

Watching the refugee situation unfold, I couldn't help but feel complicit. How might the unrest in the Middle East be playing out differently had we not invaded Iraq? Most experts agreed that the war in Iraq had destabilized the region, likely exacerbating the current crisis. That I might have somehow been complicit in that young Syrian boy drowning haunted me, especially as I hugged my young nephews Graham and Nolan that Christmas.

Dozens of organizations like International Rescue Committee, International Medical Corps, the Red Cross movement, and Mercy Corps had been spearheading efforts to assist with the suffering inside Syria and the growing refugee challenge in Turkey, Jordan, and throughout Europe. But it wasn't enough. The complexity and scale of the crisis was resulting in unimaginable suffering.

Team Rubicon had been exploring ways to get involved in the refugee crisis for over a year, and the photograph of Alan Kurdi galvanized our efforts. In 2016, Team Rubicon got its chance. An American philanthropist, Amed Khan, was funding an innovative refugee camp in Thessaloniki, Greece, called Elpida Home, and he sought out Team Rubicon to help manage it and provide medical services to its residents. Though we did not have experience in refugee camp operations, we felt that the opportunity to help with Elpida played to some of our strengths.

Unlike other refugee camps in Greece that consisted of shoddy tent cities tightly packed on muddy fields, surrounded by chain-link fencing, Elpida—the Greek word for "hope"—was a former textile factory that Khan had converted into a rudimentary apartment complex. Situated on a gentle hill, Elpida's modest three stories rose from among a smattering of trees. Its white walls were in desperate need of a fresh coat of paint, except along the ground level where its residents had hand-painted murals of their journeys to Greece. On multiple stories inside, simple, single-room units were constructed and sparsely furnished with bunk beds and hot plates. Families could live with the dignity afforded them by four walls and the ability to use the restroom without walking through ankle-deep puddles festering with disease.

There were roughly 250 residents in Elpida. The vast majority were Muslim, and most of the women covered their hair, with several wearing face-covering burqas as well. The men mostly hung out with one another, occasionally gathering outside to smoke cigarettes and argue loudly about inconsequential things. The children were like children anywhere—somehow joyful and curious and full of energy despite the horrors they had witnessed. Of course, there were exceptions. Children who were sullen and withdrawn. Children who drew planes dropping bombs rather than flowers and smiling suns. They became the focus. Elpida became their hope.

• ● •

In August 2016, Indra and I traveled to East Africa for a vacation. After several years of marriage, we decided it was time for us to get serious about starting a family. Avid travelers, we wanted to knock a few destinations off our bucket list that would be too hard to do with young children. Among those was hiking miles through dense mountain jungle in search of Uganda's endangered mountain gorillas. After two and a half weeks in Uganda, Kenya, Tanzania, and Zanzibar, I planned our flights home to go through Thessaloniki.

I rarely brought Indra on Team Rubicon's missions. For one thing, she was still in New York, most recently finishing a stint with ABC's *Good Morning America*. And, frankly, I spent so much time caring for the concerns and well-being of others that it often came at her expense. Humans have only so much capacity for emotion, and Team Rubicon alone often brought my tank up to full. I did my best to make our time together just that—our time together.

But Elpida felt different. Elpida was the confluence of my life's two defining experiences: war and Team Rubicon. Indra, despite her best efforts and sharp intellect, struggled to fully understand my wartime experience. It certainly wasn't her fault—I struggled to fully understand it myself. Like most Americans, the majority of whom have no direct connection to someone in the military, she at first assumed my experience was defined by death and killing. Naturally, to some extent it was. Blake Howey's warped face still stares at me with lifeless eyes when I close mine. Nathan Windsor's breathing, labored as he drowned in his blood-filled lungs, still fills some empty silences. The screams of Afghan children echoing off a valley wall as a Taliban fighter slumps to the earth still make my skin crawl. Those were the easy things to pinpoint, but they weren't everything. Sometimes it was the people we didn't kill who haunted us, like the Afghan man we'd observed and suspected was tracking a British unit's location. He was unarmed and not visibly speaking into a radio, but we were near certain he was reporting their movements, possibly coordinating an ambush. The Brits were not attacked that day, but we often wondered whether someone, somewhere, was killed another day because we didn't kill that man.

My mind would often drift to Ali and his family. The promise to keep them safe. The promise we didn't keep. I will never know what became of them. Often, I'm sure they're dead. For all I knew, that Mercedes returned in the middle of that very night, its passengers walking into the house and killing Ali and his family for having hosted us for dinner. If not that night, then any day during the American presence. And if they survived that, how could a family that liberal survive ISIS? The truth was that they couldn't. Ali would have been executed and dumped in the Tigris, his daughters-in-law conscripted as ISIS brides, and his beautiful grandsons handed rifles and forced to fight.

Occasionally I allowed myself to believe that Ali was alive. That he finally made the prudent choice and took his family to join his son in Europe. I imagine him running a shop on a busy tourist street, playfully bantering in English with friendly passersby. His grandchildren able to walk to and from school without fear of bombs, hopeful for a better life.

If he didn't get out before ISIS, then perhaps he made a harrowing escape like the thousands of others. Perhaps he would even be at Elpida, and I could embrace him and apologize for lying to him a decade prior. I could sit in his room and break bread and drink tea and give him all the bullshit excuses for why I couldn't keep my promise. I'd ask for his forgiveness. But I knew better than to dwell on that fairy tale.

Team Rubicon's mission at Elpida would not help Ali and his family. But there were tens of thousands of families like Ali's, and Team Rubicon's veterans were committed to helping as many of them as we could.

• • •

SEPTEMBER 7, 2016
ELPIDA HOME, THESSALONIKI, GREECE

Indra and I rode in the back of the compact car as it snaked its way through Thessaloniki's narrow streets. We had landed the day prior and spent the afternoon at Elpida's medical clinic, getting to know the Greyshirts on the ground and touring the facility. I spent most of my time asking questions, wanting to understand the friction points of the operation so I could return to the U.S. and ensure better support for the effort. There were plenty of things to improve. The pharmacy was short on medication. The rotation of volunteers every two weeks created massive inefficiencies and at times led to inconsistency of care—and consistency was something Team Rubicon prided itself on. There were concerns about the logistics and legalities of transferring patients to and from the local government hospitals, something that took place about every other week. None of them insurmountable, all of them in need of solutions.

Now we were going to visit with the residents, the part of the trip I most anticipated. We spent the morning with Omaid and Marwan, two teenage brothers serving as interpreters. They each wore secondhand American and European clothes littered with logos and pop culture references, which seemed somehow appropriate as they appeared to have learned English courtesy of Taylor Swift and *Star Wars*. Omaid and Marwan fawned over the American women working in the camp, flirting in a way they never could with a woman on the streets of Damascus. With Indra's blond hair and my height and size—plus word having gotten out that I was Team Rubicon's CEO—Omaid and Marwan were soon attached to us at the hip.

The boys guided us through the camp as if they were the mayors, introducing us to families and commenting on interpersonal dynamics. Indra asked them where they hoped they would end up in Europe. Belgium and Paris were shouted by each. And what did they want to be when they grew up? Doctors, both of them.

Around noon, Marwan and Omaid led us to the third floor of the building and then turned to us excitedly. "Come and meet our mother!" Omaid said.

Marwan and Omaid led us down the hall and through one of the dozen doors evenly spaced along the left-hand side. Inside was a simple one-room apartment, maybe fifteen by twenty feet in size. On one side stood a bunk bed, opposite it a wooden chair. A picture of Mecca hung on one wall. In the center of the room their mother, Farah, sat cross-legged on a mat, her ten-year-old daughter plopped on her lap.

"*Salaam alaykum,*" I said, putting my hand over my heart and lowering my eyes. "*Alaykum salaam,*" she responded warmly. She gestured to the floor and Indra and I took a seat opposite her, tucking in our feet as was customary.

We learned that she was a French-language professor at a university in Damascus. Early in the Syrian civil war, her husband had fled the country for fear that he would be conscripted into Assad's army and sent to the front lines to be massacred. He was working in Turkey, sending every dollar he could to Farah to support his family.

"We had a beautiful apartment, many floors up. From window I see smoke rising from the bombings a few miles away." She pulled her cell phone out from between her legs. "Then one day this happen." She turned her phone to face Indra, whose eyes grew sorrowful. Farah then showed it to me. On it was a photo taken from inside an apartment, or what was left of one. The blue Syrian sky poured in through a ten-foot hole punched through an exterior wall, the floor inside caved into the apartment beneath it. "This was my living room. We eat dinner one night when artillery bomb hit apartment. We lucky no one killed." She put her phone away and sighed.

The war had arrived, and she was likely only days away from having either Assad's people or the rebels drag her sons away to force them to fight. Out of good options, Farah took every dollar she had and paid a smuggler to put Omaid and Marwan in the trunk of a car and drive them to the Turkish border, where she'd try to follow them a few days later with her daughter. The pain and fear of that decision still lingered on Farah's face. She knew that the smuggler was just as likely to pocket her money and turn the boys over to Assad to be tortured.

Once in Turkey, Farah reunited with her husband. There they made another excruciating decision. They only had enough money left to send four of them on to Europe, the only place they believed their children had a future. One night, Farah, Omaid, Marwan, and her daughter stepped into a rubber boat on Turkey's moonlit coast. The boat was overcrowded and had no life preservers. Shoving off from shore, Farah said she watched until she could no longer see her husband waving. That was when her nightmare truly began. Harsh seas nearly capsized the boat several times, and it was clear the smugglers had no experience navigating the waters. She was terrified that the smugglers were the types rumored to throw passengers overboard if the waves got too rough, making it easier for them to return alive. Eventually the sun rose and the waves calmed, and soon Greece could be seen faintly on the horizon. "I rejoiced and praised Allah," Farah said, but it was too soon. The motor ran out of gaso-line, and the boat drifted listlessly in the Mediterranean. None of the refugees knew how to swim, but it didn't matter as even an accomplished distance swimmer wouldn't make it across the open expanse. With no drinking water on the boat, the situation grew desperate. Eventually the Greek coast guard spotted them and rescued all the passengers, bring-ing them safely to Greek soil. "It was Allah's will that we get here," Farah said, tears in her eyes.

I found my arm wrapped around Indra's shoulder. We thanked Farah for her time and told her that she'd raised a wonderful young family. That Omaid and Marwan were critical to the camp's operations. As Indra and I rose to leave, Farah reached out and grabbed my forearm.

"Why do all your country think we are terrorist?" she asked. "We not terrorist. We good people. We families with sons and daughters trying to escape." Her voice was equal parts confusion, frustration, and sadness. "I am professor!" she added.

I was unsure how to answer. The rhetoric surrounding refugees in general, and Muslim refugees in particular, had become increasingly toxic. America was divided. One side wanted to open America up to any refugee who raised their hand, while the other was calling for a "Muslim ban." Neither option was practical, and the latter seemed un-American. Even more frustrating, few Americans wanted to accept our complicity in the current Middle East crisis. They washed their hands of responsi-bility and probably cared little whether Farah and her children sank to the bottom of the sea. I couldn't answer for America, only for myself. I put my hand on Farah's and responded. "I don't feel that way. That's why we're here."

I needed to speak to more residents. We went next door to meet with a twenty-year-old Iraqi man from Mosul who was living in a room with two brothers, a sister, his parents, and his aunt. His name was Yusuf and his English was just good enough to make conversation possible. We removed our shoes and joined him in the center of the room. My joints groaned as I lowered to the concrete floor. It was clear that Yusuf's family was conservative, as his mother and aunt avoided eye contact and stayed huddled in the far corner of the room. Yusuf sent his younger brother, Mustafa, to go and get his father. Minutes later a tall, brooding man with a thick mustache entered the door and sat down opposite me.

"This my father, Hussein," Yusuf stated.

Hussein stared at me with a mix of respect and contempt. His attitude instantly brought me back to every sit-down I'd had with an Iraqi elder a decade prior. The conversation started off a bit rocky, with Hussein rattling off a series of questions in harsh Arabic that Yusuf translated. Why didn't the clinic have an ambulance? What happens if someone has an emergency? How long will you be staying? None of our answers seemed to suffice, and for a while I thought that everyone was wasting their time.

Hussein looked at his wife and muttered something in Arabic. Minutes later the wife and aunt poured hot chai into cups placed in front of us. Hussein's smaller sons were crawling all over him, and though he pretended to be annoyed, you could see the love flash briefly across his face. I took a sip. I couldn't escape the feeling that I was back in Iraq. I smiled at Hussein. He didn't smile back. That made the feeling even more real.

I knew that Iraqi men respected strength. I sat up a bit taller, lowered my voice, looked him more intensely in the eye, and relayed stronger answers back through his son. There was a glimmer of amusement in Hussein's eye. He enjoyed seeing this American work for his respect. The banter got friendlier.

I asked Hussein what he did back in Mosul. He responded that he managed a trucking company that moved material back and forth from Baghdad to Mosul. "I had a very big desk," he added, holding his arms out wide.

"What did you do before you ran this Rubicon-Team?" Yusuf asked.

I hesitated. I had not spoken to an Iraqi since leaving the country ten years prior. Part of me worried that if Hussein and Yusuf knew I was a Marine who had served in the war, they would become angry. But another part of me needed to connect with them somehow, whatever the consequence.

"I was a *jundi*," I replied, using the Iraqi word for the lowest rank in the military. Both Yusuf's and Hussein's brows furrowed, unsure what I meant. Was *jundi* an American word they were unfamiliar with? Finally, Yusuf leaned in.

"You were America Army?" he asked, incredulous.

I decided it wasn't the time to lecture Yusuf on the ego-driven rivalry between the Army and Marine Corps and nodded my head. Yusuf leaned back, he and his father both silent for a moment. Hussein chewed on a toothpick, his mustache undulating like a centipede. Finally, he responded in Arabic, yet to show any real emotion.

Yusuf faced me. "He says to tell you he a nurse and driver in Iraqi army. But before America invaded. My father fight Iran." Hussein just stared.

I broke the silence and pointed at him. *"Jundi?"* I asked. Hussein erupted in laughter, throwing both hands in the air. *"Jundi!"* he exclaimed, grabbing my hand and shaking it.

When the laughter died down, Yusuf settled forward with his elbows on his knees. In his broken English he told me that he was six when the Americans invaded his city. With a stern face he told me he had no love for the American military, but he knew there must be good *jundis* like me. He then told me that his neighborhood was now controlled by ISIS and that he didn't know what had happened to many of his friends. The girls were probably raped and the boys . . . He made a slash across his throat. He described fleeing Mosul with his family as ISIS entered the city and then, with a pained smile on this face, Yusuf told us that if I listened to his stories I would cry.

I looked at Yusuf and told him I was sorry. I wasn't apologizing for myself, or for America. I was simply sorry that such a kind young man had been forced to live a life of unspeakable violence for fourteen years.

"Why did you fight Iraq?" Hussein asked.

It was a simple question. It deserved a simple answer. "I guess I wanted to keep America safe." Hearing the translation, Hussein piqued his eyebrows.

"He want to know if you think you keep America safe," Yusuf asked.

There it was. The real question. The one I had grappled with for so long. Was the mission worth it? I thought of ISIS's emergence and the horrors it brought. I thought of the increased terrorist attacks on U.S. soil. Of the trillion dollars spent and all the blood spilled. I took a sip of tea. I imagined Howey and Windsor. Was their courage and sacrifice cheapened if it was all for naught? No. Their country asked them to go to war, and they answered the call honorably. They didn't pick the mission, but they executed it.

"I don't know," I answered, not proud that I couldn't give them a better answer. I looked at Yusuf and then Hussein, knowing that I just told them I'd invaded their homeland and couldn't even justify it.

Hussein said something, speaking with real warmth for the first time. "He says, 'You not worry about this, you just *jundi* then,'" Yusuf translated. "Now you no longer *jundi*. Now you help people like us."

Hussein and Yusuf insisted that we stay for lunch. Knowing that each family was apportioned specific rations, spending out of their own pocket for additional food, I tried to refuse. But Hussein insisted and soon we were served spiced lamb, rice, and *khubz* bread.

The mood lightened and the conversation was full of laughter and jokes. "What do you want to study at the university?" I asked Yusuf.

"I want to be a doctor," he proudly proclaimed. He pointed to his eyes. "I want to be a doctor for the eyes, because the eyes, they are, how you say? They are the gateway to world."

It wasn't lost on me that all the young men I'd met in Elpida wanted to become doctors. I thought about Yusuf wanting to preserve sight for others, even after he had seen such horror and tragedy himself. He seemed to sense what I was thinking and smiled and shrugged his shoulders.

"Where do you want to be placed permanently?" I asked. The refugees at the camp were all awaiting decisions on which EU country would accept their asylum requests. Yusuf turned to his younger brother, Mustafa. "Where do we want to go?" he asked him.

"Austria!" he shouted.

The answer surprised me. Austria was not a common destination for refugees. I looked at young Mustafa and drifted back to my time in Austria twenty-six years prior. Where my own journey had begun. That moment at Mauthausen had discretely set my life on a path that had brought me to this very moment. Everything in my life seemed stitched together by a common thread.

"Have you been to this place, Austria?" Yusuf asked.

"I have," I replied. "It is beautiful and you will make a wonderful life there with your family."

We went outside and played basketball on a cracked asphalt court, Hussein mercilessly swatting his sons' jump shots into the bushes. Other kids joined and laughter filled the air. An hour later, a Greyshirt came and indicated to Indra and me that it was time to go. We had to head to the airport to catch our flight home. Indra, seated off to the side with Hussein's daughter in her lap, stood to leave. The little girl began to cry, and Indra scooped her up into her arms.

"Please, stay for dinner," Hussein asked. I told him that we couldn't, that we had to fly back to America. Hussein, disappointed, reached out and embraced me. *"Salaam alaykum, sadıqı,"* he said.

"Wa alaykum salaam, hajji," I replied.

Yusuf followed us to the car, where I shook his hand.

"You not forget this place when you go back to America?"

"Of course not, Yusuf," I responded.

"Promise?"

"I promise."

CHAPTER 18

WE'RE GOING TO WISH
WE HAD BOATS

SEPTEMBER 1, 2017
HOUSTON, TX

The flood had come from all directions. It fell from the sky in sheets, rose from the bayous in waves, rushed through the streets in torrents, carrying cars and mailboxes and dead animals caught in the tempest of Hurricane Harvey.

Among a graveyard of homes, 1445 Forest Bend sat like a tilted tombstone no longer cared for by the progeny of a once proud ancestor. Inside, heavy boots built for far-flung battlefields squelched as men and women in grey shirts dragged the home's contents out the front door. Blasts of exploding tile reverberated as kitchen cabinets met the business end of a sledgehammer. Elsewhere, a gloved fist punched through the drywall, ripping the sheet off its studs.

Dozer, a pint-sized Air Force vet as tough as her nickname, moved with authority from room to room. It was nearing ninety degrees out-side, which meant that inside the flooded home it was as humid as the Amazon jungle. Dozer's job was to make sure the work was done prop-erly, and that none of her fellow Greyshirts got heatstroke.

She reached down and tapped a worker on the shoulder. He was thirtysomething with a broad back that stretched the seams of his T-shirt. He stood up from his crouch. His grey uniform was three shades darker from the sweat, but below the Team Rubicon logo on his chest you could clearly make out his name, *BILLY*, alongside an identification number, known allergies, and blood type, all of which he'd grown accustomed to writing on his flak jacket and boots in Iraq.

"How ya holdin' up?" Dozer asked. Billy shrugged his shoulders. His response was muffled by the N-95 protective mask over his bushy beard. "What's that, Billy?" Dozer asked.

He reached up and pulled down the mask. "It's hotter than two rats fucking in a wool gym sock." There was a moment of suspense. Billy's eyes sparkled in anticipation. The line for inappropriate jokes was some-times toed among the ranks in Team Rubicon, and nobody liked testing the boundaries more than Billy. Finally, Dozer burst out laughing.

"Alright, everyone. Let's take a fifteen-minute break," she shouted. "Outside, now! Get some water."

Everyone huddled in the shade of a giant bur oak. A distinct water-line ran the circumference of the trunk four feet off the ground. Billy reached out to brush his fingers across the line. Sunlight filtering down through the branches illuminated his arm, tattooed from his wrist all the way up under his sleeve. A tapestry of skulls and swords and storm clouds illustrated a scene of chaos on his bicep. His forearm featured a pair of boots, behind which stood a rifle with a helmet resting on top—

an image familiar to any veteran who has buried a brother or sister on the battlefield. When Billy's hand dropped, the rest of his forearm was exposed. *For he who sheds his blood with me shall forever be my brother,* the tattoo read. Under that was a list of names and dates.

Billy reached into his pocket for a tin of Copenhagen. He poked a wad of tobacco into his cheek. A car pulled up.

"Guys, gather round," Dozer said. "That's the owner, Isabella. The fire department pulled her and her grandson out. She's living at a shelter," Dozer finished, glancing at Isabella. "Come on, let's go meet her."

Isabella stood over a debris pile—*her* debris pile—clutching a framed painting of the crucifixion, trying to stifle a gasp. Still feeling her out, Dozer draped a tentative arm across her shoulder. "Isabella," she whispered, "I have some people here who'd like to meet you."

"These are the volunteers Team Rubicon sent," Dozer said, extending her arm.

No longer able to contain her emotion, Isabella broke down in tears at the sight of the half dozen strangers who'd arrived at her home to help on her worst day. "I . . . I . . . I don't know what to say . . . What can I do to thank you?" Isabella stammered. Billy stepped forward. He had joined the Army at eighteen and spent most of his adult life in foreign lands, fighting and killing. And burying friends. Too many friends. Bearded, tatted Billy, who looked more Hells Angel than heavenly helper.

"Isabella," he said, "we are so honored to be here. Thank you for giving us the opportunity to be of service to you." His arm wrapped around Isabella's shoulder and pulled her to his chest. A muffled sob spilled out between heaving shoulders and, for a moment, the tattoo on Billy's forearm was covered up when a second volunteer stepped in to complete the hug.

• ● •

ONE WEEK EARLIER

The meeting ended without fanfare. It was Friday, August 25, and Team Rubicon's National Operations Center in Dallas, the NOC, had just conducted a mission planning update for Hurricane Harvey, which was gradually intensifying into a Category 4 storm. "I've got a bad feeling about this one," said Art delaCruz, my new chief operating officer, scratching the salt-and-pepper stubble on his chin. I nodded and bit my lip. We'd just dialed into the meeting from our headquarters in Los Angeles.

The U.S. had not sustained landfall of a major hurricane in twelve years. It was a streak that was due to end. Harvey had the potential to wreak massive damage along the coast, and experts were predicting that the worst damage could be from the rainfall, not the wind.

"I suspect that, come Monday, we're going to wish we had boats," I said. Art, an aggressive tactician like me, leaned forward.

"Want me to tell Burke to buy some? I'd rather have them and not need them than need them and not have them."

I thought about it for a moment. There was a time when I would not have hesitated. After all, I could name off the top of my head a dozen volunteers and staff members with extensive experience in swift-water rescue. But over the past several years, Team Rubicon had evolved. One evolution was the creation of a department whose sole focus was developing the doctrine, standards, guidelines, and tactics for missions that Team Rubicon undertook. The department would assemble teams of experts to research potential disaster response functions, identify the gaps in the disaster space, and determine whether Team Rubicon was uniquely suited to address them. Just going out and buying boats and throwing them full of people into a flood-ravaged city flew in the face of that deliberate approach.

"No. Let's see how this plays out. I've been around long enough to know these things often fizzle before they make landfall." Art shrugged his shoulders. We walked out of the glass-paneled conference room at Team Rubicon's headquarters. In the open office space outside, dozens of desks grouped in pods covered the concrete floors. The atmosphere buzzed as each department prepared for Harvey. The marketing team prepared social media posts and fundraising emails. The partnerships team culled lists of corporate partners, calling to inform them that Team Rubicon was standing by to assist should the storm warrant it. Everyone was making sure their checklists were executed. "It's a good buzz," I said to Art. "Most of these folks haven't been here for a big one. This will be a good test."

- - -

Hurricane Harvey made landfall near Rockport, Texas, later that evening, the strongest storm to hit the U.S. since Hurricane Wilma in 2005.* Winds over one hundred miles per hour destroyed large swaths of Rockport and Port Aransas before Harvey bounced off the coast like a pinball and crept northeast toward Houston. There it weakened to a tropical storm, but a pressure system stalled its path and the storm sat over the city for nearly four days. Hurricane Harvey dumped an estimated fifteen trillion gallons of water into Harris County, where Houston sits. That is a staggering volume—an amount that would fill 15,600 New Orleans

---

* "2017 Hurricane Harvey," World Vision, September 7, 2018, www.worldvision.org/disaster-relief-news-stories/2017-hurricane-harvey-facts.

Saints Superdomes (infamous for its role during Hurricane Katrina). It was as if God had grabbed the universe's largest bucket, dipped it in the Gulf of Mexico, and dumped it on Houston and the surrounding area like a child destroying a sandcastle at the beach.

It became clear very early that the rain and resultant flooding would be unprecedented. And indeed the economic cost would be immense, matching that of Hurricane Katrina at an estimated $125 billion.* Of that total, the Insurance Council of Texas estimated that only $19 billion in losses were insured. That meant that the estimated thirteen million people who were impacted in some way by Harvey—some of whom owned one of the approximately 135,000 homes or one million cars damaged or destroyed by the storm—were on the hook for $106 billion in losses.†

It wasn't necessarily their fault. Traditional homeowners insurance does not cover damage caused by flooding. This is typically handled by the National Flood Insurance Program (NFIP), which mandates that homeowners get insurance if they have a federally guaranteed loan and live in a hundred-year floodplain. In Harris County, which includes the city of Houston, only 15 percent of homes had flood insurance through the NFIP.‡ People living in five-hundred- or thousand-year floodplains were suddenly wondering how they'd get out from underwater, literally and figuratively.

Officials in communities throughout the coastal cities had urged

---

* "2017 Hurricane Harvey," World Vision.

† "ICT Estimates Hurricane Harvey Insured Losses at $19 Billion," Insurance Council of Texas, September 15, 2017, www.insurancecouncil.org/ict-estimates-hurricane-harvey-insured-losses-at-19-billion/.

‡ Chris Isadore, "Most Homes in Tropical Storm Harvey's Path Don't Have Flood Insurance," CNN, August 26, 2017, https://money.cnn.com/2017/08/25/news/economy/hurricane-harvey-flood-insurance/index.html.

residents to evacuate, but, as is often the case, few heeded the warning. One emergency management official in Tyler County put out a warning as blunt as it could get: "Anyone who chooses to not [evacuate] cannot expect to be rescued and should write their social security numbers in permanent marker on their arm so their bodies can be identified. The loss of life and property is certain. GET OUT OR DIE!"*

Several days after landfall, with rain still falling and thousands in need of rescue, officials in cities along the coast put out an exceptional request: they asked private citizens to put their shallow-draft boats in the water to assist with rescue efforts. With the U.S. Coast Guard on scene, the entire Texas National Guard mobilized, and local police and fire officials working around the clock, officials still could not rescue everyone clambering up onto roofs to escape the water. Water rescues in these scenarios can be extraordinarily dangerous—currents can sweep boats or swimmers away in a moment, unseen hazards beneath the surface can instantly capsize vessels, and downed power lines can kill someone instantly. The fact that private citizens were being asked to take these risks was an indication of the magnitude of the disaster.

As the scope of damage became clear, it was nearly impossible to get people into the impacted areas. Our teams at the NOC were working tirelessly to gather as much information as possible to produce actionable intelligence. They were poring over satellite imagery, scraping public social media posts, and monitoring communications from emergency management agencies. One thing was clear: we needed boats.

It was Sunday back in Los Angeles, and over the weekend I had dialed into mission planning calls every six hours. Each call had staff

---

* *Austin American-Statesman* staff, "Dire Warning in East Texas: 'Get Out or Die,'" *Dayton Daily News*, August 31, 2017, www.daytondailynews.com/news/national/dire-warning -east-texas-get-out-die/YjhDqvBMLbu615QJq6xpYM/.

and volunteers dialing in from nearly one hundred locations. Despite the chaos unfolding on the ground, the calls ran like clockwork. The agenda remained static, everyone knew precisely what they needed to brief, and the listeners knew exactly what information to expect.

After Sunday morning's call, I sat back in my chair and wrestled with a decision. Do I order the team to buy boats? To do so would be a sudden departure from our deliberate approach to launching new things, but it would also be in the spirit of Team Rubicon's culture of bold decision making. The risks of putting staff and volunteers into the water without formal standard operating procedures were high—but people were awaiting rescue. Could we really stand on the sidelines? I agonized over the decision more than I probably should have, and several hours later I made up my mind.

I grabbed my phone and called David Burke, now my vice president of Programs and Field Operations. David oversaw the NOC, in addition to many other responsibilities. David picked up after the second ring. "What's up, Jake?" he asked.

Puffing out my chest, I put my foot up on a table and dropped my voice an octave, then proclaimed: "David, get me boats!" This was it. This was my moment. The culmination of my evolution as a leader, in which I make the tough, right choice and inspire my team to follow me. The awkward pause that followed confused me. *Did David disagree with the decision?*

"Uhhh, Jake, I ordered the team to buy boats a few hours ago. We just got three with more on the way. They'll be in the water by this evening."

I burst out laughing. Of course David had already bought boats. Team Rubicon had built a culture of empowered leadership; David knew that he was the leader closest to the issue at hand, understood the risks and rewards, and felt that he had my full trust and confidence to make the tough call. Moreover, David knew that even if I disagreed with his decision, so long as he made it with the right intention and logic, I wasn't going to fire him. My moment had become David's moment, and it couldn't have made me happier.

Over the next seventy-two hours, it became clear that Hurricane Harvey would become the largest operation in Team Rubicon's history. The NOC was working to activate and organize all of our Greyshirts in the impacted areas, ensuring first that they were safe and then that they had the means to help their neighbors. Our boats were in the water, and over the course of five days they rescued seventy-two people and searched 446 structures. The NOC was drawing up a response plan that would install what's called an Area Command in downtown Houston, with satellite command posts at forward operating bases in as many as a dozen communities from as far south as Rockport and as far northeast as Beaumont. The area of operation would span over 250 miles. We estimated that we needed to deploy two thousand volunteers to execute the plan.

A year before Harvey, Team Rubicon had laid out a vision for how the organization would scale by focusing our growth and development efforts on major metropolitan areas. We believed we could build dense "centers of gravity" in these cities that would increase efficiency and impact by increasing volunteer engagement and reducing the cost of training. The vision was the culmination of years working with my board chairman, Adam Miller, on what the future of Team Rubicon would look like. It was a long-term goal we hadn't made much progress on yet.

As the chaos unfolded in Houston and it became apparent most of the rescue efforts were neighbors helping neighbors, I logged onto Census.gov and pulled up some data sets. One number I found blew my mind: 163,317 veterans lived in Harris County. I asked myself: *What if all those veterans had been organized, trained, and equipped before Harvey hit?* Imagine an auxiliary disaster response force that incorporated all the veterans across every community in America. That was what Team Rubicon was trying to build—we just hadn't gotten there in time for Harvey.

The other element of Team Rubicon's vision that I couldn't get out of my head was our desire to expand our programs into long-term recovery. After nearly every disaster, our volunteers would lament that they had to leave the community they were serving before homes could be rebuilt. The mission didn't feel complete. Our hope was to launch a program that would train military veterans in construction skills and then employ them to rebuild disaster-damaged homes at little to no cost. Unfortunately, we had been delaying the development of that initiative because it was extremely expensive to design and launch. Was this an opportunity?

I gathered my leadership team in Los Angeles. We sat in a conference room named Port-au-Prince, in honor of our seminal mission. The bags under everyone's eyes told me that the team was running at redline. We discussed the operation in big-picture terms—not the tactical level of the NOC calls. How did we need to position the organization to succeed? What kind of work-rest rotations did we need to establish so people didn't burn out? Near the end of the meeting I grabbed everyone's attention.

"Team, listen up. We've raised approximately 1.5 million dollars so far, and there's no indication things are slowing down. We could raise three million, maybe five million dollars if we play things the right way. But we have to have a plan to spend that money efficiently." We'd never executed a response operation that cost us in excess of $3 million before. "I recommend we keep our foot on the gas and accelerate the fundraising. If things go right and we raise the money, then we should be prepared to launch our rebuild initiative." It sounded like a simple suggestion, but it wasn't. Because of funding, Corey's capabilities department hadn't yet written the playbook for a rebuilding program. It would undoubtedly involve a large incremental staffing plan, and Candice, our head of people, would have to figure out how to make that work. There were hundreds of other variables to consider, but we didn't have time to agonize over them. If we lost fundraising momentum now, we would never recover it.

David laughed. "Are you asking us or telling us?" I smirked and said nothing, baiting him to weigh in with an opinion. "I mean, we wouldn't be sitting here if we didn't have a history of taking chances like this. I'm in."

I turned to Art. "If we don't bet on ourselves in this situation, then we're fools," he said.

I looked at Corey, whose team would carry a large component of the effort. As he was one of our most deliberate and systematic thinkers, I anticipated that he might lead with all the reasons it wouldn't work. But Corey was also one of our most compassionate humanitarians, and he knew that tens of thousands of people had lost their homes. He put his hands on the table and looked around the room. "I'll go make a few calls and organize the team to begin working on this." He stood to leave, turning back as he reached the door. "We'll get it done."

The next forty-eight hours were a blur, and raising money for the mission became my highest priority. One afternoon, a woman from Under Armour named Stacey contacted me. We had not spoken in several years. She said that Under Armour's founder and CEO, Kevin Plank, wanted to speak to me. I paced back and forth in my room for twenty minutes waiting for his call. Plank was a legend—the kind of relentless David-versus-Goliath entrepreneur I fashioned myself after.

Kevin rang. "I love what you're doing with Team Rubicon," he said.

"It's just incredible the work you guys are doing. All of us want to help. What can we do, send clothes?"

I delicately told Kevin that sending clothes after an event like this caused a disaster within the disaster, and politely told him that the most effective help at this moment would be sending money. "Okay, you got it. Under Armour is going to send you $100,000 right away, and I'm going to personally match it." I thanked him profusely before he continued. "And I want to fly down and see your operation on the ground."

I pumped my fist in the air. Getting donors on the ground to see our teams in action all but guaranteed that they would be lifelong supporters. The work was simply too powerful not to become hooked. "Kevin, that's great. These are still the early phases of the operation. It's total chaos down there. I would expect we will have things stabilized within about seven to ten days."

"No, I want to go now. My plane can get me to Houston tomorrow. That's where you are, right?"

Shit. I wasn't there. My best use at the moment wasn't gutting homes; it was raising money. Still, Kevin's request didn't surprise me. He was who he was because of his relentless go-go-go attitude. I took half a second to analyze my options before responding. "Of course I'm in Houston. I'll see you tomorrow." After all, you're not an entrepreneur until you've bluffed your way into a big deal.

I was at the airport within an hour, booking a one-way ticket from my phone on the way. The following day I met Kevin, Stacey, Kevin's son James, and a few other members of his crew at the airport. We drove into Houston toward the downtown convention center, which had been converted into a massive shelter. As we drove down the wide Texas freeways, Kevin marveled at how much water still remained. Looking down gentle slopes into some neighborhoods, we saw flood levels were still at the midway point of many one-story homes. Elsewhere, the waters had receded only to reveal the devastation left behind. Kevin pinned his cell phone to the inside of the car window, taking photos and filming the gut-wrenching scenes.

Parked outside the convention center, we gathered out front. I wanted to let them know why we were there and what they would see.

"A few things. First, many people who arrive at these shelters are the most economically disenfranchised. They are here because they have no other options—they cannot afford hotel rooms or even the gas money to drive to another city, or they have no extended family that can take them in. Second, you'll see just how vulnerable people here are. Women, young children, and those with disabilities can very easily be taken advantage of or harmed, despite everyone's best efforts. Finally, Kevin, you'll see why I told you sending trucks full of clothes wasn't a good idea."

We toured the facility, which was housing thousands of displaced Houstonians. Cavernous rooms lined with simple cots—the same kind Team Rubicon volunteers slept on—were filled with anxious and grieving people wondering what would come next. Queues of people stood at folding tables waiting to speak to representatives from FEMA and learn how they could start the process of applying for aid. They would be devastated a year later to learn that, though FEMA's maximum payout to an individual was around $30,000, the average payout after Harvey was well below $10,000. That was if they received anything at all. Many received nothing. Considering a single inch of water in a home can cause in excess of $20,000 in damage, and many of the homes would be condemned, FEMA's aid would be too little, too late.

Finally, we arrived in the center room. Rising before us was a mountain of clothing, a fifty-foot pile of cotton, polyester, and wool. Shirts and pants and socks and coats. None of it arranged by garment type, none of it arranged by size. Some of it clean, some of it dirty. Some of it useless, like the truckload of winter jackets sent from a well-meaning group in Minnesota. Houston didn't need jackets in August. "I guess this is why Jake said don't send clothes," Kevin said.

We loaded back into our vehicles and drove toward the Friendswood neighborhood. Dozer and her team, working on a different house at this point, were the perfect group to take Kevin and his crew out to meet. An elderly couple owned the house and lived with their daughter and grandchild. As with Isabella, the water had risen quickly in their home in the middle of the night and they had to be rescued. "One more thing," I said. "We don't believe in disaster tourism at Team Rubicon. If you come to a job site, you come to work. That's what those Greyshirts over there are expecting. Before we get out of the car, I need to know that you guys are willing to get dirty."

Kevin looked offended. "Dude, what do you think I came down here for?" His door was halfway open before he finished. Kevin and his group worked all afternoon with Dozer's crew. At one point I saw Kevin speaking to the grandfather. He learned that the grandfather only had enough money left for two more nights at their hotel. After that, he might have to take his family to the convention center. Kevin shook his head in disbelief.

By the end of the day, Kevin's clothes were covered with filth and it was time for his crew to leave. They loaded up in the SUV and departed, Kevin committing to partnering Under Armour with Team Rubicon in a big way. An hour later, Kevin's SUV returned. The driver stepped out of the car and asked if the homeowner was still on the site. I pointed him out and the driver handed me a thick envelope. "Here, give this to him. Kevin made me stop at a bank on our way to the airport." With that, he turned and drove away.

I opened the envelope and peered inside. It was a stack of cash, probably more than I'd ever held at one time. Kevin didn't want that man's family to have to go to the shelter.

A few days later, another business leader joined me in the field. Howard Schultz, who built Starbucks into a global behemoth, had supported Team Rubicon along with his wife, Sheri, for many years.

When we brought Howard to the Area Command Post downtown, one of the volunteers presented him with an honorary Greyshirt, *HOWARD* stenciled neatly into the white bar. She even took the time to put a messy cup of coffee on it, leaving an artfully placed circular stain.

Howard asked thoughtful questions, but one thing in particular seems to have stuck with him. When he asked about the impact disasters like Harvey have on economic inequality, I offered him a staggering fact. The U.S. Federal Reserve estimates that 40 percent of Americans do not have access to $400 in case of an emergency. That meant that after a disaster in a metropolitan area like Houston, millions of residents would not have enough cash for two or three nights in a hotel, let alone to fix a damaged car so they could get back to work. Even more tragic, it meant that they were likely to spiral into further financial ruin. Later, when Howard explored a run for president of the United States, I often heard him cite this statistic.

Howard seemed impressed by the scale and complexity of Team Rubicon's operations, and he and Sheri continued their financial support for the efforts. Resources were pouring in, but it was obvious that our battle lines with Hurricane Harvey were just being drawn.

CHAPTER 19

CLAY WOULD BE PROUD

Back at our operations center in Dallas, Art, David, and the rest of the operations team worked with me to develop plans for Team Rubicon's largest-scale response ever. By now, our boat rescue teams were returning from Houston, their crews cold, wet, and tired. At the same time, hundreds of Greyshirts were being sent forward and the NOC was loading trucks and trailers day and night to reinforce them. Our initial plans estimated we would need thousands of volunteers to deploy along the coast. However, unlike during Hurricane Sandy, we were confident we could do it. By now the organization had nearly fifty thousand volunteers registered in its ranks. But there weren't enough in Texas to man this kind of response. We would have to mobilize nationwide.

The problem was that planning two thousand individual flights across hundreds of dates and points of origin would be a coordination quagmire. We had to reduce the complexity of the effort, and fast. Art, who had been a senior Navy officer with a background in aviation, had an idea. Let's conduct an airlift, he said. We would plan a mass mobilization from ten major cities. Waves of volunteers would fly in on chartered aircraft departing and returning on specific dates. That would meter our inbound volunteers so that we could realistically process and employ them on the ground, while ensuring we had sustainable volunteer levels present for the duration of the response. It was a brilliant concept with only one problem. We needed really big airplanes to make it work.

We decided we would pitch American Airlines, headquartered in Dallas. Two of our board members, Chris Perkins and Bruce Mosler, began working their channels to get to the right people at American. Art took the lead on building out a presentation. Meanwhile, I went back to manning the phones and raising money. PricewaterhouseCoopers called and donated $500,000. Alex and Steven Cohen called and pledged the same. Our incredible partners in the insurance industry—Farmers, Travelers, and USAA—called to commit even more. Home Depot, Target, and Walmart each chipped in. General Michael Linnington, the CEO of the Wounded Warrior Project, one of the country's largest veteran charities, texted me and said they'd be wiring a million dollars. "Keep inspiring our veterans to serve," he added.

Then my phone rang from an unknown Arizona number. I answered it and learned it was Laura, who ran the Bob and Renee Parsons Foundation. Bob was famously the founder of GoDaddy.com, which he sold for several billion dollars. What most people didn't know was that Bob is a Marine veteran from Vietnam. I caught Laura up on Team Rubicon's response. She indicated that Bob was interested in supporting our efforts. As she was speaking, a gruff, booming voice drowned her out on the phone. "Hey, Marine! What she's trying to say is I like what you're doing. I'm going to wire you a million dollars. You just let me know if you need more." Apparently, Bob was on the line. We chatted for several minutes, one-upping each other in Marine Corps bravado.

When I finally hung up the phone, I looked at Art, who was putting the finishing touches on the presentation. "I think I've raised $3 million in the last thirty minutes."

"Well, hopefully your luck isn't about to run out. We have the American Airlines call in five minutes."

The call with American went well, the folks on the other end of the line eager to help. They needed to run it up the pole internally but hoped to get back to us within a couple of days. But an hour later they called back. They were in. They would dedicate two MD-80 aircraft and execute airlifts from our ten cities. They'd ask pilots from their crews who were military veterans to volunteer to fly them. Enthusiasm ended up being so high they had to turn people away. Combined with Southwest Airlines' contribution of five hundred individual tickets, Team Rubicon's mass-mobilization vision was becoming a reality.

The NOC was humming around the clock. Trucks and trailers pulled in and out of the warehouse, driving in empty, driving out with critical supplies. The planning team was poring over satellite images of the damage, looking for locations to house teams. Meanwhile, the mobilization team was battling the limitations of our technology infrastructure, struggling to sort through tens of thousands of rows of data while trying to track the vetting and dispatch process for Greyshirts being deployed. *We're going to have to build a new system when this is all done,* I thought. In the background, a reporter on one of the televisions caught my attention. *"As Texas battles the devastating impacts of Hurricane Harvey, residents in Florida should begin preparation for Hurricane Irma, which has just been upgraded to a major hurricane and is bearing down on their coast."*

Within the next week, Irma would slam into Florida's coast. With it, Team Rubicon would be fighting on a second front. And in ten days more, yet another storm would form east of the Lesser Antilles in the Atlantic Ocean. It became Hurricane Maria, and on September 20 would slam into Puerto Rico, becoming the worst disaster to ever hit that island.

Team Rubicon was about to get tested in ways we had never imagined. For me, it was time to get back to Houston.

• • •

HOUSTON, TEXAS

The large bus idled quietly. Looking across the asphalt plain, I could see waves of heat rippling upward. Every few minutes a giant shadow would roll past our window as an airplane taxied down the runway. We were sitting on the tarmac at Houston's Hobby Airport awaiting the first wave of volunteers to arrive from Los Angeles.

Over the next several weeks, ten chartered flights would arrive from cities throughout the U.S., every seat filled with a Greyshirt or veteran volunteer from a corporate partner. Once they were on the ground, we loaded the volunteers onto buses and transported them a short distance to a facility owned by Southwest Airlines, which we'd set up as a reception and processing center. There, they would get their personal safety equipment, initial mission and safety briefs, administrative processing, and, finally, their FOB assignments. By the end of the day, each one would depart for one of nine forward operating bases in Houston or along the Texas coast.

Soon an airplane approached, its silver fuselage marked with the unmistakable red, white, and blue stripes of American Airlines. "I can't believe this is happening," I said to Art with a grin. The plane's wheels were chocked and the ground crew positioned a stairwell outside its door. Walking across the tarmac, I couldn't help but feel a growing sense of pride. In the seven years that I'd been running Team Rubicon, I never thought I'd see the organization execute a mission on this scale. An American representative walked up the stairwell and peered in through the oval window, giving a thumbs-up to someone inside. Soon the door clicked and swung heavily on its complex hinges. A tall, trim man—the pilot, judging by the epaulets on his shirt—emerged. He was wearing a red Team Rubicon baseball hat and sunglasses. Behind him, I could see the first of nearly two hundred Greyshirts eager to deplane.

I stood with Art at the bottom of the stairs, shaking the hand of every volunteer who stepped off. It was a parade of sturdy work boots, heavy canvas work pants, and military-style packs slung over shoulders. And a grey shirt on every one of them.

• ● •

Back at Area Command in downtown Houston, I struggled with a decision. The organization had always prided itself on its commitment to direct its efforts to communities most in need. That meant that we didn't necessarily work where the damage was the worst, but where it was most likely to economically cripple survivors. Two inches of water in the home of an elderly couple on a fixed income without flood insurance was a higher priority than three feet of water in the home of a middle-class family who could file a claim and hire professional restoration services.

That's what made my struggle so difficult. I knew our process and priorities because I helped design them. And I believed they were right. But I couldn't shake a feeling in my gut.

I navigated the cubicles in the windowless room Team Rubicon was borrowing for its command center from a local veterans organization. The air was stale. Unshowered volunteers and trays of hours-old food created a musty odor. Bob was somewhere, and I needed to find him. Stepping over a sleeping bag, I was startled when it rolled over underneath me. It was noon, but the Greyshirts who were working through the night were stealing naps whenever they could. The volunteer looked up at me with tired eyes before pulling the bag back over his face.

Bob, in his late sixties, was a member of our Incident Management Team, a group of highly trained volunteers who deployed to operations to mentor and assist leaders on the ground. They were like an internal consulting and advisory practice. Bob was an Army veteran of Vietnam who'd come home and built a successful career in human resources at a Fortune 100 company. Full of energy, he joined Team Rubicon when he retired and was one of our most frequently deployed members. His enthusiasm was infectious, and volunteers couldn't help but gravitate toward him.

"Bob, can I speak with you?" I asked, nodding toward a corner. "I have an issue, and I want your input."

"What's the problem, boss?"

"I know we don't make exceptions to our work order prioritization process. No special favors. But . . . I'm considering putting together a special detail to go execute a muck-and-gut on a house that we're otherwise not going to help."

Bob knew that, as the CEO, I could grab whomever I wanted and go do whatever I cared. But that wasn't the culture we'd built. Rank had no privilege. "If you don't mind me asking, whose house is it?" he said.

"Susan Selke," I said. "Clay's mom."

Bob threw up his hands. "Why are you even asking? If we don't have that house done by sundown tomorrow, I quit!"

I smiled—his reaction confirmed what I had felt in my gut. There was the correct thing to do, and there was the right thing to do. We would do what was right.

The next morning, I briefed a dozen Greyshirts on the job. They didn't need me to explain who Clay was. He had become something of a tall tale within Team Rubicon, partly because so many volunteers saw themselves in his story. As I'd learned, many veterans joined Team Rubicon in search, like Clay, of a mission that gave them purpose, a community that felt like a tribe, and a sense of identity that made them proud. Five years earlier, Team Rubicon had also launched a fellowship program aimed at helping small cohorts of veterans become stronger leaders inside and outside the organization by exploring themselves in a deeper and more meaningful way. It was the type of guided self-discovery that would have helped Clay. Fittingly, it was called the Clay Hunt Fellows Program, and selection was highly competitive. Some veterans applied three or four times before getting chosen.

We loaded into trucks and made our way west toward Katy, Texas, a nice suburb of Houston. Nearing our destination, we turned onto a boulevard that skirted a large park on one side and a neighborhood on the other. A median cut down the center of the road, and standing water was everywhere. Every few hundred feet, abandoned cars sat with doors flung open, reminders not to get overconfident in our ability to ford the flooded parts of the road. In parts, the standing water would rise to our doorjambs, and the water crashing into the floorboards sounded like a car wash. We hopped the curbs in search of higher ground.

A car pulled over just in front of our truck. The door opened and Richard, Clay's stepdad, stepped out, wearing a faded University of Texas T-shirt, swimming trunks and athletic shoes, and a smile on his face. Richard had the disposition of a preacher—warm, genuine, and gentle—

though he hardly looked like a preacher at the moment. I noticed a waterproof pouch with his cell phone and wallet. Richard had clearly learned his lesson—water destroys everything.

Susan emerged from the passenger side. Her knee-high rain boots splashed in a puddle as she stood to face me. She wore a bright pink blouse, the kind someone would wear on a fishing trip or safari. Susan's dark hair was stuffed under a baseball cap, which cast a shadow across a somber face, broken, eventually, by a smile. "I'm so glad you're safe," I said. Theirs was a common story. They didn't evacuate because the flooding was not supposed to be bad where they were. Eventually, the Army Corps of Engineers made the tough choice to release water from a nearby reservoir to prevent its dams from failing—which would have led to even more catastrophic damage. The released water flooded straight into their neighborhood. As the waters rose, they realized that they would not be able to ride out the storm in their home. They had neighbors down the street with a second story who were kind enough to invite them in. They waited it out there until a boat came and rescued them the following day.

The rest of the team joined and I made introductions. Richard told us that their home was only a half mile away, so we loaded back up and drove farther down the street. Richard pointed out his window toward the entrance to a neighborhood and slowed to a stop. The roadway itself was invisible under a pool of water. A white sedan sat cockeyed on the curb, its back half underwater and its windshield pierced by a street sign, the glass spiderwebbing out. A low-slung brick wall on either side of the entrance likely once proudly displayed the neighborhood's name, but its words were now covered in filth. "This is it!" Richard shouted.

It didn't take an engineer to know that Richard's vehicle could not navigate the water at the entrance, so we sent one of our drivers forward to see if the rest of our trucks could. He edged forward cautiously until his engine was at risk of going under, then backed up to try another approach. We ruled out driving too far off the roadway for fear of hitting underwater hazards—running a truck into an invisible fire hydrant would be a disaster. There was no way we were driving the last half mile to Susan and Richard's home. It left us only one option—we would carry all our gear and supplies on our backs.

The team dismounted and emptied the beds of the trucks. Then a convoy of Jeep Wranglers pulled up alongside the team. Each one was highly customized, and all sat high on huge after-market tires, easily thirty-seven inches in diameter. A driver leaned out of the lead Wrangler. "Y'all need assistance?" he asked from behind mirrored sunglasses.

The group was a part of a local Jeep Wrangler affinity club. After the storm, they realized their vehicles were uniquely suited for navigating the flooded streets, and so they self-organized to help homeowners get in, but more importantly out, of flooded neighborhoods. We soon had our gear loaded into the backs of the Jeeps. I put Susan and Richard in the front Jeep and stood in its rear, holding on to its roll bar as it lurched forward.

We entered the devastated neighborhood, which now resembled Venice, Italy, more than Katy, Texas. Our Wrangler plowed through the water, at times feeling more like a fishing trawler than a four-wheel-drive vehicle. To our front, a mother duck led her ducklings in a line across the canal, as casually as if on a water hazard at a golf course. *Nature doesn't care about our problems,* I thought.

The red-brick home was one story, nicely constructed but modest in size. Large windows bore the mark of the flood line, three feet above the ground. We unloaded the vehicles and energetically thanked the drivers, writing down their cell phone numbers so they could help us get out of the neighborhood at the end of the day.

I led Susan and Richard inside. It was not the first time they'd been back, so the destruction inside was not a shock. Nonetheless, Susan was crestfallen at the sight of her entire world covered in bayou filth. I put my arm around her shoulder and pulled her close, realizing that much of my day would be spent in that exact pose.

We caught a distinct smell—the beginning stages of mold. I noticed that all the windows were tightly closed and locked. Richard told me they were worried about looters and had closed everything up when they left after their first return. I looked around at the contents of their home, nicely furnished and carefully adorned. And completely destroyed. I delicately told Richard that most of what they owned would have to go to the landfill. The thing that mattered most at this stage was salvaging the home itself, which meant preventing mold from making the situation worse. I saw defeat enter Susan's eyes for the first time. This woman who had lost the most important thing in her life—her son—was now beginning to realize she had lost all of her earthly possessions as well.

After opening all the windows and doors, the team moved in, respirator masks covering their faces, sledgehammers and crowbars slung over their shoulders.

As a first order of business, each Greyshirt was told to pull any salvageable items out of the house and onto the back porch. There, Susan would determine what she would save and take to a storage facility, and what she would have a Greyshirt take around front and dump on the growing pile of debris in their front yard. Plates and silverware and pots and pans that could be cleaned were stacked along the fence in the backyard. Medication bottles from a bathroom cabinet were dumped in a duffel bag and set aside to take away. Other, more sentimental items began making their way out. A crucifix that had been hanging on a wall, along with a family Bible, some of its edges damp. Photo albums with pictures of birthdays and Christmases and trips to Grandpa's ranch. Occasionally, Susan would grab something from a Greyshirt and cradle it, not ready to accept that it was gone.

Meanwhile, Greyshirts hauled carpets and drywall and furniture and mountains of clothes out the front door. Among the clothing was likely buried the black dress Susan wore at Clay's funeral. Perhaps it was okay if that one left.

I saw one of the volunteers carrying out a picture frame. Suspecting what it might be, I snagged it and turned it over in my hands. Looking back at me was a photograph of Clay in his uniform. Handsome with sandy hair and a strong jaw, Clay shot the camera a frank, spirited look. "You got it?" the Greyshirt asked. I blinked away tears.

"Yeah, I got it. Thanks, Rob," I said. Clay had been gone for six years, and not a day had passed without me thinking about him. For a while I thought back to our time together in the Marines, a lifetime ago. I thought of the missions we ran. Like that time Clay was shot through the arm and, high on morphine, all he could talk about was going home and drinking dollar beers at the Hermosa Pier. I remembered the conversations we would have between missions, when doubts about the war were gradually creeping into his mind. In many ways Clay had served as my conscience overseas, never letting me become something I was not.

Inside and outside the Marine Corps, Clay was a man in search of meaning. He'd seen some of the worst of humanity and wanted to make sense of it. Admittedly, back then I thought Clay was maybe a little naive for believing that we could make the world a better place if we simply tried. He would implore his fellow veterans to find a way to help someone, somewhere. To serve. But looking around Susan's home, and knowing that thousands of Greyshirts were en route to Texas to help, I knew now that Clay was right. He just didn't live to see it.

293

I turned and handed the frame to Susan. Her shoulders stopped slumping. "I always loved this picture, Jake," she said. "I miss him so much, but this picture puts all of this"—she waved her hand at the destruction around her home—"into perspective. None of this stuff matters. We've got our faith. We've got insurance. We'll get new things." She sighed. "And we'll always have our memories."

I tried to busy myself with work. I needed to sweat and strain. I found a room in the corner of the house that hadn't been touched. After snapping the baseboards off with a prybar, I set to work pulling up the waterlogged carpet. The carpet was so thick and heavy with water that I had to cut it into narrow strips. Each strip I peeled back was only a foot wide by a few feet long but weighed nearly a hundred pounds. By the time I was finished, I was soaking wet from head to toe, uncertain how much of it was sweat and how much was that filthy bayou water.

I wandered down a hallway, followed by the deep thuds of sledge-hammers crashing into cabinets. Two doors were open, their rooms occupied by Greyshirts destroying walls. To my left was a closed door. I opened it. Inside was a small room, a den or home office. A heavy couch, sopping wet, sat along one wall. Opposite the door, the entire wall was built out with shelves and cabinets. The cabinets along the bottom had all been pulled open by the retreating water, spilling their contents onto the floor. I scanned the shelves above. Books and crosses and picture frames were sporadically placed, interspersed with Hallmark mementos.

Sitting on the shelf were two other items. The first was a wooden shadow box shaped like an octagon. It was large, maybe eighteen inches across. The felt behind the glass looked soft and was a deep navy blue. Pinned to the felt were Clay's medals and marksmanship badges alongside a series of photographs. All the contents aligned and spaced with military order and discipline. The top two photographs were of our platoon in Iraq and our sniper team in Afghanistan. The brothers Clay served with. Below them were photographs of Howey, Windsor, Washington, and Crass. The brothers Clay lost.

I knew that shadow box. It once hung in Clay's apartment in Los Angeles. When he first hung it up, I asked him about the photos; it wasn't common to put pictures of the fallen in a military shadow box. He pointed at the medals and then to the photos. I've got to make these mean something for them, he said. He meant making their sacrifice worth it. It sounded familiar.

Next to the shadow box in the den sat another wooden display case. This one a triangle. Inside this case was an American flag, crisply folded to show the blue and white field of stars. It was the flag that had draped Clay's coffin.

I leaned against the doorjamb and stared at the flag. I didn't fight the tears, but, truthfully, not many came. It had been ten years since I'd returned from Iraq, when Clay waited at the parade field for me to come home. A decade since I first stood at a military memorial service in front of a row of rifles thrust into sandbags, topped with helmets and framed by empty boots. Six years since I handed the very flag I stared at to my best friend's mother. It just didn't seem like I had many tears left.

Maybe the mission I had now helped me make sense of it all. The losses were no less tragic. The aching no less dull. But they were buoyed by a new sense of purpose and hope for a better tomorrow.

An arm twisted around my waist. "I thought I might find you back here," Susan said, working her way under my arm. She didn't look up at me and I didn't look down. Instead we just stared forward and thought of Clay.

A few minutes passed. Finally, I squeezed her shoulder. "Come on, we've got a job to finish."

EPILOGUE

Nearly two thousand Greyshirts deployed into Texas for Hurricane
Harvey. It was a remarkable logistical feat that demonstrated just
how far Team Rubicon had come. In all, Team Rubicon gutted 1,078
homes, each of those jobs potentially keeping the homeowner from spi-
raling into homelessness or financial ruin. At the same time, we also sent
hundreds of volunteers into both Florida and Puerto Rico, and in the
latter deployed our medical teams for the first time in a domestic capacity. As with Hurricane Sandy, these hurricanes were a watershed moment
for the organization. New resources and volunteers flooded into the
organization, nearly doubling its size in a matter of months. We launched
a multiyear, multimillion-dollar partnership with Microsoft, which promised to help us build customized solutions to the technology problems
that plagued our early efforts during Harvey. T-Mobile shot a Team Rubicon commercial that aired throughout that fall's World Series, a seven-
game classic between the Dodgers and Houston's very own Astros. And
Team Rubicon further cemented itself in the upper echelon of disaster

management, becoming a sought-after voice at industry conferences and in the news media.

But as Harvey's spotlight faded, we knew that the work was just beginning. Early in the effort, we hatched a plan that had figuratively sat on our shelf for nearly five years. During those first two weeks, we hustled to raise as much money as possible, knowing that in order for the plan to be successful, it would have to be well capitalized. It worked. Team Rubicon raised an incremental $10 million and set it aside to launch the organization's next evolution: community rebuilding.

We had a crazy idea: find military veterans transitioning into a new phase in life, train them in construction skills, and give them a one-year fellowship to use those skills to rebuild homes in Houston. It was a solution that would tackle two problems: ineffective recovery efforts and a rising shortage of skilled construction labor across America. We looked around the organization to determine where to position the pilot program and fellowship, and only one department made sense. We folded it into the Clay Hunt Fellows Program.

About six months after the decision to launch the program, I was there for the Fellows' first "Welcome Home" party in Houston, where Team Rubicon turns over the keys of a refurbished house back to its owner. I met the diverse crew serving in Clay's honor, including Brian, a chatty helicopter pilot who reminded me of Clay himself, and Teaira "T-Bone" Johnson, a petite African American woman and Army veteran who credits Team Rubicon with getting her off the streets.

The Fellows were giddy preparing for the homeowner's arrival. Courtney, the Fellow who had served as supervisor on the home, frantically wiped down every surface she saw, making sure there were no smudges on the crown molding. There was a cake. And music. A red ribbon was tied across the modest porch. When the car pulled up, all the Fellows and some of the local volunteers lined up from the passenger door to the home's steps, like a basketball team during the announcement of the starting lineup. When the homeowner, Estella, exited the car, they began clapping and whistling, welcoming her home.

Courtney walked her up to the porch, where they both broke down in tears. Courtney spoke first, clearly uncomfortable with the spotlight. She turned to Estella. "Thank you for giving me the opportunity to help you," she said. They embraced.

Within two years, Team Rubicon's nascent program would rebuild 100 homes in Texas, 41 in Florida, and put 504 roofs back on homes in Puerto Rico. The gamble had paid off, and Team Rubicon made plans to dramatically expand the program in the coming years.

Three months later, I was back in Los Angeles. It was July 18 and I was seated alongside Indra in the 7,000-seat Microsoft Theater, site of the 2018 ESPY Awards, held annually by ESPN to celebrate excellence in sports performance. Indra was seven months pregnant with our first child, and looking at her, I knew just how lucky I was. A year prior, Indra had walked away from her career as a broadcast meteorologist, intent on starting a family. I still wondered how a beautiful, talented, and successful woman had fallen in love with a Marine sergeant with no money and no plan a decade ago. I owed her everything.

When the narrator announced my name as the recipient of the Pat Tillman Award for Service, I rose and turned to hug Indra. "I love you," I whispered as I reached down and touched her belly. For a moment, I paused and considered the decade-and-a-half journey I had been on. Being there in that moment, accepting an award named for Pat, was the most unexpected outcome I ever could have imagined back when I first looked in the mirror after his death and made the choice to join my fellow Americans at war.

In my acceptance speech that night, I spoke of seeing hardship bring out the best in people. I relayed a saying that Team Rubicon has: "If people acted every day like they do after a disaster, we'd live in a truly special place." So then why is it that once a disaster fades from memory, we retreat into our corners? What if Americans rose to the occasion every day? Yellow ribbons and *COEXIST* bumper stickers are not enough. Nor is dropping off canned goods at a food bank, anxiously hustling in and out so you never have to interact with one of the people arriving down on their luck and hungry. Clicking "share" on an inspiring social media post doesn't move the needle, although spreading hate and conspiracy certainly can.

Throughout history, Americans have risen to the occasion. We overthrew a monarchy and built the world's greatest democracy. We weathered the Great Depression and conquered the Nazis. We promised to put someone on the moon within a decade and we did. But the threat of apathy and division might be our next existential challenge.

Today, as we mark the tenth anniversary of Team Rubicon's founding, our mission is by no means accomplished. In the next decade we have a chance to weave our story into the fabric of America. We are bold (or foolish) enough to believe we can help restore the meaning of citizenship for ourselves and other Americans, while tackling *real* national crises—our veterans returning home after our nation's longest wars and the terrifying increase and cost of disasters. We envision a future in which every military veteran can continue their life in service to others. A future in which communities turn to veterans to lead them through times of crisis.

It won't be easy. The notions of service, sacrifice, and citizenship can sound antiquated in today's me-me-me America. But I believe that Americans are yearning for a cause worthy of our history and values, yearning for inspiration to rise and be better. We can—we must—reframe what it means to be an American and a patriot. And in doing so convince a new generation that with citizenship comes a shared responsibility to serve a common cause: life, liberty, and the pursuit of happiness. Not just for ourselves, but for others.

For me, this crusade is deeply personal. I have spent nearly my entire adult life traveling to far-flung communities whose residents lack life's most essential virtue: hope. I have seen young girls forbidden from attending school, resigned to a life of subjugation. Young boys conscripted into an evil ideology, rifles thrust into their resistant clutch. I've strode through the streets of once vibrant towns, now nothing more than rusting skeletons of former glory, and witnessed the dreams of a better life slowly recede with a flood's water. And watched as the line between haves and have-nots gets drawn even starker by the cruel destructive path of a tornado. For the first time in history, we might leave the world worse for our children than we found it. For many Americans and citizens of this planet, hope is quickly fading. Can service help restore it?

A year ago my first child was born, a baby girl. Holding her immediately put everything I'd ever done in my life into perspective. That first night in the hospital, anxiously watching every breath, I paused to reflect. Those children on the battlefield in Afghanistan—where were they? Had my actions improved or destroyed their lives? And what of Ali? The parents of the children who perished in the school in Moore, Oklahoma. Have they ever muted that pain? All the children in all the communities we've served, who watched as their already economically fragile existence was swept away in a storm—do they have hope?

For communities across the United States, the now iconic Greyshirt of Team Rubicon is a symbol of hope. Amid the chaos and destruction and despair of a disaster, men and women from across America drop everything to deploy to communities they've never visited, to help people they've never known. In a way they are like Patton's army marching into Mauthausen in 1945, the source of my inspiration so many years ago. Only this army doesn't need guns and tanks. They only need each other.

Just then a nurse walked into the room to check on Indra, asleep on the bed. She looked at me and then to our child. "Congratulations," she said. "What's her name?"

"Her first name is Valija," I replied, never breaking my gaze from the crib. "Her middle name is Hope."

ACKNOWLEDGMENTS

Though this book is a memoir, my hope is it serves as a fitting tribute to the people I have been fortunate to live and serve alongside throughout my life.

To the men of the 2nd Battalion, 7th Marine Regiment, who chewed sand with me on distant battlefields in Iraq and Afghanistan, thank you. Together we endured more than most Americans can imagine. Some of us didn't come home. Still others have been lost since. For those who remain, I promise you this: our best chapters are ahead of us, if we choose to write them. We will always be warriors—remember that.

To all the men and women of the military across service branches and generations, thank you for your service. You donned our nation's cloth and served something bigger than yourselves. Everyone should be so lucky.

I am forever indebted to the Greyshirts of Team Rubicon, past, present, and future. I have the joy of waking up every day and working for you and the communities we serve. You inspire me with your selflessness, enthusiasm, and relentless commitment to the mission. There is nothing you can't do if you do it together. Mission first, Greyshirts always.

There are too many staff and volunteer leaders over the past decade who have left their mark on this organization to name them all. Each of you are plank holders in an organization that will outlive us all. Take pride in what we've built. One day you'll be able to tell your grandchildren about your contribution to this world.

Of course, there would be no Team Rubicon if there wasn't the initial team. Thank you to Jeff for answering the call and saying yes, William for responding to the Facebook post, and to Mark, Dave, Jim, Craig, and Eduardo for joining along the way. The odds were stacked against us, but we overcame them.

And none of it would be possible without the individuals, foundations, and corporations that invest in our work with their philanthropy. You invested in our vision, and our success is your success. A special thanks to our Support Squad, who donate to us monthly, and our Ready Reserve, whose substantial annual gifts enable us to respond anytime, anywhere.

Thank you to Coach Alvarez and Coach Hueber, who took a chance on an undersized offensive lineman and brought him to the University of Wisconsin. If I have an ounce of grit or tenacity in my body, I owe it to playing football.

Writing this book was a decade-long goal, one that seemed out of reach when its original proposal was rejected thirty-seven times back in 2015. I couldn't have made it happen without my agent, Lucinda Halpern, who managed to wrangle a hard-charging Marine twice her size and convince him that she knew best (she did). Or without Connor Eck, her right-hand man, who could delicately tell me when my writing was terrible without stoking my ire.

Thank you to Kevin Cook, who helped get me through a proposal process that felt disorienting and archaic. And a mountain of gratitude to Will Murphy, who suffered through draft after draft, always willing to get on the phone and listen to me vent.

To my editor, Leah Trouwborst, and publisher, Adrian Zackheim, at Sentinel, I want to say thank you for believing in the vision of this book and helping shape it into something we can all be proud of. I'm sure I can be hard to work with! And to Bria, Chase, Tara, Mary Kate, and Jamie, my gratitude for helping position this book to influence the public narrative around veterans and the mounting toll of natural disasters.

Special thanks to Art, Mike, Corey, Nicole, David, Tim, Shawn, Susan, Richard, Lissie, and Top for reviewing early drafts and confirming details that tend to fade with time. And for helping me avoid putting my foot in my mouth. Oh, and for pointing out that I use too many adverbs. I really, really like them.

Words cannot express my appreciation to Adam Miller, who has served as Team Rubicon's chairman for six years and has been an invaluable mentor throughout that time. The same goes for everyone on Team Rubicon's board of directors, which at present includes: Chris Perkins, Mary Solomon, Jonathan Smidt, Michael Stern, Joe Marchese, Christina Park, Clay DeGiacinto, Sam Greene, Edward Sassower, Duncan Niederauer. Just as important is our general counsel, John Pitts, and his colleagues at Kirkland Ellis, who have always kept me and the organization well advised.

I would be nothing without my family. My mother has been a source of love and compassion my entire life and is a rock for us. My sisters, Erin, Sarah, and Meghan, sometimes made my life miserable, but we can't think about those teenage years without laughing. I'm a better father for having watched them raise their own children. And a special thank-you to Sarah, who through her talent provided Team Rubicon with a visual identity that is now inked on hundreds of bodies—including her own.

And of course, my own father, who left us all too early in 2015. He always challenged me to be more and be better, but I really just wanted to be him. I still find myself asking his advice when I face a challenge, and I like to think I can hear him whisper his wisdom in my ear. Dad, thank you for everything; I promise to keep chasing the blue vase.

Indra, before I say anything else, I love you. Thank you for helping me navigate the last decade. You have given up so much so that we can raise our family together—it's a gift that I'll never be able to repay. There's nobody I'd rather traverse this world and the coming decades with. And thank you for not complaining when the alarm went off at four a.m. each morning so I could get up and write.

And to my dearest Valija Hope. Your laughter has made it all worth it. I hope you grow up believing that I did the best I could in the circumstances I faced.

I INVITE YOU TO JOIN THE TEAM

Near the conclusion of writing *Once a Warrior*, the novel coronavirus, also known as COVID-19, had spread like wildfire across the planet. As I write this afterword, 90 percent of the United States population is under state-mandated shelter-in-place orders. The country's number of coronavirus cases has eclipsed 5,500,000, and more than 170,000 Americans have lost their lives.

As you might expect, Team Rubicon has sprung into action. Federal, tribal, state, and local agencies across the United States have requested Team Rubicon's assistance executing missions ranging from the command and coordination of quarantine shelters, to managing all personal protective equipment collection and distribution for the city of Chicago, to operating a federal medical station in the Navajo Nation. In nearly one hundred cities, Team Rubicon has launched operations to support local food banks with operational planning, logistics, and manpower. And in an effort to support our country's most vulnerable populations, Team Rubicon launched a #NeighborsHelpingNeighbors campaign, which mobilized its more than 120,000 volunteers to safely help those who needed assistance getting food and medication while sheltering in place.

All of this was possible because of volunteers who give their most precious resource—their time—to serve their communities. If you are a military veteran, medical professional, or first responder, I challenge you to join Team Rubicon and become a Greyshirt. If you have someone in your life who fits the bill, please pass this book on to them and encourage them to join the team.

Interested in joining Team Rubicon? Text WARRIOR to 87872 to learn how.

Perhaps you're more inclined to cut a check than rip through a tree with a chainsaw. No worries: In Team Rubicon you've found an organization relentlessly committed to transparency and accountability. Our commitment to our donors is sacred. We strive to maximize the impact of every dollar contributed, treating each as though our own mother had given it. With you on our side we'll continue to scale our impact into every American community and corner of the globe.

If you want to support Team Rubicon's mission, text BOOK to 87872 to learn more.

STAY CONNECTED

Twitter and Instagram: @JakeWoodTR | @TeamRubicon | #OnceAWarrior
www.jake-wood.com | www.teamrubiconusa.org
Did you love the book? Email me! book@jake-wood.com

SELECT LIST OF TR SUPPORTERS

Our deep gratitude to the individuals, foundations, and corporations who have donated over $100,000 to Team Rubicon throughout the years (list current at time of publication).

AbbVie Foundation

Acorn Hill Foundation

Activision Blizzard

Adam and Staci Miller

Adam Yarnold and Laura Hunt

Adolph Coors Foundation

ADP Foundation

Aetna Foundation

Airlink

ALE Solutions, Inc.

Alice L. Walton Foundation

American Airlines

American Express Foundation

AQR Capital Management

Ariat International

AT&T Foundation

Balyasny Asset Management (BAM Funds)

Bank of America

Baron Weather

Berges Family Foundation

Bernice & Milton Stern Foundation

Biella Foundation

Big Wood Foundation

BlackRock

Bob Woodruff Foundation

Born This Way Foundation

Box.com

Bridgeview Bank Mortgage Co., LLC

Bristol-Meyers Squibb Foundation

Carhartt

CASE Construction Equipment

CBS EcoMedia

Center for Disaster Philanthropy

Christina Park & Jim Seery

CITI

Clear Channel Outdoor

Cliff and Laurel Asness

Cornerstone OnDemand, Inc.

Craig H. Neilsen Foundation

Cynthia and Clayton DeGiacinto

David M. Solomon

Dell Giving

Diageo North America Foundation

Don Engle

Dupont

Edison International

Everbridge

Farmers Insurance

FCA Foundation

FedEx Corporation

Ford Motor Company

Fossil Group

Fox Networks Group

Fundación Abertis

GAF Materials Corporation

Garrison Brothers

Goldman, Sachs & Co.

Goldman Sachs Gives

Google.org

Got Your 6

GreaterGood Network

Gregg & Kate Lemkau

Harry and Jeanette Weinberg Foundation, Inc.

Harvey Schwartz

Hearst Foundation, Inc.

Heinz Family Foundation

Hertz

Hilton Hotels Worldwide

HISTORY Channel/ A+E Networks

Holland Partner Group

J.A. and Kathryn Albertson Foundation

Jack Link's

JIB Fund

Joe and Christie Marchese

John and Karen Beekley

John and Laura Potocsnak

John R. and M. Margrite Davis Foundation

Jonathan and Claire Smidt

Kendeda Fund

Kirkland & Ellis LLP

Kristie Feinberg

La Quinta Inns & Suites

Laura and Lloyd Blankfein

Laura Conigliaro

Macy's

Madelaine Rapp Einbinder

Major League Baseball (MLB)

Marika Alzadon and Samuel Cole

Mary Solomon

MassMutual Foundation

May & Stanley Smith Charitable Trust

McJunkin Family Charitable Foundation

Medieval Times Dinner & Tournament

Mello-Hill Charitable Fund of the Community Foundation of New Jersey

Mercury One, Inc.

Metabolic Studio

Microsoft

Mountain Dew

Newman's Own Foundation

Northrop Grumman

One Hope Foundation

Palantir

Parsons Xtreme Golf (PXG)

PepsiCo Foundation

Pliny Jewell

Prudential Foundation

PwC Charitable Foundation

Qlik

Quantum Energy Partners

Robert and Rowena Zimmers

Robinson Foundation

Salesforce Foundation

Samuel Greene

San Manuel Band of Mission Indians

SBP

Schmidt Family Foundation

Schneider Electric Foundation

Schultz Family Foundation

Silicon Valley Community Foundation

Soundtoys

Southwest Airlines

Starbucks

Steven and Alexandra Cohen & Steven and Alexandra Cohen Foundation

Target

The Ahmanson Foundation

The Brin Wojcicki Foundation

The Carbaugh Family Foundation

The Community Foundation of Middle Tennessee

The Cupid Foundation

The Dennis & Phyllis Washington Foundation, in conjunction with Kevin and Chelsea Washington

The Dow Chemical Company

The Grover Hermann Foundation

The Held Foundation

The Home Depot Foundation

The Joseph and Mary Cacioppo Foundation

The Marcus Foundation

The Moody's Foundation

The Riley Family Foundation

The TK Foundation

The USAA Foundation, Inc. & USAA

Thomas & Susan Fuller

T-Mobile

Travelers

Tucker and Susan York

Tuft & Needle

Under Armour

University of Kentucky Athletics

UNOPS

Veronica Atkins

Veterans United Foundation

Walmart

Wheeler Family Foundation

Wipfli

Wounded Warrior Project[*]